PENGUIN BOOKS

# The Rev. Diaries

Rev. Adam Smallbone is the vicar of St Saviour's in Hackney. He studied History at Bristol University, and was ordained in 1999. He is married to Alexandra, a solicitor. He was a curate in the Ipswich Diocese before becoming the vicar of St Peter's, Gromford, where he was able to be alseep most nights by 9 p.m. His busy life in London has led to a more metropolitan bedtime. This year he helped man the C of E stall at *The Wedding Show* (O2 Centre), served on the Churches' Funerals Group, helping re-write its Culture of Death project, and he has been a strong campaigner for equal pension provision for those in civil partnerships. He has appeared on *The One Show* and been undeservedly nominated for a *Pride of Britain* award. He supports charities including Don't Forget the Kids and The Monkey Sanctuary. He is in favour of women.

Jon Canter studied law at Cambridge before becoming a scriptwriter and novelist. His TV credits include *Not The Nine O'Clock News*, *Posh Nosh* and *Live At The Apollo*. He was a script editor for *A Bit of Fry and Laurie* and wrote stand-up comedy with Lenny Henry before writing *Seeds of Greatness*, *A Short Gentleman* and *Worth*, leading James Kidd in the *Independent* to call him 'arguably the finest comic novelist working in Britain today'. With John Lloyd, he wrote *Afterliff: The New Dictionary of Things There Should Be Words For*. His Radio 4 series *Believe It* won Best Scripted Comedy at the BBC Audio Awards and his journalism has appeared in the *Guardian*. He lives on the Suffolk coast with the painter Helen Napper and their daughter Nancy.

# The Rev. Diaries

## JON CANTER

with help from
Tom Hollander and James Wood

PENGUIN BOOKS

# With thanks to the Reverend Philip North

PENGUIN BOOKS

Published by the Penguin Group

Penguin Books Ltd, 80 Strand, London WC2R ORL, England

Penguin Group (USA) Inc., 375 Hudson Street, New York, New York 10014, USA

Penguin Group (Canada), 90 Eglinton Avenue East, Suite 700, Toronto, Ontario, Canada M4P 2Y3
(a division of Pearson Penguin Canada Inc.)

Penguin Ireland, 25 St Stephen's Green, Dublin 2, Ireland (a division of Penguin Books Ltd)

Penguin Group (Australia), 707 Collins Street, Melbourne, Victoria 3008, Australia
(a division of Pearson Australia Group Pty Ltd)

Penguin Books India Pvt Ltd, 11 Community Centre, Panchsheel Park, New Delhi – 110 017, India

Penguin Group (NZ), 67 Apollo Drive, Rosedale, Auckland 0632, New Zealand
(a division of Pearson New Zealand Ltd)

Penguin Books (South Africa) (Pty) Ltd, Block D, Rosebank Office Park,
181 Jan Smuts Avenue, Parktown North, Guateng 2193, South Africa

Penguin Books Ltd, Registered Offices: 80 Strand, London WC2R ORL, England

www.penguin.com

First published by Michael Joseph 2014
Published in Penguin Books 2014

001

Copyright © Big Talk Productions Limited, 2014

Typeset by Penguin Books Ltd
Printed in Great Britain by Clays Ltd, St Ives plc

A CIP catalogue record for this book is available from the British Library

ISBN: 978–1–405–91368–3

www.greenpenguin.co.uk

Penguin Books is committed to a sustainable
future for our business, our readers and our planet.
This book is made from Forest Stewardship
Council™ certified paper.

# The Rev. Diaries

## 2nd January

I've just survived my first Christmas at St Saviour's. I was battered and bruised and frequently distraught, but I didn't end up in hospital. Either in A & E or as an inpatient in the psychiatric ward. That's an achievement in itself.

I started the year as I meant to go on, by smoking. The first step to quitting is to want to quit. And I don't. I need whatever support the fags give me, even though I know they're killing me and Alex doesn't like them. She thought I was giving them up for New Year. I said she'd misunderstood. After all the excesses of New Year's Eve, my resolution was to give up smoking for New Year's *Day*. Which I did.

The girl in the shop was on the phone. In the two months I've been going in there, she's never *not* been on the phone.

'Then she goes, I fucking hate you, Lisa, so I go, I fucking hate you too, Martine, and I fucking hate your mum and all.'

She broke off the call to take my money. I thought now was the time she and I should have our first proper conversation.

'Keeping up your New Year resolutions?'

She didn't reply, which made me feel I should have said nothing. But she lives in my parish. I have care of her soul. She fucking hates Martine, and for good measure she fucking hates her mum and all. Why can't she fucking love Martine? Or at least fucking tolerate her? I'd like to think I could help Lisa not have all that hate in her heart. That's my mission, isn't it, Lord?

I never want anyone to think that my collar means I'm earnest and pious and they can't say what they like, but that's what happened with Lisa. She gave my collar a little look and just couldn't speak.

I stood outside the shop, smoked a fag and looked at my reflection in the window. It brought back what Gran used to say when I was little.

'Look at Adam. He's pretty as a girl! Pretty as a girl!'

She wouldn't say that now.

My once cherubic face was looking all puffed and blowsy. The festive season will do that to a man. But the good news was, my black eye was fading.

Basically, for Christmas I got given a headbutt. There were moments of extraordinary grace and transcendence. It wasn't all headbutts. But when I look back on last Christmas, it's the headbutt I'll remember.

I suppose I should never have moved to a new church in November. It was an invitation to craziness, given that Christmas is the busiest time in a priest's calendar. Like starting a new school just before exams.

Advent, 'Stick a Candle Up an Orange', Christingle, the Bring a Toy Service, Carols at the Crib, Carols at the

Christmas Tree, Carols by the Cashpoint, the Perpetuity Bank Carol Service and being Father Christmas. Plus the usual routine priestly tasks – the regular services, the home visits, the school assemblies and classes, the old people's home and hospital visits, the Bible study groups, the committees, the fund-raising events, the night shelters.

I needed all the help I could get. And one man helped me a lot.

It was my second day. Night Shelter at St Saviour's. I could barely find my way from the pulpit to the lavatory and there I was, cooking bacon, eggs and beans at 6.30 in the morning for 15 people sleeping on the floor of the church, all of them strangers, to me if not to each other. But one guy, a Mancunian with a beard, went out of his way to befriend me. He was evidently a veteran of these nights and offered himself up as my assistant chef. (He called me 'Vicarage', which I actually quite liked.) I asked if he'd wake everybody up, which he did by aiming the odd kick at some duvets and shouting, 'Come on, scumbags, doss time's over.' Zealous was the word. He had no finesse but plenty of zeal.

Everything about him suggested he was no stranger to A & E, the police station and probably prison – he'd definitely seen the inside of a few municipal buildings. He had a ravaged face full of broken blood vessels and a smoker's cough. For all that, there was something childlike about him.

When everyone left and he'd helped me clear the breakfast, he asked if I'd like to join him on the bench outside the church for a fag. When he offered me one, I took it.

'You're on the fags too, Vicarage. I knew it! We're outcasts, you and me. People are always throwing us out.'

That was my introduction to Colin. He's a mainstay of the church, coming to every service and helping out with anything that has to be done, in his keen but cack-handed way. That's great. But he's also a mainstay of the vicarage, which is not so great. Colin's a serious drinker who tends to think of my home as a pub, The Reverend Adam. He doesn't really have a home of his own, so I don't want to judge him. The church itself is sort of his home, which is as it should be, that's our purpose. Rev Roy, my mentor, used to call the drinkers who came to his church 'alcoholys'. They were people in need of booze and God, and a priest was there to minister to human need. Alcoholys were trouble but a priest didn't flinch. 'Jesus *loved* trouble,' he told me.

People in need. That's always the problem. There's the lost and the lonely and the sick and the dying and the homeless and the unlucky. But there's me too. And Alex. We have needs as well.

It was the First Sunday of Advent that the trouble started.

I've always loved Advent. 'Almighty God, give us grace that we may cast away the works of darkness, and put upon us the armour of light.' I lit the flame on the first candle of the Advent Wreath and thought about the coming of Christ. There was a wonderful sermon to be written comparing the Light of the World and the Christmas Lights on Oxford Street, how the yearning

6

for the arrival of the Messiah was being obscured by rampant commercialism. And then I thought, No, that sermon's predictable. Think of something original.

On the bench after the service, puffing away, Colin was in sombre mood. Christmas was coming. There was no stopping it now. It was miserable if you had no family. The best thing was to stay pissed till it was all over.

Here he was, this man who'd helped me, who'd offered me fag after fag. He'd be alone at Christmas, while I had a wife and a home. I had to do it. I had to share.

I told him my wife and I were planning a Christmas lunch at the vicarage for people who'd otherwise be on their own, and that he was welcome to join us. He was touched. He thanked me, said he'd love to come. Then he said, in a wary way, 'It's not you cooking, is it? You murdered those beans.' I should have been offended but I wasn't. He was just being open with his feelings, in that childlike way.

As soon as I'd invited him, I felt bad, because Alex and I weren't planning that at all. My parents were going to my brother's, her dad was going to her sister's, and Alex and I were having Christmas lunch on our own, just us, in the new home the church had given us, with its rattling fridge, leaking roof and toilet-brown wallpaper.

What would Alex say now that I'd put Colin's needs above hers? I said I was sorry, it wouldn't happen next year, and did she understand why I'd done it? She did. She was gracious.

'It's ministry,' she said ruefully. 'You don't leave your work behind when you leave the office.'

The trouble started with Colin, but it didn't end with him. On the second Sunday of Advent, I told the congregation I was bringing back Midnight Mass.

Why had my predecessor cancelled it? We had it in my last parish and everyone loved it, and that was in Gromford, a quiet Suffolk village that by 9 p.m. was actually asleep. So how could we not have Midnight Mass in a vibrant inner-city hub like St Saviour's?

We had to take every opportunity to get people into the church and celebrate its presence in the community. I mean, the fact there was still a church on the site was amazing in itself. It's inner inner city, minutes away from the City of London and Liverpool Street. Eleven buses pass the door and about a million cars. St Saviour's is the only church I know with a double yellow line outside it. You'd expect it to be an investment bank, a block of flats, a luxury gym, a two-storey lobster and burger restaurant for hedge-funders and software designers. But no, it's a draughty old church that sometimes has asylum seekers asleep on its floor.

I told Nigel, my pastoral assistant, that I was re-introducing Midnight Mass. He wasn't keen. We'd be the place where revellers went before they lurched home: 'The religious equivalent of a kebab.' He pursed his mouth in a disapproving way – he's got a gift for disapproval. Nigel's a tall bearded man in his late twenties, who seems to have a mental age of 59. He works part-time for Transport for London (on roundabouts, I think) but feels his mission in life is to be a priest. So he wants to help me, which is great, but mostly he wants to help me realize that he's right.

But I knew he wasn't right about Midnight Mass. I told him not to be negative. It would be a lot of fun.

'I trust you've informed the police,' said the Archdeacon, who turned up at the vestry, out of the blue, a few days later, as I was counting my Midnight Mass mince pies. Months went by in St Peter's, Gromford, without a visit from my Archdeacon, whereas this Archdeacon pops up all the time.

There's definitely a touch of the Cardinal Wolsey about Archdeacon Robert. He looks like he's on the point of being amused but then he turns scornful. He's commanding and sly, withering but brilliant, and he has a mesmerising quiff made of very few strands of hair, which looks like a tiny arrow he's aiming at your head.

He said restoring Midnight Mass was a brave but probably foolish decision. However, this was now my parish to do with what I wanted and he'd support me in my endeavour. However, there was something unsupportive about the way he said it – like a man who stands behind you and tells you to fall backwards, but then takes a step to the side.

He asked how much I'd spent on mince pies. When I told him they were £3.50 for 6 and that I'd bought 24 packets, he said, 'Well, let's hope they're delicious,' in an equally worrying way, as if it might be my parish, but he'd be micro-managing it every step and pie of the way. Is the man on my side or not?

*

And then came Christmas Eve Eve. Which I'll always think of as Black Friday. Short, of course, for Black Eye Friday.

The day began badly and got worse. I was due to see Mr Summers at Mulberry House, the local old people's home. His daughter had been killed in a car accident and the poor man was very low. I'd been due to see him ever since I arrived in the parish. (Then again, I'd been due to spend an evening at home with Alex, and I hadn't done that either.) Once he'd had to cancel because he was in hospital and twice I'd had to cancel because I had so much other stuff to do. But on Black Friday, I just plain forgot.

At the time I was meant to be seeing him, I was lugging the mince pies back to Waitrose. They were luxury ones and I thought I'd exchange them for the cheaper 'essential' ones. But then I thought again. Why shouldn't the congregants at Midnight Mass have a luxury mince pie? Yes, some of them would probably be pissed, and others would be there to get out of the cold because they had nowhere else to go. Did that mean they weren't worthy? Were the only people who deserved luxury mince pies people who could afford them? Of course not.

So I lugged the pies back from Waitrose to the church and then I went home. By that point I was frazzled, so much so that I called out to Alex from the hall, 'I'm totally knackered. Any chance of a Christmas blow job?'

'Yes please,' replied a man from the living room. That's when I learned my father-in-law was coming to ours for Christmas.

It turned out he couldn't go to Kate's because her daughter Alice had measles. Was it possible she'd given his granddaughter measles just to get out of seeing him?

OK, the man has qualities. He cooks an excellent roast beef lunch. He serves on a lot of local committees. He really looks after his chickens. Plus he's Alex's father, so there must be something wonderful about him. And his wife died a year ago, and he's just had a knee operation. It's just, I'm not the man he would have wanted for his elder daughter.

It was fine when I was working for the Bristol City Council Housing Department. He and his wife could tell their golfing and bridge-playing friends that I worked in property. But when I realized I wanted to devote my life to God, everything changed. Basically, their hearts sank as mine lifted. What would they tell their friends now?

They reacted to the news of my revelation as if I'd had a stroke. How long would it last? What were the chances of my making a full recovery? Their daughter would have to look after me for the rest of my life.

It didn't turn out as badly as they feared. I've clearly 'made a go of it'. I have a job, a free house, a pension. Nevertheless, he doesn't think being a vicar is a job for a man with ambition; not like a Barclays Bank manager, which he was for 26 years. He thinks we're fine for 'hatching, matching and despatching', but unwise to bang on about religion, as that just upsets people, even if it's supposedly our core business. He finds me a bit embarrassing.

When I got the job at St Saviour's, in a working-class

district of London, his comment was, 'Maybe you should get a guard dog.' I don't want to reduce him to a stereotype just because he's a retired bank manager from Ipswich who reads the *Daily Mail*, but he relishes the stereotype, he plays up to it, so who can blame me?

While he went off to find the Glenfiddich, I went into the kitchen with Alex. Our plans were ruined. How could we have a waifs and strays Christmas lunch with him there? There was no way Martin was going to sit in our dining room and pull a cracker with a Somalian asylum seeker. The man was a social hand grenade.

I told her I didn't want to cancel the lunch, not on his account. All those poor people with nowhere to go. 'But he's my dad,' she said. Which was unarguable. He wanted to have Christmas lunch with his daughter. Her dad had needs too.

And then we heard him shout, 'HELP ME!' and there was Colin in our living room, in a filthy red Santa's hat, with his arm around the terrified Martin's neck.

'Call the pigs, quick!' said Colin. 'I found him half-inching your Glenfiddich!'

'That's my dad!' shouted Alex.

'Yeah, right,' said Colin. 'Like your own dad would break into your home and steal your booze.'

'Colin, let him go!' I shouted.

'You *know* this psychotic tramp?' said Martin. It was more of an accusation than a question.

'Colin, you've got to stop this, this is terrible!'

With great reluctance, he let go of Martin. I took

Colin off to the doorstep. What the hell was he thinking of, breaking into our home and attacking the first person he saw? He (sort of) apologized for the 'misunderstanding'. He'd popped in for a dump and found the old man there. Could he have his dump now?

'We're not a public toilet,' I said. 'Just go, all right, just go away.'

Drunk as he was, he made an innocent face and said he'd only been trying to protect my Glenfiddich, and could he come to Christmas lunch early? Say, a day early? He'd just been thrown out of The Three Greyhounds, so that was one less place he could go.

I couldn't believe what he was asking. He'd just attacked my father-in-law and now he wanted to move in with us.

I told him, as calmly as I could, that we weren't doing Christmas lunch after all, not now that Alex's dad was staying. But the Winter Shelter Charity were putting on a lunch at the church. I suggested he went to that.

'You turning me away, too?' asked Colin.

I said I was sorry, but I wasn't sorry, not after what he'd done. And he could tell I wasn't, of course he could, so he threw his Santa hat at me, which angered me even more.

And then he pushed me, so I pushed him back.

'I thought you were my friend!' he shouted.

And then he headbutted me in the face.

I lay on the ground. I felt sick. So many things I'd never done before. Never been the vicar of an inner-city church in London, never shared 20, maybe 30, fags with a childlike Mancunian alcoholy who I thought was my friend. Never been headbutted.

My eye hurt so badly I howled like an animal, and Alex rushed out to see what had happened. Colin had fled. Alex asked if she should call the police. Martin appeared behind her and said, 'Maybe you should get a guard dog.'

'Stay there,' said Alex. 'I'll get you an ice pack.' But I told her not to bother, I was fine, don't call the police, don't do anything.

'It's Christmas,' I said. What was I talking about? How did the birth of Jesus, the coming of the Light of the World, explain a headbutt?

All I wanted was to get away, get on with things, just get down to the old people's home and see Mr Summers. He was the next thing on my list. Nothing stopped for the list.

The trouble was, I was trying to get away from my own eye.

I staggered to my bike and put my right foot on the pedal. I went forward 6 inches then the bike and I fell over. After that, I went back into the vicarage and lay on our bed with the ice pack. The room got dark – half of it was dark already, since one eye was virtually closed. I prayed.

When I pray, it's like a silent chat. I think of the things I want to say to God and I feel him hearing my thoughts. Christmas can make people behave in extraordinary and desperate ways. A time of extremes, Lord. Extreme anguish, extreme buying, extreme anticipation.

It was so important, at this time of extremes, not to neglect the basic Christian principles, such as thinking of those less fortunate than ourselves. Colin, a man without the ties of family, work or home. Un-tied. Loose. Wild.

And then, when I stopped chatting to God, I chatted to myself. I resolved to tell nobody how I got the black eye: not the police, not the Archdeacon, not Nigel, nobody. I'd make a joke of it, a Christmas joke. I'd say, 'That's the last time I stand behind a reindeer,' or, 'There were three of them and they were all on camels.' Ho ho ho. Or I'd say I fell off my bike. I'd turn the consequence of my black eye into the cause.

The following night, I was in church for Midnight Mass. Alex stayed behind with her dad. It was the first time since I'd been ordained that Alex had missed Midnight Mass. Was this what my new life was going to be like? So many tensions and so little relief.

I watched Adoha mulling the wine. I'd never met a Nigerian woman with 4 daughters and a son and 19 grandchildren before. Suffolk's devoid of them. Already it was obvious that Adoha was as much a mainstay of St Saviour's as Colin, except that she loved cyclamen and begonias, not lager and fags. I could tell she was competitive with Colin, feeling that the church wasn't big enough for both of them. Each made it clear they weren't keen on my liking the other. I definitely mustn't like the other more than I liked *them*. So when she looked at my black eye and asked who did it, I went for the three men on camels.

'If I find the person who did it, they will have a piece of me,' she said. Adoha has a big maternal bosom, a real bosom of God, and the thought of her butting Colin in the face with it gave me some much-needed joy.

Then Nigel came up and gave me some terrible news: Mr Summers had just died. I'd never even met the poor man for long enough to give him the Last Rites. I failed him. As a priest. As a man.

I nipped out to the pub, just to be on my own, and I found myself, with two whiskies inside me, blaming the seasonal madness for my failure to see Mr Summers. And then Colin appeared, the embodiment of that madness. I hadn't seen him since the headbutt, and now, of course, I could only half-see him. I walked out of the pub and he followed me. He told me my eye looked terrible, which was meant to sound regretful but didn't.

He demanded my forgiveness, which outraged me. He told me I had to turn the other cheek, as Jesus had done. A priest was obliged to do that. I'd be 'court-martialled' if I didn't. So I did. I presented him with my left cheek and I screamed at him, 'Hit me again!' What was I doing, outside a pub, screaming at Colin? Alone in my bedroom, with an ice pack on my eye, I understood how needy and desperate he was. Why couldn't I understand that now?

Colin didn't know what to say. He was full of self-disgust and confusion. So he backed off. He literally went back into the pub. I'd vanquished the most vunerable soul in my care.

I was guilty about Mr Summers and now I was guilty

about Colin. I knew I had to forgive him sooner or later. I just didn't want it to be sooner.

I went back to St Saviour's and had a mulled wine chaser. For the first time since I'd arrived at St Saviour's, the church was packed. Six teenagers sat side by side, all wearing bowler hats. There was a young woman with purple hair and a baby in a sling, next to a man with a nose ring. When had I ever seen a nose ring in Suffolk, except on a pig? There were half a dozen Santas, maybe more, laughing and joshing with people wearing reindeer-style horns. The Christmas spirit had come to St Saviour's. There was joy all around. I was right and Nigel was wrong.

I went up to the pulpit and gazed out at them. This was going to be fun. I wasn't drunk or out of control, just filled with a warm and boozy benevolence that was absolutely right for the occasion.

I greeted everyone and told them they were a wonderful sight. 'Our opening carol is one of my personal favourites,' I said, even though it isn't, and we launched into 'While shepherds watched'. The volume was tremendous. Raucous but heartfelt. As we got near the end, a few people – some holding cans above their heads, like candles made of lager – sang:

> While shepherds washed
> Their socks by night
> While watching ITV,
> The angel of the Lord came down
> And switched to BBC.

But that was all right. That was fun. Ish.

At the start of the Eucharistic Prayer, I said, 'The Lord be with you,' and a man shouted, 'You too, mate.' That wasn't fun, but it was just one man, being stupid. I could easily ignore him. I carried on.

And then a man came in and shouted from the back, 'Taxi for Bob! Anyone called Bob?'

At that point, I stopped. I couldn't compete with that. I simply had to wait until Bob left the church. But the taxi driver had got it wrong. There was no Bob. One man got up and pretended to be Bob, but then he sat down. So I waited for the driver to leave the church which, after much laughter, he did.

I consecrated the bread and wine, facing the altar, my back to them all.

'Take, eat; this is my body, which is given for you; do this in remembrance of me.'

That's when they started singing 'Jerusalem'. It sounded like maybe half a dozen, soon joined by half a dozen more. All men. Making an ugly sound. Did they actually think it was a carol?

Communion's our participation in the blood and body of Christ. There's no compromise with that. It's sacred.

Did they think it was a pub? Or a football terrace? It's Christmas. A time of extremes, Lord. Was I meant to stand there and take it?

I turned round and shouted at them. My temper, my dignity, my authority – I lost them all. I shouted at my own congregation, in my own church. When I think of it now, I feel ashamed. But standing in front of that congregation, I felt my anger was righteous and just.

I told them 'Jerusalem' wasn't a carol but an indictment of the godless abomination that was the Industrial Revolution, sung in celebration of an England that never really existed. If they wanted a carol, I'd *give* them a carol.

It was an outburst, and it couldn't be stopped, I had a kind of crazed momentum. I could no more stop my outburst than Colin could stop his headbutt.

I sang, solo and fearless and shaking with anger, 'On the first day of Christmas my true love sent to me.' I wanted to explain that 'a partridge in a pear tree' symbolized Jesus, as sent to us by the one true God, my true love. But the West Ham boys came back with, 'Five gold rings.'

Well, OK, if they were going to get the words wrong, I'd show them how to do it. And suddenly I was off. Everything that was in my head – all the anger, frustration, exhaustion and guilt – came out. And it came out to the tune of 'Twelve Days of Christmas'.

I sang 'one black eye' instead of 'five gold rings'.

I sang, not caring that it didn't scan: 'And then before I could get to the old people's home Mr Summers died and I didn't even get to administer the Last Rites.'

And then for 'six geese a laying' I did a weird sort of Christmas jig and sang, 'Six mince pies for £3.50 from the luxury Waitrose range more expensive than the essential but why not.'

Silence in a church is usually beautiful; it's deeper than silence anywhere else, because it's not an absence of noise, it's a presence. A communion, if you will. The congregation communing with each other in silent contemplation of the Lord. But the silence that followed my outburst wasn't that. It was more like the silence that comes when you're in shock.

I shouldn't have done it. It was a bad thing to do. But I was provoked. I was under attack from godless piss-taking bastards. Nigel had been proved right, as had the Archdeacon. The Church of St Saviour's had become a sort of religious kebab house, invaded by drunk revellers on their way home. So what I did was bad, but not mad. It made a sort of Christmas sense, which meant that everyone would write it off, the same way they wrote off snogging the boss at the Christmas party. It was just something that happened. Then you both went home to your wives.

This wasn't what the new vicar was like. It was just what he was like at Christmas.

'Oi!' shouted a guy at me as I walked down Hackney Road at half-past one that night. I couldn't face it, I just couldn't, not after everything I'd been through. I thought of breaking into a run, but he had one of those big, fast athletic voices – that's how it sounded to me – so I just carried on walking naturally, pathetically trying to pretend he wasn't shouting at *me*.

'Oi, Vicar!' he shouted again, much louder, so I turned and looked at him. He was on the other side of the road, an enormous black guy, standing outside a club, looking very much like a bouncer. He ran across the road to me. I was so frightened, I couldn't move.

'Why you wear that collar then, Vicar?' My heart was pounding. 'God take you for walks?' Please, I thought, if you're going to headbutt me, choose the other eye.

Then he laughed, took a wad from his pocket and stuffed it into my hand.

'Give *that* to baby Jesus. Sixty quid. Merry Christmas!'

Then he hugged me, so hard he actually lifted me several inches off the ground, before dumping me down and running back to his club and waving at me from the doorway. It was wonderful. A moment of grace in a season of madness. It restored my faith – not in God but man. Specifically, Hackney man.

I told the story of this encounter at Christmas breakfast, just for the pleasure of Martin not being able to say, 'Maybe you should get a guard dog'. He contented himself with, 'Why anyone would choose to move from Suffolk to heroin alley is beyond me.'

Despite everything, or because of everything, I wanted to spend as much of Christmas Day at the church as I could. So I suggested to Martin and Alex that the three of us went to the Winter Shelter Lunch, which followed Morning Service. Alex was keen. To no one's surprise, Martin wasn't. He didn't want a Christmas lunch that was 'Amnesty International, *Guardian*-reading, low carbon and politically correct'. He wanted 'a family Christmas with my daughter and the Queen and spuds and turkey and cranberry thing'. Cranberry Thing was part of his family. But evidently I wasn't.

I said nothing. Then Alex, darling Alex, said she'd come with me, to support me, and it was up to him if he came or not. My wife chose me over her dad. I love her.

He said he'd stay at home and have fish fingers and watch *Wallace & Gromit*.

As it happened, there was nothing politically correct about the Winter Shelter Lunch. They'd cooked a traditional Christmas turkey, fit for the Queen and readers of the *Daily Mail*. What a wonderful thing to see in a church, a turkey on a long trestle table, for people who might otherwise go hungry.

And then, in a true display of Christmas spirit, he turned up.

'Hello, all,' he said. 'I'm Martin.'

He'd trudged from the vicarage to the church, on his own, swallowing his pride all the way, knowing he'd be having lunch with the needy and dispossessed, some of whom probably smelled, but also with his daughter and son-in-law, with whom he belonged. Alex asked him to carve.

'Must I?' he said. But he was delighted. He'd managed a bank for 26 years, he could certainly manage a turkey.

This was it. This was Christmas. It felt heroic that we'd got there. I heard a treble voice in my head, singing a carol I knew well but couldn't put a name to. It was inspirational. It told us all to be merry and look to a future that had just begun.

I looked at the doors of the church, to see if anyone

else was going to join us before we all sat down, and through the glass panels I saw a dirty Santa hat, a cigarette and a beard. It was Colin. He was loitering outside, not sure if he was welcome.

I went out and asked him if he was coming in for lunch. He asked if I'd forgiven him and I said, sort of jokingly and sort of not, that I hadn't, but it was lunchtime and it was Christmas, so was he coming in?

He said he wasn't worthy to set foot in the church. 'I'm worse than a prossie and a tax inspector'. I told him to shut up and come in, but he wouldn't, not till I said I'd forgiven him.

'Oh all right,' I said, 'I forgive you.' And he followed me into the church, shouting out that he'd been forgiven, and we'd all been forgiven.

'Well, that's good to hear,' said Martin.

'It's Christmas' excuses a multitude of sins, from headbutts to vicars shouting at their congregation. But it also excuses – or at least explains – a fluffy blanket of benevolence settling over everything and everyone, like snow, only warm.

Next year there'll be no Midnight Mass.

This morning, as I was shaving, I heard that carol again in my head, and I realized. It was Slade.


## 4th January

'For All The Saints' – words by William W. How, music by Vaughan Williams. I've always loved the way the Lord morphs from rock to fortress to might to captain to one true light.

> Thou wast their rock, their fortress, and their might;
> Thou Lord, their captain in the well-fought fight;
> Thou in the darkness drear, their one true light.
> Alleluia, Alleluia!

We sang it this morning, despite Nigel protesting we should only sing it on All Saints' Day. The man's a world-class pedant. Though being a pedant he'd probably say he's not a pedant exactly, since that means someone who's excessively concerned with minor details, when he's just *appropriately* concerned.

At the service I thanked the whole congregation for making Alex and me so welcome in our new parish, and invited them all for a glass of something this evening at the vicarage. The whole congregation was 18 people, if you include me, which I do, as during my sermon I had the unmistakeable feeling I was talking to myself.

All the regulars were there, though, sitting in their usual places. If nothing else, I can always look forward to talking to them afterwards. Adoha; Colin; Ellie, the head teacher of the C of E school. My head teacher, as I think of her. Ellie's a smart woman with a very clear gaze. Almost frighteningly clear. Mid-brown hair, thirties, double-breasted fawn mac. Sometimes, head teachers of C of E schools are dowdy. Not this one.

## 5th January

I woke up with the mother, the Father, the Son *and* the Holy Ghost of all hangovers. Strangely, of the 18 people in the congregation I'd invited back for drinks, 40 turned up.

The party was obviously a great success, judging by the number of fag ends and crushed cans on the bird table in our kitchen. We'd never had a bird table in our kitchen before. Alex told me this morning that it was a 'gift' from Colin. He'd nicked it from next door's garden. I mentally added 'nicks bird tables' to the list of Colin's issues. When the doorbell rang at breakfast, I promised Alex it wasn't him. He turns up unexpectedly so often that she expects him now. Sure enough, it was him. Frantic. There was a 'scandal' at the church and we had to get there quick.

When we got near St Saviour's, some workmen on scaffolding on the building next door started shouting at me. 'Oi, Vicar, where's your dress?'

This wasn't like the bouncer shouting at me after Midnight Mass. For a start, there were three of them.

It took me back to the Westleton Primary playground, with Mark Morgan and his two henchmen. I always knew the henchmen wouldn't hit me, but I knew Mark Morgan would. And he did. He told me I had 'girl's eyes'.

'If someone strikes you on the right cheek, turn to him the other also.' That's what I did with the men on the scaffold. By contrast, Colin offered to 'do' them. Colin, as I know too well, is more of a striker than a turner.

In the church there were shards everywhere and a hole in the stained-glass window above the apse. Nigel treated us to a mercifully brief but still far too long lecture on the influence of Burne-Jones on the design of the window, which was broken and therefore didn't really have a design any more. Colin went very CSI, detecting some bits of broken brown glass, which weren't stained glass at all – they were glass from a bottle. He concluded that a beer bottle had been thrown through the window.

He offered to 'get to the bottom of it'. I pictured him in full eye-for-an-eye striker mode, tracking down the guilty man and smashing all his windows with a beer bottle. So I fudged it. I told Colin I'd be grateful for any 'help'. The thing about him is, he does want to help. The church means a lot to him. It's his rock and his refuge. Yes, he's aggressive. Yes, he's done time. But the man has a soul. It just needs watering and fertilizing. And maybe, just to be safe, it needs a chicken-wire fence put round it, to protect him from predators and, of course, to protect predators from him.

I lead the three of us in Morning Prayer, Colin, Nigel and me. Toning down my volume dial so as not to disturb my hangover.

Roland Wise entered my thoughts, which annoyed me. I was trying to tune into God's will and there was Roland. It was probably the hangover, or the presence of bits of beer bottle. The Reverend Roland Wise, aka

TV and Radio's Reverend Roland Wise. I thought of Roland holding court in The Bat & Ball in Cuddesdon. We'd only been at theological college a month and already he was known as Roland Wise Superstar.

His theme that night was bus drivers. The Bishop of Peterborough, Donald Fairless, had been our guest lecturer. He was a hopeless sort of man, completely bald, so with our infantile student wit, we'd renamed him Donald Hairless. Desperate to be 'modern', Hairless had told us that the college was preparing us to be 'bus drivers for the Lord'. The church was the bus, the Gospel was the engine, the congregation were the passengers. In The Bat & Ball, Roland was having a lovely time mocking the Hairless metaphor. What did it say on the front of this bus? Heaven? Were we supposed to drive to Heaven and back, several times a day? Did the passengers get off or did they just get on?

Fifteen years on, Roland himself is addicted to cack-handed metaphors. Last time I heard him on the radio, he was banging on about the way we're all 'chained to the radiator of life'.

He was right, though, the bus driver metaphor doesn't work. Here I am, the driver of St Saviour's. Someone's broken a window. The Archdeacon will now tell me I have to raise the funds to restore it. Whereas the owner of the bus company never tells the driver he's got to raise the money to fix the broken seat on the number 149.

Another thing about The Bat & Ball. Roland kept getting the drinks in and shouting, 'Put it on my tab, will you, Seamus!' What kind of theological student has a tab in a pub? A student who's going to end up as the Archbishop of Canterbury. Roland was (and is) unstoppable. I just want to make a success of St Saviour's. That will do me.

Though I'd quite like, just once, to be on 'Thought for the Day'.

## 6th January

Epiphany.

Matthew just says that 'wise men' came from the East. He doesn't give names or even say how many there were. We deduce that from the number of gifts. Three wise men, three gifts. Gold, frankincense, myrrh. They're not remembered for their pilgrimage, which was remarkable and brave, but for their gifts.

Sometimes I find that a bit depressing. 'You are what you give' is a bit like 'You are what you buy'. There aren't many people in my parish who could afford to take gold as a gift, though a lot of them would do it anyway. They'd just borrow the money at extortionate rates.

## 7th January

Lunch at The Monarch.

Gemma the barmaid and her boyfriend Vincent want to get married in St Saviour's. And they want to do it on

12 February, the same date her parents got married. Gemma knows her dad, who died a few years ago, will be 'looking down'. She hoped I'd go, 'Aaah!' and possibly, 'Bless!' But I don't see Heaven like that. In fact, I don't *see* Heaven at all – it seems to me to be a state in which we're united with God's mercy and eternal love, not a fluffy cloud on which we have an endless tea party and 'look down' on the living.

I didn't say that to Gemma, though.

I want people to like me, Lord. If I'm to do your work, I *need* them to like me. Isn't that right? So sometimes I have to pretend to like them, in order that they like me.

Gemma told me that before he died her dad gave her a beautiful book called *The Prophet* by someone Gibran. Had I heard of it? I told her I had. For some reason, everyone thinks that no one's heard of *The Prophet*, whereas it's been scientifically proven that everyone alive has heard of *The Prophet* by someone Gibran. There are babies being born as we speak who've heard of the frigging *Prophet*.

Gemma's going to do a reading at her wedding. 'Beauty is eternity gazing at itself in a mirror. But you are eternity and you are the mirror.' If that's the bit she wants to read, she can do it outside.

She can seriously stand outside my church and read it to those bastards on the scaffold. That kind of stuff is not WORSHIP. It doesn't teach us to love God or each other. It's not doctrinal or theological. It's not the fruit of hard-won wisdom. That kind of stuff is . . . 'Wow!' That's all it is. It's just a big 'Wow!'

I understand. I mean, we've all smoked the odd bit of dope. We've all smoked a spliff and gazed at the stars over Glastonbury, as REM take their place on the Pyramid Stage at midnight. We've all done that and gone 'Wow!' But that's just a physical reaction. It's not reflective or humble or connected to the love of God. 'Wow!' should never be confused with 'Amen'.

There was more. Gemma asked if I'd heard of Robbie Williams, as the groom wanted to sing 'Angels'. Of course I've heard of him, he's like Kahlil Gibran, only he was in Take That. I didn't say that. Nor did I say what I really felt, that this was a wedding service not a talent show. I couldn't recommend that instead of 'Angels', Vince should sing 'For All The Saints', with music by Robbie Williams' immortal ancestor, Vaughan.

I smiled and was kind and then I was saved by the bell, because my mobile rang and it was the Archdeacon, calling me away. He'd tracked me down. Did I want to meet him in his cab, which was waiting outside? The answer was no but I said yes. This is what he does to me, he calls me out of the blue and then drives me round London in a cab, like a parcel.

He told me (as I predicted) that I'd have to raise some funds as there was nothing in the diocese budget for replacing stained-glass windows. Then (as I didn't predict) he asked me for 'the numbers'. How many in my congregation last Sunday? I told him the Church wasn't just about keeping score. He agreed but asked me to guess. I cracked and said 60, which he thought meant 20.

I denied there were as few as 20, which he thought meant 22.

How do you measure success in a church? St Saviour's will never be Holy Trinity, Brompton. It's not fashionable or exciting or in a beautiful part of London. It doesn't appeal to the rich. Does that mean St Saviour's is less 'successful' than HTB, even though we're as present and engaged with our community as they are with theirs? Is it only, and always, about numbers? Or is it about spiritual succour, which can never be measured?

No. Let's face it, it's about numbers. Especially when the Archdeacon's talking numbers in the back of a cab. (Does he ever use a bus? I think not. He's just not a bus person.)

Then he changed the subject. That's another of his features. He's got a devilish knack of changing the subject when you least expect it, though somehow he makes it very hard for *you* to change the subject. It's as if all the subjects belong to him and he can pick whichever he wants. He asked if I was 'still managing to resist Adoha'. Apparently, she's not just known for loving flowers. She's a famous 'cassock-chaser', notorious for looking as if she's having an orgasm during the service. I've been warned. (On no account must we ever sing 'O Come All Ye Faithful'.)

Our cab meeting was over, so he ordered me out. He asked the driver to stop, right there, where we were. In the middle of nowhere. No. Not even the middle. It looked more like the edge of nowhere.

Perphaps it's no more than I deserve. I must make St Saviour's a success.


## 10th January

I woke up buzzing with fund-raising ideas.

The bring-and-buy presents sale was a huge success when I was at St Peter's, Gromford. As was the skills auction.

I got in touch with the Archdeacon and arranged to see him on the 20th to give him my ideas.

'How very pro-active of you,' he said. I think he was pleased. It's hard to tell, as he can make 'good morning' sound sarcastic.

I wish he could have been in church today to see the numbers. It was a very gratifying sight. The word, it seemed, was out. St Saviour's had a new priest and he was worth coming to see.

I was about to get into the Prayer of Preparation when they all flocked in. Not the usual flock, who'd flocked in already (all 22 of them, or possibly 18). No, this was a whole new herd. They were families, though, people with children – this wasn't a repeat of Midnight Mass. Half a dozen families, all entering slightly late, much to Nigel's irritation. I've never seen a man har-rumph like that. I mean it really did look like he was saying, 'Harrumph.'

The Yam family was the first to arrive. Patrick Yam, our local MP, with his scowling wife and his sulking little boy. He walked all the way down the aisle, as if he owned the place, then plonked himself in the front pew, which I suppose reminded him of the front bench. How come some people always draw attention to themselves? I'm the vicar, it's my church. Why don't *I* always draw attention to myself?

Yam's a tall man in his mid-forties. A shiny sort of bloke, who was probably a public school prefect. I can imagine the click of his heels as he walked down the corridor, then put you in detention for some bogus offence like 'having a nose that doesn't accord with school regulations'. His expression is part chummy and part nasty, and his smile is like a warm sneer.

His little boy asked – far too loudly – what they were doing in a church, as it wasn't Christmas. For that, Patrick confiscated his Game Boy. Quite right, too. The church is no place for high-tech gadgets. Unfortunately, a minute later, Patrick's mobile went off. In an ostentatiously 'holy' way, he switched it off without answering it, then looked at it as if it had sinned.

'Let's pray quietly for a moment,' I said, which cued a lot of movement from the man whose pals probably call him the Yamster. He fell to his knees, as if he'd been shot, then – realizing genuflection wasn't the thing – he sprang to his feet and found he was the only man standing. Finally, with all eyes on him now, he sat down calmly. I'm surprised he didn't get a round of applause.

No matter. I wasn't going to ask him to leave. After all, the theme of my sermon was that every one of us is acceptable to God, and therefore to each other. To reject another person is to reject Christ.

In fact, I addressed most of my sermon to Yam and his family, to reassure them they were welcome, and also to avoid looking at Adoha, just in case there were visible signs that she was having an orgasm. When I finished, I did hear a little 'mmm' from the back. Was that orgasm or agreement? Maybe it was both.

She came up to me afterwards and said how much she loved my words. And my voice. And my eyes. Apparently, my eyes make her tingle. But lots of things make you tingle, don't they? Alex and I once swam off the Suffolk coast on New Year's Day. That made us tingle, but it wasn't sexy.

I thought Ellie my head teacher would be impressed by the numbers, which she was. She was very impressed, with reason, as it seems she was responsible. It was 'the sniff of a good Ofsted report' that made Patrick and the rest flock to St Saviour's. Rumour is, the school will be judged 'good with elements of outstanding'. Our new worshippers, said Steve Warwick (who's got kids there, so he should know), were 'school whores', queuing up to prove they were Christians so Ellie would take their kids.

I'd thought, wrongly, that they were there because of me, the new vicar in town. 'Don't take disappointments personally,' as my dad always says. As if there's any other way of taking disappointment.

Ellie said there was a meeting next week for prospective parents. Every year it's the same, apparently. There's always a raffle and Ellie can bank on the parents outbidding each other ostentatiously, in the hope of getting their kids a place. She told me this like it was good news and all a bit of a joke. As if they were welcome to use their money to buy a place at a C of E school.

Did she think I was going to stand there and say nothing? I mean, I'd very much like her to like me. But just because she's a youngish, reasonably attractive woman doesn't mean I'm going to suck up to her. That's the curse of being an Anglican vicar: no one thinks you have real convictions, which you're going to express, with force. They think that's the province of evangelicals. And, of course, Dawkins and the other neo-atheists, who are themselves evangelical.

So, I told her giving places to the highest bidders was no way to run a C of E school. Places should go to the children of believers. She gave me one of her ferociously intelligent extra-withering looks and asked me who in my congregation actually believed in God.

With perfect timing, Patrick Yam bowled up, oozing fake bonhomie. Thick-skinned as a crocodile, he was entirely unfazed when Ellie introduced him as the man who'd 'closed our local swimming pool'. He told me he'd loved my service. He said, 'We must do this again some time,' as if he and I had just played squash. Ellie was much amused.

I couldn't help noticing that all the school whores were giving generously to our Window Restoration Fund, stuffing Nigel's collection box with fivers and tenners. They were giving that money in bad faith. But the money was good.

Maybe I can turn these school whores into believers. Today, they came to the right place for the wrong reason. Surely over time they can come to the right place for the right reason?

Hypocritical congregants are better than no congregants at all. Isn't that right, Lord?

## 16th January

It's 1.09 a.m. and I'm still up. Still worrying about fundraising and getting the Archdeacon off my back.

In the study I can hear all the London street sounds. So different from the night sounds of Gromford, Suffolk, as heard from my old vicarage. Fewer owls. More barking dogs. Night buses. (In Suffolk, we barely had day buses.) A sort of plip-plap noise which, by looking through the curtains, I've worked out is the door of Tony's Kebabs, opening and closing.

There's the odd ambulance but no gunfire, which is nice.

Some giggling and screaming teenage girls who've probably not spent the last few hours doing their homework.

Alex is next door in our bedroom, sleeping. Alex, I don't know if you'll ever read this, but I love you. It's not just because I've been drinking. It's because of your beauty, your values, your strength, your integrity. You will never understand what you do for me. Especially when we're apart. I'm always thinking, what would Alex do? Or I'm wishing, too late, that I'd done what you'd have done if you'd been me. Which you are. We're one flesh.

You're my rock.

I might pop out now and get a Tony's Kebab. The night is cold and the journey, though short, is paved with dogshit. But that's what I'm going to do.

## 17th January

Out of the blue, a couple called Tessa and Paul Connor sent Alex and me a crate of wine to thank us for our work in the community. It's Pinot Noir from Martinborough, New Zealand. Alex says it must have set them back over a hundred pounds, so they want something.

I say they don't. People don't always want something. Some people give away millions of pounds without wanting something.

Who's right? The worldly wise lawyer or the priest who has faith in the goodness of Tessa and Paul? I sent them a thank-you note.

## 18th January

The school entry guidelines clearly state that parents must be 'regular and committed worshippers'. I woke at 6 with those words on my mind, fretting about the school whores trying to exploit my church.

I dozed and fretted till the radio alarm came on. 'Thought for the Day' was on the theme of hypocrisy, which was perfect.

Jesus, the speaker said, points out to his disciples that hypocrisy is futile, because the hypocrite knows what he really thinks. And the Lord knows it, too.

That inspired me to get my Bible out of the bedside drawer. Alex says keeping a Bible there makes our bedroom like a motel in Nebraska, but I pointed out that also in the drawer is *Under the Ivy: The Life and Music of Kate Bush*, which the Gideons definitely don't distribute.

The speaker was quoting a passage from Luke 12:2:

There is nothing concealed that will not be disclosed, or hidden that will not be made known. What you have said in the dark will be heard in the daylight, and what you have whispered in the ear in the inner rooms will be proclaimed from the roofs.

I wanted to shout that out of my window at any passing school whores. It was one of those rare 'Thought for the Day's that truly spoke to me. Shame the speaker was TV and Radio's Reverend Roland Wise.

'You jammy bastard!' I shouted as James Naughtie said his name. 'Why are you always on "Thought for the Day" and I'm never on it?'

At least no one can accuse me of being a hypocrite.

My blood was up. I went to work and stormed into the vestry, demanding Nigel's help in weeding out the hypocrites. Nigel was up for it, relishing the chance to disapprove of other human beings, so we role-played. He was a prospective parent and I was the one asking the religious knowledge questions.

I can't remember all of it, but I do remember asking him who wrote the Epistle of Philemon and where. 'Saint Paul, in prison,' he said, which was right.

Then I asked who the Gospel of St Luke was addressed to. 'My dear Theophilus,' he said. Right again. Then I asked, 'Where today would you find—' and he said, 'In modern day Iraq.' I hadn't even got to the end of the question and he'd got the answer right.

Whenever I get infuriated with Nigel's need to be right, I remind myself that his previous job was for a quango called Transport Solutions, of which we all know there are none. He wasted those years being totally wrong. Definitely. For sure.

The upshot of our role-play was, Nigel's definitely got an imaginary place at the school for his imaginary kid. And I'm even hotter for hypocrites' blood. Bring it on.


## 19th January

The first people I met at the prospective parents' meeting were Tessa and Paul Connor. They loved the school and were so keen to get their daughter in. Had I received their crate of wine? Damn. Alex the worldly wise lawyer was right.

I told them I'd sent them a thank-you note, which I now wanted back. They smiled, not really listening, which is another curse of my calling. People assume you're about to say something churchy and bland, which they don't actually need to hear, because it's just verbal muzak.

Everyone and his pushy wife and 'gifted' children were there, all of them hosing me down with smarm. Did I know they'd bought all the green raffle tickets? Just to help out the school? The Yamster, desperate to get his delinquent into Ellie's 'outstanding' school, actually offered to sign a cheque for our entire window restoration, till I told him it would cost 30 grand and his warm sneer cooled.

Alex, meanwhile, was being felt up by a sweaty-palmed chiropractor, which isn't in her contract. Sometimes she finds it burdensome to be a vicar's wife. People have (wrong) expectations of what a vicar's wife should be and do, whereas, as she has often remarked, no one has any expectations of a 'lawyer's husband'.

Tonight she told me she hates it when I wear my collar in bed. It's like I've got no cock. Which is strange, because a lot of people think the opposite. They only have to see a collar to think of sexual crimes.

One day soon, I just know it, those three men on that scaffolding rig – the three unwise men from the East – are going to shout that I'm a paedophile. Dog-collar equals priest equals paedophile.

# 20th January

As soon as the door of the cab was slammed, I pitched the Archdeacon my funding ideas. The bring-and-buy presents sale was perfect for Jan and Feb, with all those unwanted Christmas presents. Here was a chance to donate them to a terrific cause. And the skills auction. We couldn't go wrong!

He was deadly. No one wanted a bring-and-buy sale. No one wanted to pay to have Nigel and his skills for the afternoon. They'd sooner pay *not* to have Nigel and his skills for the afternoon. My ideas might have worked in Suffolk (he pronounced it 'Sussex') but they wouldn't work here. I had an inner-city church with inner-city problems, which needed an inner-city solution.

To show me what inner city meant, he kicked me out the cab on the Old Street roundabout, which has about nine exits, on any of which you can be killed from five directions. It was like being in a video game.

Does the Archdeacon actually have any belief in my abilities? I'm not saying he fucking hates me like Lisa fucking hates Martine. I'm actually pretty sure he fucking quite likes me. But does he respect me? Probably not I think, more than anything, he likes toying with me.

On the other hand, he is dynamic. He's keen to get results. If the Church of England had more people like him, we'd all be better off. He may toy with me, but it's only to provoke me into being more like him.

I must assert myself more. Alex asserts herself. When I go to her office, I can see the respect radiating from her colleagues and her boss.

## 22nd January

I met Patrick Yam in church this morning. He and I shared a pew. It was the second time I'd seen him in St Saviour's and he still seemed out of place. He kept looking round, like he was wondering where the bar was.

To put me at my ease, he asked me, man to man, what I thought of Ellie. It was as if we were in the changing room after our imaginary squash game, within sniffing distance of each other's jockstraps.

'She could stick me in detention any time!' said Patrick. I said nothing. But he wouldn't let it lie, oh no. He's good at not letting it lie.

'Bet you get women after you the whole time, don't you? Bit of authority.' He gestured to my dog-collar. 'Girls love it.' I said nothing again, only louder.

Then – bam! – Patrick Yam, MP, got down to some serious horse-trading. He'd been speaking to his mate Sir Jeremy from the Foundation. (Lunardi? Lombardi?) Sir Jeremy was passionate about Burne-Jones-style windows. He liked all the Pre-Raphelite boys who looked like girls. Patrick was sure Sir Jeremy and his Foundation would fund the restoration. Completely. All 30 grand.

In return, all I had to do – I really liked that 'all' – was put in a good word with Ellie for his little boy Luke. He said Luke had 'a lovely nature at heart', which of course made him sound like the sulking, Game Boy-playing little tit I knew him to be. If I made sure his Luke got a place at the school, he'd make sure we got our window.

I pointed out, not unkindly, but not kindly either, that it would help me write a good referral for Luke if Patrick actually came to church like a regular and committed worshipper. Patrick had no problem with that. He knew the deal. 'On your knees and avoid the fees!' His sneer had never looked warmer.

So. We had a deal. Patrick and me. Was it wrong to make that deal? 'For the love of money is the root of all kinds of evil.' I wasn't driven by love of money though, Lord. I didn't make the deal because I love money. It's money for the church. To restore an artistic creation dedicated to your greater glory.

As I walked into church to help prepare the meal for the homeless (tonight we finally introduced a vegetarian option) the scaffold bully boys had another go. One of them shouted that he had something to confess, then turned round, took down his pants and 'confessed' his bum. He thought I was too kind and nice and tolerant and meek to object.

He was right. I was too meek. Outwardly. But inwardly I was seething. I was furious that he spoke to me with such contempt, though I hid that from him. 'There is nothing concealed that will not be disclosed, or hidden that will not be made known.'

## 23rd January

School day.

I went in determined to make Ellie like me. I know she likes Alex and Alex likes her – they were gabbing away at the parents' night. Women's talk, I suppose.

I decided to talk women's talk with Ellie. There's no reason I can't do that, just because I'm a man and/or a priest. What is women's talk? Emotions? Clothes?

I steamed into her office, full of the joys of spring, even though it's winter. Ellie was wearing a pink cardigan that matched her lipstick. A pink cardigan with big buttons and a sort of ribbing thing down the front. She looked very nice, so I went for it. I talked about her clothes. I told her the cardigan looked great and was it Boden? No, she said. That was it. Just a crisp no.

Straight to business, she asked what I wanted. I said I was thinking of giving Patrick's son Luke a good reference, given that the boy would benefit enormously from an education at her school.

Ellie gave me a big smile, withering in the Archdeacon style, but more attractive. Quite knowing and intuitive, as if she understood what I'd been through, which she did. She's really very bright. She knew Patrick had offered me money and it wasn't any use my saying the money wasn't for me, it was for the window, since basically she thinks Patrick's a despicable hypocrite with a horrible son. It was hard to argue with her about that.

All (30 grand) seemed lost. But no. She said she'd find a place in the school for Luke if I found her sister a half-term slot for her wedding date. Saturday, 12 February. Noon. Could I do it?

I wasn't going to say I'd already given that slot to Gemma, or add that the date really mattered to her because it was the same date her parents had got married, which would make her dad very, very happy, even though he's dead.

I just said yes. Ellie and I had a deal, just like Patrick and I have a deal. There seem to be a lot of deals in the life of a London priest. Up the road, in the Square Mile, City boys are making deals all the time. I'm God, they're Mammon. That's the theory. It hasn't quite worked out.

This evening in our kitchen I put the deal to the committee, i.e., Alex and Nigel, who we'd invited round for a drink, out of kindness, hoping it wouldn't lead to anything more. I laid out the advantages.

1. Yam gets his delinquent son into a good school.
2. Ellie's sister gets married at half term, which makes everything easier for Ellie.
3. I get the Archdeacon off my back.
4. Everybody wins.

'Everybody wins apart from Gemma and Vincent,' said Alex, who's trained to fight for justice for underdogs *and* pick holes in arguments.

I know that he who is slow to anger is better than the mighty. I also know that he who rules his spirit is better than he who captures a city. But sometimes the

45

spirit rules you. That's what happened in the kitchen this evening.

I told Alex she didn't understand what my working life was like. All day long, people wanted things from me. Fine. That's my vocation. But who did I have to help me? Just a bunch of volunteers who couldn't wipe their own arses. I had to wipe Colin's arse, I had to wipe Adoha's arse, I sometimes had to wipe Nigel's arse.

I found myself going on and on about arses. Why? Maybe it was brought on by seeing that scaffolder's bum.

I stormed out of my own kitchen, saying I was off to the pub to tell Gemma and Vincent they'd have to move their wedding date, which was a small sin for a greater good.

## 24th January

I'm sorry, Lord, I shouldn't have talked about arses like that. It was a grotesque succession of images. I'm just finding everything a bit difficult. 'On your knees, avoid the fees!' How did I get into this situation? I'm supposed to walk with the broken, aren't I? Not horse trade with an admittedly rather pretty head teacher, that toxic MP and Gemma the barmaid, who worships the naff. And why do you want me to be a fundraiser the whole time? Why've you given me this huge, crumbling building and now this window to deal with? It's such a burden. Let's face it – it's not a terribly good window, is it?

Speak to me, Lord. Your servant listens.

## 25th January

I studied the history of our church. It's extraordinary.

There's been a church on this site since 1174. Always at the heart of the community. As the Spanish Armada was coming up the Channel, St Saviour's was giving out bread and coal to the poor.

The starkness and beauty of that. The sense of mission and ministry. From bread and coal to the poor, to trading a school place for cash, even if the cash is to restore a broken window. That can't be right can it, Lord?

I'll tell Patrick Yam we don't have a deal. Which means I won't have a deal with Ellie.

Alex was going to do good in the world by being a lawyer who did legal-aid work. Meanwhile, I would do good by being ordained. That was our deal, Lord. Mine and Alex's. That's the important deal in my life.

Nat Jones, our pal from uni, was the first guy I knew who went on about deals. Tuscany, summer 1998. We were only two years out of Bristol, but already Nat was knee-deep in money, high on the fact that he was spending all day with deal-makers. Nat said I'd love it. Financial PR. I should think about it. He'd help me.

Nat was offering to help me get a job in his financial PR firm. To this day, I don't know why. Because we both had history degrees (only mine was better)? Because we'd shared a flat in our final year at Bristol? Because we both liked Kate Bush? Probably it was because I hadn't yet found my vocation. Basically, I was available.

Nevertheless, I was offended that Nat thought I should hang out with deal-makers. That was the last thing I wanted to do with my life. So I told him I'd think about it. I couldn't tell him I hated the idea, not when the trip to Tuscany was his wedding present to Alex and me. Why didn't he just buy towels from John Lewis like everyone else?

I saw his name only last week in the *Daily Telegraph*'s 'Top 100 Great British Entrepreneurs'. Chairman of Waddington PR. Up 10 places from last year to number 24. Nat won't like that. Only 10 places. That'll really piss him off. I remember what he was like when I beat him at croquet.

Nat Jones. As Alex once said, even his *name* is fast-moving and dynamic. (Unlike, say, 'Adam Smallbone'.) I bet he's a mate of Roland Wise.

I don't have a deal with *you*, Lord, because a deal implies rights and obligations on both sides and I have no rights where you're concerned. What I give is given freely and infinitely with no obligations on your part. No contracts. No sub-clauses. No percentages on the back end. Sorry, Nat.


## 26th January

Why's it called Mulberry House? I haven't seen a mulberry tree. Probably they knocked it down when they built Mulberry House.

I met a lovely woman there today called Joan. She's taken over Mr Summers' room. She grew up in Whitechapel. At the start of the war, her mother refused to let her and her sister be evacuated. She wanted her family to live or die together.

In October 1940, there was an air-raid warning, so the family took refuge in St Mary's Whitechapel, an underground station that no longer exists. Joan's little sister Barbara didn't want to go because she couldn't find her teddy bear Ted. Joan held Barbara for hours because Barbara wouldn't stop crying. When the all-clear sounded, they came out the shelter and found their house was rubble. But Joan found Ted, which made Barbara very happy, even though Ted was charred all over. Barbara died last year from multiple sclerosis but Joan still has Ted. She showed me.

Joan was very gorgeous when she was young and could have been a film star. I know this cos she told me. Next time I visit, she'll show me a photo. She'll get her daughter to bring one.

She said she doesn't want to die, she feels she has a lot to live for.

When I was leaving, she took my hand and said how much she'd enjoyed my visit and how much she looked forward to seeing me again. I said, likewise.

As I walked out of the room she called after me and said, 'You're a nice man, Alan.' Alan must be her husband, who died 6 months ago. That's why she called me that, because she's so used to saying his name. Plus, I'm sure she used to tell him he was a nice man. Doesn't matter what she calls me. I made her feel better, whoever I am.

I cycled back to the vicarage and found Mick outside. He's a slightly alarming black crackhead who takes a bit of getting used to, though I'm trying as hard as I can. He looks like a child's drawing of a man, done in a hurry. Wonky teeth with a gap in them. Big staring eyes. His movements are cartoonish, too. But that's probably the crack.

Mick doesn't turn up as much as Colin but he still turns up at least once a week, always with a hard luck story. Today he wanted money to get to his granny's funeral. I seem to remember that story from before, but every man is entitled to have two grannies. It was such an obvious lie that I couldn't believe he was lying. I mean, I couldn't believe he'd insult my intelligence with such a cliché.

Anything But Cash. That's the rule. Bus tickets, yes, food, yes, knitwear, yes, money, no. So I offered to drive him to the funeral but he didn't want to put me to any trouble.

## 27th January

This morning my cassock felt like the full armour of God, which doesn't happen every day. But today I was off to meet Patrick Yam in The Monarch. I needed to feel fully armed against the schemes of the devil.

I thought he'd be more at home in the pub than

St Saviour's, but he still didn't look right. He's simply not an East End-pub man. Patrick's more of a Chelsea-Notting-Hill-Kensington kind of a guy. He needs to be in a pub where all the women are rich and speak Russian.

I told him straight that I wasn't prepared to offer or trade a school place for cash.

In return I got scorn. Scorn for the school. Scorn for the rumours that Ofsted would call it 'good, with elements of outstanding', when they'd more likely say it was 'poor, with elements of shit'. He bet Ellie had started those Ofsted rumours herself. Only he didn't call her Ellie. He called her 'that posh totty you've got a rod in your cassock for'. The warmth was gone. He was all sneer. Sneer and smear.

Maybe he's right, though. Maybe Ellie did start those rumours. She's clever and ambitious. But is she that ruthless? I hope not.

Yam threatened to start some rumours of his own, such as that the school was an educational car crash. We'd soon see whose rumours won. Then he asked me what I'd like to drink, which surprised me. I said a pint of bitter. He said, in that case, I should go to the bar and buy one.

He was angry, but what made him *very* angry was all the time he'd wasted coming to our services. I pointed out that he'd only come once, which didn't placate him. Hell hath no fury like a hypocrite scorned.

In a gentle way, suspecting the answer, I asked the angry slimeball if there was any chance Sir Jeremy from the Foundation would still send the cheque for the window.

He thought about it for less than two seconds, said no and stormed out of the pub, disappearing from my life. Possibly for ever. Hopefully for ever.

Then Gemma appeared, like some angel, and showed me the collection box she'd started for our Window Restoration Fund. It already had 90 quid in it. Before my very eyes, she made it 100.

Then she said that after her wedding we should talk. She'd like me to help her get her little girl a place in Ellie's school.

There we are then. The struggle continues. But I mustn't feel sorry for myself, Lord. I have to be strong.

## 28th January

Thomas Aquinas' Feast Day. Great theologian, but a very fat man.

## 1st February

1.32 a.m. Elated. Just finished my sermon. Took me four fags but I did it. It's all in there. The futility of hypocrisy, since you know and the Lord knows what you've done. (I'm as free as Roland Wise to quote that passage from Luke.)

That idea – we're all transparent in the eyes of the Lord – led me on to think about the window. Typed 'DONNE

HERBERT RELIGIOUS POEM WINDOW' into Google in the hope of finding something relevant.

And there it was. This poem by George Herbert.

'The Windows' by George Herbert (1593–1633)

Lord, how can man preach thy eternal word?
He is a brittle crazy glass:
Yet in thy temple thou dost him afford
This glorious and transcendent place,
To be a window, through thy grace.

But when thou dost anneal in glass thy story,
Making thy life to shine within
The holy preachers, then the light and glory
More reverend grows, and more doth win;
Which else shows waterish, bleak, and thin.

Doctrine and life, colours and light, in one
When they combine and mingle, bring
A strong regard and awe: but speech alone
Doth vanish like a flaring thing,
And in the ear, not conscience, ring.

The light of Christ in us, the light that shines through the stained-glass window of the holy preachers – when it hasn't been smashed by blokes – that light radiates into people's lives and leads them to God's grace and mercy, more than a preacher's words ever can. In a way, that means the stained-glass windows are more important to our church than I am.

Isn't it wonderful? And wouldn't it be wonderful if

that poem could be used to raise funds for the window restoration? I could print 30,000 copies off and sell them for a quid each.

No. That's not going to work, is it? That's the kind of thought that sounds great at two in the morning but crap at breakfast.

Must get some sleep. I'm delivering the sermon in less than 10 hours. Nigel always says I write them at the last minute. Just because he always has to be right doesn't mean that sometimes he isn't, in fact, right.


## 2nd February

My sermon yesterday was marvellous. Adoha said so.

There were 17 in the congregation. One down on last week.

I felt angry and useless as I set off for work this morning. The scent of dogshit, smack, garbage and unemployment was in the air. Can you smell unemployment? I really think you can. People on the street, giving off the odour of uselessness and despair.

Alex and I had just had a row. She said I was too preoccupied with my job. I said it wasn't a job, it was a vocation, and she told me not to be so pompous. Which was fair enough, because this morning my vocation absolutely felt like a job.

Then it happened, as I knew it would. The paedophile shout.

'Oi, Dibley! You off to bum a choirboy?'

St Paul believed he'd become a fool in the eyes of the world. He was mocked and misunderstood, but because of his foolishness, the Corinthians had acquired the wisdom that comes with faith.

'We are fools for the sake of Christ,' said Paul. Holy fools. 'When reviled, we bless. When persecuted, we endure. When slandered, we speak kindly.' Yeah, right.

Apart from anything else, did those scaffolding bastards not know Dibley couldn't bum a choirboy, because Dibley was a woman? Dawn French gave years of her life to that show. Wasted on them, wasn't it?

Speak kindly. Turn the other cheek. I knew what I had to do. But I'd had enough. I just couldn't stand there and watch a man in a hard hat with a big grin all over his idiot face miming me bumming a choirboy. So I took it off. Forgive me, Lord, but I ripped off my dog-collar and revealed myself as an angry man. A mortal angry man. And I stared up at those scaffolders and shouted, 'WHY DON'T YOU JUST FUCK OFF?'

They were stunned. Speechless. They didn't know what to say. Or who to say it to. I mean, who was I, now that I didn't have my Dibley collar on? They didn't know anything about me.

I admit it, Lord. I was stunned, too. I didn't know I was going to do it till I did it, if that makes sense.

It was Midnight Mass all over again, wasn't it, Lord? Every so often I blow my top. I wish I had an inner core of calm that was unshakeable.

I went inside St Saviour's and put my collar back on.

## 3rd February

It's 5.17 a.m., Lord. I couldn't sleep. So I came in here and put on Bach's cantata 'Ich Habe Genug', sung by Dietrich Fischer-Dieskau. Very loud. Fear not, though, for Alex or the neighbours. I've got headphones.

I feel your presence in the beauty of the voice and the oboe. And the music is sublimely appropriate, given that Bach composed it for Candlemas. It's powerful and salutary to sit here in the dark and think about Simeon holding the baby Jesus and calling him a light to the world.

The broken window is much on my mind, Lord. Help me find the criminals who threw a beer bottle through that window. They deserve justice. I mean proper justice. Not a headbutt from Colin.

## 4th February

This afternoon, smoking on the bench as per usual, it occurred to me that maybe Colin is a holy fool. He's foolish, we all know that, but he's also intense in his holiness. Extraordinarily open to the Word of God. He wants to believe and he truly does.

He told me he'd like to kick Richard Dawkins in the bollocks for writing *The God Delusion*, a book Colin takes personally. As a true believer, he's not happy with Dawkins saying believers are 'irrational nutters'. (Colin's words, in fact, not Richard's.) I told Colin not to let Dawkins worry him. The professor can only believe in things if they're scientifically proven. Where does that leave all the things we still don't understand? To illustrate which, I picked up a snail and we marvelled at its perfect mathematical golden spiral. Why was it so beautiful? It didn't *need* to be so beautiful. What was the purpose of its beauty, if not divine? At which point, Colin gave me a swig from his bottle of beer.

Then he asked what I was going to do about the window, which is sort of where we came in, all those weeks ago, when he turned up at the Vicarage and dragged me off to church to see the 'scandal'. So I gave him the classic vicar answer: I was going to ask ordinary people for money and hope the Lord would provide. Then I asked him if he ever found out who broke it. He said it was a total mystery. He'd asked everyone in The Monarch, he'd asked all the people he knew on all the estates near the church, he'd asked Joseph Foggett, who'd done time with him and always knew everything. (Actually I might have misheard that name. It could have been Joe the Fuckwit.) Nothing. No one knew anything.

To me, it all seemed commendably zealous, but Colin felt his whole investigation had been a waste of time. He'd decided to give up solving crimes as 'no one owns up'. Which is probably right. Especially if Colin's the investigating officer.

All that remained was for us to dispose of the beer

bottle, thoughtfully, and go our separate ways. Colin showed me this game he plays where he sees how far he can chuck empty bottles. He leaned forward and hurled the bottle backwards, high over his head. I watched it as it soared towards the heavens. But it didn't reach the heavens. Instead it hit the boarded-up bit of the stained-glass window.

You didn't need to be Inspector Morse or Professor Richard Dawkins to work out how the window got broken.

Colin gave me that look he does when he knows he's done something wrong. It reminds me of Basil, the springer spaniel we had when I was a kid. 'Sorry, Vicarage. I don't remember doing it, honest. I must have been pissed.'

What I'd say to Dawkins is this: how come the bottle hit the boarded-up bit, rather than a previously unbroken bit, thereby adding not a penny to the cost of restoration?

It was a miracle. A minor miracle. Which science is powerless to explain.


## 5th February

Mick hasn't been round for days. I hope he's all right. Was I too harsh with him the last time? I don't want him to feel he can't come round. But I don't want him to come round either.

## 6th February

When I was little I felt sorry for the old man outside the Co-op in Beccles. I didn't understand why he was talking and no one was listening. Was he mad? Mum said no, he was a member of the Plymouth Brethren. Which means nothing when you're four. I stopped and stared at him till she tugged on my hand and moved me on. He had white hair and a thin bony face. He didn't look at me. In fact, he didn't look at anyone. He sort of looked into the middle distance. Like he was testifying to the buildings and the air.

That's how I felt this morning. There were five people in the congregation. Most of the church was air. Is it me, Lord? Is that why people aren't coming?

Then the Archdeacon walked in. Of all the services in all the dioceses, the Archdeacon had to walk into mine.

He definitely thought it was my fault, because afterwards he said he was worried about me. Where was my congregation? Nigel unhelpfully agreed that the congregation was upsettingly small, when what he should have done was just say yes when I asked him if there was a Tube strike. He then proceeded to list the whereabouts of everyone known to be missing. Nigel's one of those people who feels obliged to impart his knowledge. His defence is always the same: he says it because it's true. Why couldn't he keep the truth to himself? Who needed to know that Mike Swan had a cheese stall at the farmers' market? Or that Margaret had gone to visit her mother just outside Hove?

Then the Archdeacon's conversation turned to money, as it always does. He pointed out that we're late paying our Parish Share, and the wealthy parishes grumble when their money subsidizes empty churches, blah blah blah.

Of course the wealthy parishes grumble. Wealth and grumbling go hand in hand. Ask anyone rich and they'll tell you, one of the things money buys you is the right to grumble.

'From each according to his abilities, to each according to his needs.' I wish it weren't Karl Marx who said that. I'd love to stand up in front of my congregation and say it was from the Gospels.

What was your congregation plate this morning, asked the Archdeacon. We did our usual verbal dance. I said £60, he said that means 20, I said no, 40. Then Nigel the Imparter steamed in and said it was £24.07, which didn't sound too bad. But annoyingly the Archdeacon had seen me put in 20 myself. I pointed out this wasn't against the rules. And I promised our numbers would be up next week.

I'm thinking about numbers all the time. Numbers and money. The world I always wanted to avoid, the world of Nat Jones. It's unavoidable. That *is* the world.

I offered the Archdeacon some instant, but he's not an instant man. The Archdeacon's definitely Costa Rican High Roast.

To be fair to him, as he left the church he matched my 20 with a 20 of his own. But somehow that made what we'd collected seem even less.

## 7th February

I was reading a paragraph of Rowan Williams' book in bed. I got to the end of that paragraph and went back to the beginning. I mean, I didn't even notice I'd just read it. And even after reading it again I knew I hadn't taken it in. So I went back to the paragraph before that one, to give myself a run at it.

Rowan Williams is a great man so I'm not going to skim his work. Even if I just do a page a day I'll have finished it by Christmas.

'Leaflet drop'. Those were the words that kept coming into my head as I tried to read the paragraph. I asked Alex what she thought. Wouldn't that get my numbers up? Leaflet the estate. Leaflet the pubs. Leaflet Tony's Kebabs. No point in being shy.

She said sometimes weeks go by without us having sex. That wasn't an answer to my question. Far from it. But it was the truth. One of us is always too tired or distracted by work. She's right, we need to rekindle things.

She wants some excitement. She wants to be seduced. As do I. But I also want to get my numbers up.

Hearing the truth from Alex is so different from hearing it from Nigel. I love Alex and I want to have sex with her. No one wants to have sex with Nigel.

After she turned the light out, I asked her in a sexy voice if she wanted me to dress up as a vicar. I thought it was quite funny but it didn't go down well. Didn't go down well at all. Humour. So important in a relationship.

## 8th February

No sex.

## 9th February

Dear Lord, if you don't mind me bringing this up, could you give me more energy in bed. I'm so exhausted all the time and it's not fair on Alex. She deserves to be happy. Please help me find more time and energy for her. And it.

Why do you make finance such a constant daily issue for us? Shouldn't I be spreading your Word and building the Kingdom rather than worrying about money? I gather wine's a good investment at the moment. And property in Hunan Province.

Kindly remember, Lord, that I turned down the chance to work in financial PR.

## 10th February

I was praying that the Lord didn't find the size of my flock insultingly small. I was actually asking Him if he had any ideas now to fill the place when in came Darren.

Darren strode into St Saviour's in a shiny black sleeveless puffer jacket with a zip. Sort of a puffer jerkin thing. Pink and black tartan shirt, sleeves rolled up to show his biceps. Tattoo on his right wrist, which I didn't read because I thought it would be rude. Darren. A great big mountain of a man. He towered over everything. He told me I had an awesome organ. I said it was broken. (None of this was double entendre.)

He turned out to be the Vicar of St James in Fulham. That took me aback, on account of the tattoo, jerkin and shirt. But really it shouldn't have surprised me. He's charismatic with a little 'c' and Charismatic with a big one too.

So. There he stood, exuding success. That's what Charismatics always make me think of – not divinity, not ministry, not community but success.

He said his church was undergoing renovations. His congregation, 400 strong, had nowhere to go on Sunday. Could he bring them to St Saviour's? There he was, large as life, guaranteeing to up my numbers by roughly 1,000 per cent, with worship he said was 'evangelical in a kind of chilled, friendly way'.

I wasn't sure that was my kind of way, though. I told him I had a problem with worship that was more emotion than theology. He said he had a problem with it too. As if that got rid of the problem.

He said he'd bring his 'cool bunch' to us on Sunday and we'll see how it goes. If it's good, we can hook up more often. If not, no problem. Absolutely not a problem.

Did he really think all 400 would come? He did. He really believed that. Which amazed me. I mean, Fulham's nowhere near Shoreditch, is it? It's a long way on the

Tube. Maybe Darren will charter some buses. I can see him driving a bus, very fast, while singing the praises of the Lord, in true Donald Hairless style.

I had prayed for a way to up my numbers, and up turned Darren. So in that sense I'm grateful. It behoves me to be grateful.

I can't wait to see the Archdeacon's face when he eyeballs the 400.

Nigel agreed to replace me for tomorrow night's homeless meal, despite the clash with his badminton. I want to spend the night at home with Alex. Sofa, bottle of wine, mushroom risotto (my signature dish), DVD. Maybe we'll have another go at *The Wire*. Perhaps this time we'll understand a word they say. And maybe, just maybe, when the DVD's over, we'll eject it, put it in its box-set case and have sex.

## 11th February

After the risotto, and during the wine, she asked me what my fantasies were. All I could think of was a full church with a heaving congregation plate.

Stalling for time, I told her I had the normal male fantasies. All involving her. But it's no use saying that to a lawyer, even if she is your wife, because she pointed out that they couldn't be fantasies because she's not a fantasy, she's real, and you can't have a fantasy about something real. What about fantasy fantasies?

I told her to go first. And she did. She was astonishingly well prepared.

There was doing it in a shop, dressing as a stripper, dressing as a prostitute, doing it in a hotel corridor, being tied up by someone famous, doing it in a lift. It was a sexy but intimidating list. The lift featured more than once. She wanted to be serviced in a lift by faceless men. Or have I got that wrong? Maybe it was the *lift* that was being serviced by faceless men.

There were just so many fantasies. No one could remember them all. Apart from Alex, obviously. But she was keen to reassure me. These were all fantasies, they weren't meant to happen. Except some of them. Maybe the doing it in a shop one. I pointed out that this didn't sit well with my vocation. Then the doorbell rang. She knew it would be Colin. I said it might not be, knowing it was. But it wasn't, it was Mick.

Mick offered to clean our windows. He even showed me his bucket. I said we didn't want our windows cleaned. For a start, it was dark. Alex, pissed off by the interruption, said she was off to watch telly. I feared that the moment had passed. The sex moment. As they so often do.

I told him to come back tomorrow. I shut the front door on him and walked away. Then I heard a funny sort of whooshing sound. He'd sloshed the contents of his bucket over the glazed bit of our front door, dowsing it in a browny liquid.

That was sort of a free sample. Mick was apparently intending to clean our windows with sewage.

## 12th February

Sex turns up when you least expect it. As I walked towards Colin on our beer and fags bench, he told me to watch out for the used condom left by the Goths. Goths had been shagging in our churchyard, apparently, though it's not a Gothic church. I found myself telling Colin I'd never had sex al fresco. And we were off. Me and Colin. Talking sex.

He told me he hadn't had it in years. He said nobody loved him. That brought back a conversation I'd had with Alex, when I first told her about me and Colin meeting on our bench. She asked if I actually liked Colin and I said no, I loved him. Which is true. I do. I love him and God loves him.

So I told him we loved him. That didn't make him happy. He said he wanted sex not love. Would God be cross with him for 'wanting to get my balls wet'? Not wishing to bother God with that question, I said no on His behalf. But I reminded Colin that God's love was powerful, ceaseless and ineffable, more profound than physical love.

He said he just wanted to 'stick it in'.

I thought I'd enlighten him, as a minister should. I'd explain that the purpose of marriage was procreative, but this applied to the whole relationship, not individual acts, thereby allowing for acts of love that were subject to contraception. I'd reassure him that no Anglican teaching ruled out the pleasure of sex. But I knew that at some point he'd say 'stick it in' again and I just couldn't face it.

## 14th February

I was woken by a passing car playing 'Easy (Like Sunday Morning)' by The Commodores. It was a merciful change from the usual hip-hop that blasts out of cars round here, people shouting at terrifying volume about bitches and motherfuckers and hoes, a weird word that makes you think of a prostitute on a lawn.

Sunday morning's never easy for me. There's too much to do. I suggested to Alex she might come to the service. She asked if that was my 'alternative to sex'.

There's nothing in that, nothing at all, though it's true that this morning I felt excited, not sexually but almost, thinking of the Darren exodus from Fulham to Shoreditch. The journey of the 100, and what that would do to the numbers in my church. Whatever my reservations, there was no denying the evangelical capacity to make new Christians and draw young people to the faith.

I arrived at St Saviour's unprepared for what Darren had done. He'd installed a big screen. He'd added white sofas. There'd been a church on this site since the 12th century, but this was the first time it had looked like Ikea. There was no faculty permission for any of this, but Darren wasn't fazed. He promised that after the service, he'd put it back to the 'cold barn' it was before.

Alex said the place looked friendlier. She asked

Darren, in a teasing way, if everyone was allowed to watch telly during the service. That definitely fazed him. He patronized her briefly, thinking she was the little vicar's wifey who did the flowers, then flounced off to set up the smoothie bar. (We really did have a bar now. Shame Patrick Yam wasn't there.) 'Knob-end,' said Alex, like she loathed him. Then she added, 'but very good-looking.'

I kept telling myself it was only for a day. By lunchtime, Darren and his world would be gone. That was what I hated – the sense that he'd come to our church and created his own world. This brashness and whiteness and fakery were all Darren's doing. The church itself, and what went on inside it, which should all feel like a gift from God, now felt like a gift from Darren. Ephesians 2:8: 'For by grace you have been saved through faith. And this is not your own doing; it is the gift of God, not a result of works, so that no one may boast.'

Darren – for some reason I want to call him Dazza – manhandled me to the bar and introduced me to a girl called Pip, who was in charge of making the smoothies. She was blonde and smiley and blissed out, like a girl who comes out of a tent at Glastonbury and gives you a flower. You think she likes you but actually she's done Ecstasy and likes everyone.

Dazza recommended a smoothie made from blackberries and blueberries called the Merry Berry Jesus Explosion. So to spite him I had the Creamy Jesus Tropical Splash, made from pineapple and guava.

Everywhere I looked there were things I'd never seen

before in St Saviour's. Hundreds of young people smiling and hugging. Archdeacon Robert, on a white sofa, sucking a smoothie with a young man in shorts. I had to admit that it was, in its way, awesome. I was worried the Archdeacon would want St Saviour's to be like this, always.

I went to the pulpit, smoothie in hand, and welcomed everyone to the service. But no one wanted to be welcomed by me. It was Darren they wanted. The awe was for him.

Darren welcomed Jesus to the church, as if Our Lord had been waiting backstage for his Darren introduction. And then, within 30 seconds, he was talking about filling in standing-order forms and direct debits. All very straightforward, said Darren.

I walked away from my own pulpit and sat in a pew with Colin. I took a slug from his miniature vodka bottle and turned my smoothie into a Creamy Jesus Bloody Mary. A man called Ikon, in a baseball cap and tracksuit, stepped up to the mic and started rapping about 'not liking his behaviour/Till he found Christ was his saviour'.

Everyone got up to dance. Or leave. Mike Swan, Margaret – out they went. Colin didn't, though. Colin embraced the new way with all his heart. He looked at Pip and he was all smiles, as open and credulous as a little kid, leaping around like our church was the Lord's bouncy castle.

Everyone sang along when Ikon got to the chorus: 'Love me take me Jesus, make me feel brand new/Love me take me Jesus, our resurrected Jew.'

I hope I forget those lines soon, but I fear I never will.

The lights. The drinks. The sugar rush. Four hundred people, all of them high, on their feet and dancing. This wasn't praying, it was clubbing.

I found myself abhorring Ikon's performance with a Puritan zeal. But I love performance. It's key to good ministry. I've performed in choirs since I was 8. Where would I be without performance? I'd never have met Alex. Bristol Dramsoc, *The Importance of Being Earnest*, 1994. Me as Jack, Alex as Lady Bracknell. She thought she looked ugly in that hat. I found her sexy.

But that was a play, a show we put on to entertain an audience and yes, OK, to try and get off with each other. A church service should never be a performance and nothing more. It's a liturgy.

As soon as it was over, I said all that to Darren. I told him it wouldn't be right to have him back next week. Our congregation didn't come to church for a show. They wanted a sacrament. He stared at me with contempt.

We withdrew to the vestry to continue our 'discussion'. The Archdeacon came in and asked how we were getting along, in a headmaster-in-the-playground sort of way, and *The Darren Show* kicked off again. How he'd said to the Father during the service, Father give me all you've got. (I think he was getting confused with Father Christmas.)

Then he asked the Archdeacon if he'd 'experienced Jesus?' Several times, replied the Archdeacon, in a way that reminded me of Lady Bracknell. It was great to hear him deliver a withering line to someone else. I was sure he'd loathed the hysteria. The infantile 'Wow!' He'd have loved the increase in numbers, though.

Then Darren produced a donation cheque, made out to St Saviour's, for £10,000. What do you say to a cheque for £10,000, Lord? The Archdeacon said thank you. Then he fixed me with his steely Archdeacon gaze and said the Area Dean would be delighted. He hoped the Diocese would see 'some of the fruits of it', as if the cheque was a great big smoothie.

I thanked Darren, too. And he left.

I got 10 grand towards the Parish Share and the Window Restoration Fund. And what's more, I got rid of Darren.

Well done me. Can I say that? Yes, I can say it. I can shout it if I want. The gamble worked.

In all the excitement, I nearly forgot it was Valentine's Day. About four, I went to the shop for some stuff, intending to stop at the garage for some flowers on my way home, so Alex wouldn't think her Valentine's gift was toilet rolls.

Then this fantasy woman appeared in the aisle, out of nowhere. Black belted mac, pink wig, matching pink bra. What a show.

This fantasy woman was my wife. But she also wasn't my wife. So when I said her name she said no, she wasn't Alex, she was Vivienne. 'V' for Valentine. 'V' for very sexy. Then she asked me who I was and I said, by mistake, Darren, because his name was on my mind and so it just sort of came out.

She gave me a flash of suspenders. She rubbed up against a red pepper with a don't-squeeze-me-till-I'm-yours pout. Then she glanced towards the exit. The message was clear. See you at home, fast as you can get there. Try to keep your clothes on till then.

I rushed off to pay for my stuff, but Lisa was on the phone, of course. She kept talking even when I said, please, quick as you can. So I scanned my own stuff. I actually mounted the counter and scanned my own toilet rolls.

Back at the vicarage, we went at it on the kitchen worktop. *They* went at it. Darren and Vivienne. Nothing could stop them. When the doorbell rang, Vivienne shook her head and said, 'Me!' and Darren knew what she meant. Then there was the sound of squeegee on glass. Mick had come back. He was inches away, at the kitchen window, watching Vivienne polish the kitchen worktop with her bum. He told us not to mind him, then offered to 'do round the back'.

I admit it. I did a bad thing, Lord. I paid him to go away. That's not ministry, is it, Lord? That's bribery.

I don't know why I'm telling you this, Lord, but my wife now calls my penis my *darren*.


## 17th February

Colin turned up in the vestry and said, 'Hello, Vicars.' I didn't correct him. That's an easy mistake to make. Even I often have to remind myself that Nigel's not a vicar, he's a pastoral assistant, who may or may not be ordained in the future, which means he's not on my level and doesn't have the power or status to annoy me, even when he does.

Just before Colin arrived, Nigel was singing the hip-hop hymn 'Love Me Take Me Jesus'. To himself. But loud enough for me to hear. I acknowledged it was catchy. In return, he acknowledged that last Sunday's service had been very different in style from my own. I hoped he meant different and worse, but no, he meant different and better – all that energy and pizzazz!

'I must say, Darren is very good-looking.'

Why must he say that? Because it's true.

Colin still had his bouncy-castle face. He'd just been on a 'Be Transformed' course at Center Parcs, courtesy of Darren and his charismatic crew, who'd paid for everything. There were parties. There were lectures on dealing with sex, including how to cure people of gayness.

He then produced a couple of glow-sticks from his 'Be Transformed' goodie bag. One said, 'TRANS-FORMED' and the other said, 'JESUS'. The Light of the World was a glow-stick.

It was just like watching my god-daughter Enid take stuff out of a party bag, except Enid's five and Colin is – how old is Colin? It's hard to tell because he's suffered so much and suffering ages you, but with the glow-sticks in his hand, he was innocence re-born. He'd fallen under the spell of these people. God doesn't cast a spell, though. He doesn't use magical powers to ensnare. A spell is both manipulative and finite. We all know spells are made to be broken. Whereas God's love is eternal.

Colin couldn't wait to see them all again on Sunday, especially the 'mega-hot' girls. (Evidently Colin had been totally cured of any remnants of gayness.)

I asked him where he was going to see them all again. It turned out to be my church. Colin, who now knows more about my church than I do, told me Darren was not only coming back on Sunday, directly against my wishes, he was swanning round the nave as we spoke. That made me really angry.

I confronted him. Again. He was glowing with self-righteousness. His way of worship, according to Darren, was better than mine because he filled St Saviour's and I didn't. His God was a success. And he knew that scared me. Why didn't I just admit it?

I told him that what scared me was his services, by which I meant *him*. His certainty. His views on gays and women priests, which I dreaded to know, so he told me – my pathetic liberal acceptance of gays and women priests disgusted him. To be that close to Darren's disgust made me proud to be pathetic. When you're pathetic, you arouse pity, which is so much better than what Darren arouses. Which is inadequacy. And slavish devotion. I just don't believe he ministers to human need. His own needs predominate.

Darren told me my church was now his and it was time for me to acknowledge that and be his friend. And God's friend. He actually told me to be God's friend. And then he left.

He'll return, though. I can't stop him. But I'll keep fighting him.

## 18th February

It's 11.55 p.m. Back from the night shelter. Mattresses, not white sofas, on the floor of St Saviour's. A typical homeless group – single people low on housing lists, refugees from other hostels, victims of domestic abuse, people running away from debt or broken relationships, failed asylum seekers, alcoholics off the booze for one night only. (Nigel, I must say, is rather good at being a human breathalyser.) And Coughing Jack, who always comes and never says anything. Just eats and coughs and sleeps.

I talked for ages to an embarrassingly grateful guy called Duncan. He said he'd be traumatized if he had to live on the street, he just didn't know how to do that.

Duncan had come to London looking for work after everything went wrong for him in Scotland. He kept saying it was all his fault, without ever saying what 'it' was. He told me he was a musician. I asked what kind and he said a piano player, so I offered him the use of the piano in the vestry. He shook his head. He said he wasn't good enough. Eventually, after a bit of persuading, he agreed to give us a tune. So we went in there, maybe half a dozen of us. I thought he'd play 'Roll Out The Barrel' or 'My Way' or 'Angels' by Robbie Williams, and we'd all have a sing-song.

Instead, Duncan played Rachmaninov's 'Prelude in C Sharp Minor'. We all went very quiet when he started and we stayed that way. In the distance we could hear Coughing Jack but that didn't matter. It was humbling to stand near Duncan and watch him play. When he finished, he got massive applause. I put two fingers in my mouth and tried to whistle and, magically, I could.

It turned out Duncan was a concert pianist who won second prize in the Leeds International Piano Competition in 1998. I told him how wonderful it was to hear him play, but he denied it and kept shaking his head, saying he'd made loads of mistakes and his hands no longer did what his brain told them. I didn't know what to say to that, so I apologized that the piano hadn't been tuned because we were strapped for cash.

For some reason, that amused him. He put his hand on my shoulder, when I was thinking that I should do that to him. And then he made me a mug of tea, which took him an age. At the keyboard, he was astonishingly dextrous, but away from it, even lifting a kettle seemed to give him trouble.

His kindness made me think of my favourite poem, Louis MacNeice's 'Fanfare for the Makers' in which he celebrates those minor kindnesses that transform a passing moment into something marvellous.

It gave him such pleasure to make me that mug of tea. Receiving it from him was a moment of grace.

I thanked him and returned to the others. Sadly he'd forgotten to put a tea bag in it. He'd made me a mug of boiled water.

## 19th February

Bench News – Colin's in love with Pip, the mega-hot Queen of the Smoothies. She makes him glow with an inner warmth and he's pretty sure she likes him, too.

I urged him to consider the disparity in their ages and get to know her better before making any declaration.

From the look of her, Pip makes a lot of men glow and he shouldn't take it personally. I didn't say that to Colin, though. That would have hurt him.

He says it's up to Jesus. He'll do what Jesus tells him. So all we can do is hope that Jesus tells him to keep his distance.

## 20th February

Once again it's that time of night when all good husbands should be in bed with their wives. Which I was until 10 minutes ago. We were ready to get in the fantasy lift, the one that would take us – Ping! – to sex heaven. I put the blindfold on Alex and everything. Not a proper full-length sexy one, a British Airways night-flight job from our trip to New York years ago, before I was ordained, when we stayed in that no-star hotel on East 94th. That was when we had sex all the time. On our first morning, we set off for the Empire State, but instead we bought a postcard of it and went back to the room and had sex.

I got in our fantasy sex lift and pressed all the buttons I could. A passing car played hip-hop, but it didn't get quieter because the car wasn't passing at all. It was parked in our drive. I heard 'Jesus' and 'resurrected Jew'. There was nothing for it but to pull on some pyjamas and go out there.

Darren was at the wheel, saying nothing, smirking with his mate Ikon. Darren the playground king. I was back at Westleton Primary with that bully-boy Mark Morgan. What were they doing outside my home? Praying for me, said Darren. Harassing me, more like. I told him to bugger off, which he did.

'See you Sunday!' he taunted.

Worse than the harassment and the smirking and his rampant self-love was the car. Darren drives a BMW convertible. Darren's a success and his God's a success so he drives a successful car. What's that got to do with celebrating the presence and spirit of Christ in the community? How does driving that car help him minister to the Duncans of this world with their raw human needs?

I'm under siege, Lord. I need relief. Allow me to find an untroubled time when I can make love to my wife. And reassure me that my instinct about St Saviour's is right and Darren's is wrong, because there are times when I feel he's the future and I'm the past.

The past and future should flow into one another. A continuum of worship, as in *Hymns Ancient & Modern*. But sometimes I feel – straightforwardly – that ancient is bad and modern is good and my preaching to a con-

78

gregation of 20 people in a draughty church with a broken window is hopeless. I'm a worthless relic.

I'm going out for a kebab now. You can't be angry when you're eating a kebab or the juice goes all over you.


## 22nd February

Very angry now.

The Archdeacon told me it had been agreed at the Deanery Synod that Darren should preach at St Saviour's once a month. This was outrageously presumptuous. I hadn't been at the meeting because they're excruciatingly boring and I had to watch *The Wire*. Nevertheless. St Saviour's is my church and they shouldn't have done that.

Anger made me tell the Archdeacon that Darren can't preach in my church without my approval, so I'm reversing the Deanery Synod decision. The Archdeacon recommended I didn't do that. But then he never gets angry. Or maybe he goes home and kicks the cat. Does he have a cat? There's so much about him I don't know. What worries me is, at some level, he's on the side of the Darrens, for all that his lips quivered with contempt when Darren asked if he'd 'experienced Jesus'. The Archdeacon loves successful people. He's always going to Gordon Ramsay restaurants with Simon Schama.

Once a month. How bad that can be? I have to forgive Darren, don't I, Lord? Even though his views are repellent, even though he drove his BMW convertible into my drive at midnight, just to intimidate me and show his contempt. Lord, how many times am I to forgive my neighbour Darren? As many as seven times? More. Once a month, apparently.

## 23rd February

Decision made. Or not made. Or at any rate delayed. I haven't complained to the Area Dean, so Darren and his posse will be back at St Saviour's on Sunday. But they weren't there last week and won't be there next week. Once a month is a small price to pay for a large contribution to our funds.

Joan phoned. I didn't even know she had my number. I must go to Mulberry House and see her again.

## 1st March

It was round about half-past ten this morning when Jesus told Colin what to do.

Morning Service had barely started. Darren was just about to give the congregation his top 10 tips on how to be a friend of God when suddenly Pip shouted, 'Get off me, you're disgusting,' and ran out of the church. Given that she was sitting next to Colin, I feared the worst. And the worst duly happened.

He got to his feet and hundreds of people stared at him. All those gleaming bright young things who flock to Darren stared at his grey beard and broken veins. And

Colin announced to each and every one of them that 'Jesus told me to do it!' Stretching his arms out as he said it, for the full Crucifixion effect. The only good thing about all this was we never got to hear Darren's top 10 tips. He abandoned them and went straight to the hip-hop hymn. But it was hard for anyone to concentrate. Colin had snuffed out the glow.

So. There we were again, half an hour later. Me and Darren in the aisle of St Saviour's, confronting each other as is our wont. Him on, as he saw it, the moral high ground.

Darren said Pip was so distressed she'd never be able to come back to St Saviour's again. Pip who wore a chastity bracelet. Pip who was a virgin. A born-again virgin. (Her virginity once was lost but now is found.)

He demanded that I bar Colin from my church. I told him I wasn't going to do that. Colin had been a regular for 15 years. I asked Darren to forgive him. Instead, Darren threatened to prosecute him.

Goliath had the sword and the spear and the javelin, but David had the Word of God, which meant he was no longer looking up at a giant. He was looking down on a mortal man from God's point of view.

I hit the giant with the Word of God: 'Lord, how many times am I to forgive my neighbour? As many as seven times? Seventy times seven, said the Lord.'

Darren threw the Word of God straight back in my face, screwing up his eyes and chanting 'Seventy times sair-ven! Seventy time sair-ven' like he was six. He said Pip was a vital part of his congregation, the implication being that Pip was important and Colin was not. I told him Colin wasn't vital to anyone except God and if God loved Darren, he loved Colin equally. Colin's presence was a blessing.

No, said Darren, his presence was smelly. Colin was a dangerous man who smelled funky. (Did he think Colin was deaf, too? The poor man was sitting about 10 feet away.)

Then the Archdeacon did that thing he always does. He turned up. The man's got a genius for just turning up.

Darren now had a higher authority to appeal to. He offered the Archdeacon a simple deal. Ban Colin and Darren wouldn't take his large and generous congregation to another church.

I was certain the Archdeacon would see it from Darren's point of view. After all, Darren had the numbers and the big cheques. He had the things that could be measured, the fit-for-purpose, target-exceeding outcomes.

We had Colin, who's nothing to do with success and has never even heard of Simon Schama.

The Archdeacon just stood there and said nothing, which he never ever does, not in my experience. He always knows what to say and comes out with it straightaway.

Finally he pronounced. He told Darren we couldn't be seen to bar anyone from our churches. Especially those in need.

I wanted to hug him. (I'll never do that. Ever.) The Archdeacon was siding with the funky-smelling losers.

'Even though he touched her bottom?' asked Darren.

'Even though he touched her bottom,' replied the Archdeacon. I liked the way he said it back to him. Very deliberate. Very even. He didn't condone the touching of the bottom. But there it was. That was his answer. I needed his support and he gave it. Which was great, though I won't rely on it happening again.

Darren left, taking his money and his people and his sofas with him, deaf to Colin's request that he should leave behind his smoothie bar.

I hope I never see him again. I don't want him anywhere near me. For that reason, I told Alex to find another name for my private parts.


## 4th March

NORMAL SERVICE WILL BE RESUMED AS SOON AS POSSIBLE.

Wasn't that what it used to say on the TV when something went wrong? That's what it was like today at Morning Service. We resumed and were normal. There were tens of us not hundreds, but we sang our hearts out and felt like a family again, an extended family. A family in Christ.


## 5th March

I thought enough time had passed for me to go back to the bench. I asked him if he was OK. He said he missed

Pip, he liked Pip a lot, even though she was a 'massive prick-tease'.

Whatever I am to Colin – confidant, fellow-smoker, friend, victim – I'm his priest and it's my duty to give him moral guidance. So I told him he was wrong to do what he did. Even if, in his words, he 'only pinched her arse'. There was no 'only' about it. That was a horrible thing to do to a woman. The arse-pinchers of the world deserve zero tolerance.

He understood. My work was done. Now it was time to relax. So I told him that if he hadn't done it, that dreadful mob would still be coming to St Saviour's. Well done, Colin. Thanks, Colin. Nice one, Colin, the headbutting arse-pincher. He said I could always count on him.

Shortly after he quit the bench, my darling wife rang. Only it wasn't my darling wife. It was Vivienne, asking for 'the man whose private parts once began with D'. I went back home and we made love.

Lord, I think you should know that the sex was unprotected. It's been that way for a while now. Alex is desperate to have a baby. She feels incomplete.

Help Alex get pregnant, Lord.


## 6th March

A cassette arrived in a jiffy bag from Mum. It was marked 'ADAM, ALDEBURGH CHURCH 1.9.85'. There was a note saying she'd found it under the sofa in the living room, which they're having re-carpeted after 47 years. They moved the sofa and there it was, this cassette of me aged 10, singing a solo in Britten's *Ceremony of Carols*. 'That Yonge Child'.

I rang Mum to thank her then put it in a drawer, as we have nothing to play it on. Alex is now keen to track down a cassette player. She's curious to know what I sounded like 'before your little testicles dropped'.

Was I infused with the Holy Spirit that day in Aldeburgh Church? I certainly remember the thrill of the moment and the elation when it was over. I'm sure that being a chorister was the first step to ordination, though I didn't know it then. All that singing softened me up. It made me at home with the Liturgy. Sometimes, when I stand at the pulpit, just about to speak, I have the urge to burst into song. Instinctively I know that music conveys the Holy Spirit better than words. In some ways, it's a pity I can't sing my sermons.

At the end of our conversation, Mum asked if there was 'any news about grandchildren', which she sometimes asks and sometimes doesn't. Embarrassing as it is, it's almost better when she asks. When she doesn't, the grandchildren thing lurks there all the time beneath our conversation.

I told her Alex and I were 'trying', which I regretted immediately. That's not a word I'd naturally use. It's got an air of doom about it. Also, it's incredibly unsexy. I mean, I really don't want to go to bed with my wife for a session of trying.

## 7th March

Funeral service for Steve Warwick's mum. There are lots of funerals at St Saviour's, but hardly any weddings. Is that something I should worry about? Probably. But I'm not sure what I can do. There's just something about an inner-city church, hemmed in by traffic. Newlyweds want rolling fields in sunlight. A grassy path, strewn with confetti. Confetti just doesn't look right outside our church. They should throw little bits of kebab.

For Steve's mum, Adoha had chosen a beautiful wreath of hyacinths, narcissi and sweet peas, over-ruling the florist, who called her an amateur. Apparently, there was a bit of a scene and Adoha won. She asked me what I thought of the narcissi. I said, 'Wonderful,' though I wasn't sure which ones the narcissi were.

Steve gave a very touching eulogy, saying what a wonderful mother she'd been and talking about the love between his parents that had brought him into the world. That was brave, as most people in the church knew that his mother and father hadn't spoken to each other for over 20 years.

You could see on the faces of Steve's girls that they'd never been to a funeral before. Maybe the next time I go into school I'll talk about death. Nobody ever talked to us about death when I was at school. Simply by opening it up for discussion, I can help them deal with it when it comes into their lives. Ellie will appreciate that, I think.

When we came out of the church, two men from the council were towing away the hearse. I tried to reason with them. Yes, it was parked on a double yellow line but where else was it meant to go? One of them wouldn't even talk to me. The other said that rules were rules and there was an underground car park 'two minutes' walk away'. I told him, with all the calm I could muster, that the dead found it hard to walk. Then the silent one spoke and wasn't as much of a jobsworth. In fact, I think he felt quite bad, because he couldn't look at me when he talked. He told me if they made an exception, other vehicle users might complain and they'd get in trouble with their bosses.

'We've got gods, too,' he said. That flummoxed me. Gods, plural. As in Mars, god of War. Zeus, god of Thunder. There's a great theological and philosophical gulf between those Greek and Roman gods and *God*. But this wasn't a good time to discuss it. We were all in the grip of Clampus, god of Parking.

In the end, we got a minicab and put Steve's mum on the back seat. The driver couldn't have been more helpful. He was Polish or Lithuanian or Ukrainian or something. A great big bearded bear of a guy. Very humble. Kept crossing himself.

I really missed Suffolk. You could have parked a hearse outside St Peter's, Gromford, and left it there for a week. No one would have complained.

That said, it's good to be a vicar in the inner city. Alex always talks about my move from Gromford as a 'promotion'. It's good as in good for my career. But in terms of being buried or getting married or being christened – or even simply praying – it's easier to get close to God in the country. Your view of Him is less interrupted.

## 9th March

Went to Mulberry House and saw Joan again.

She showed me a photo of herself in the Fifties. Very attractive. English rose. She looked a lot like the woman in the film Mum and Dad always took us to see at the Aldeburgh Cinema when we were little. It seemed to be on whenever it was raining. A whimsical comedy called *Genevieve*, about a vintage car race to Brighton, with a beautiful actress called Deborah Kerr, whose name was actually pronounced 'car', which I always found very amusing.

Joan told me she was brought up to be a lady and to dress tastefully and be polite and make sure men respected her, which meant all the men she knew when she was young were 'very dull'. She didn't meet a black man till she was 24. He was called Alan (all the men in Joan's life seem to have been called Alan). Alan was stationed at the local American airforce base. He was very tall with beautiful manners and used to take her to concerts at the base. All the great singers used to fly over from the States to serenade 'the boys'. She saw Ella Fitzgerald and it was incredibly exciting and afterwards she and Alan had their first kiss and she couldn't stop thinking about him for days. But then she broke it off because she was worried they'd get serious and she'd have to take him home, which would have killed her mother. I doubted that her mother would actually have died, but Joan said no, if she'd appeared on the doorstep with a black man, her mother would have dropped down dead before he got inside. Or if not, she'd have gone upstairs and taken an overdose.

Joan said I was much more the kind of man her mother would have liked. Though she'd have worried about my financial prospects. But she'd certainly have thought me very nice-looking. For a vicar.

Now she'd said vicar there was no stopping her. She wanted me to go through all the Sunday school stories she remembered from her childhood. What was that one about the judgment of Solomon? I told her. It went very well, as she said it meant more to her as a woman who'd had children than it did when she was a girl. I then told her David and Goliath, trying not to think about Darren and me. She thought it was a story about magic. She didn't know it was really about the power of the Word of God.

Then she asked whether everything would have been different if Jesus had been black. I told her it wouldn't.

'Goodbye, Joan,' I said.

'Goodbye, Vicar.'

'Call me Adam.'

'No I won't, dear. I'll only forget it.'

## 10th March

Would everything have been different if Jesus had been black? It's all very well my saying no. I was brought up in a Suffolk village. When I was eight, a black dinner lady started working at our school and Mark Morgan took a photo of her because he'd never seen a black person. He said it was a black and white photo and laughed at his own joke for weeks.

Basically, I've lived a very white life. I have so much to learn. We're the C of M-C E, the Church of Multi-Cultural England.

Alex told me in the kitchen this morning that her colleague Faiza wanted to use St Saviour's for her children's Koranic classes, as the community centre they were using has shut down. I said I wasn't prejudiced (though I am a bit) but I was worried about other people who might be, like Colin, who came into the kitchen as we spoke. In fact, Alex had found him there when she came down from the shower in her towel for breakfast. He claimed to have let himself in through the back door, on the pretext of making sure I got to Morning Prayer on time, but it turned out he'd spent the night on our couch. And had eaten all the bread and cornflakes.

'How can we have a man on our couch who nearly put you in hospital?'

I told her I'd forgiven him, which is true. She told me I didn't have a choice, which is also true. But wonderful, no? How may occupations have 'forgiveness' in their job description?

'He'll never hit me again,' I told her, which I believe.

Alex keeps saying there are three of us in this marriage, which is harsh and unhelpful, but not entirely inaccurate. She could be talking about her, me and Colin; or her, me and God; or her, me and the Church. Perhaps there are five of us.

On the way to Morning Prayer, Colin and I explored his feelings about Muslims, which pretty much boiled down to women in burkas looking mysterious and therefore sexy. I knew what he meant. But then he went bizarre on me, by saying that a burka was a good cover for armed robbery. And suddenly he was off on an anecdote about men in burkas robbing a betting shop in Camden Town.

When we got to St Saviour's, we discovered that robbers had nicked the lead off the roof. Churches, which are meant to be islands of peace, are now basically crime scenes. Some South London vicar in this week's *Church Times* had drawn up a list of all the things that had been stolen from his church in the last 18 months:

A baby Jesus from the crib set.
A man Jesus from a crucifix.
Three camels.
Money from the candle boxes.
Lights from the Christmas tree.
The bell he rings (rang) at the start of Mass.

Does it matter that these things disappeared? If the money went to the poor and the lights from the Christmas tree went to a family that couldn't afford to buy them?

I thought of Matthew: 'If thou wilt be perfect, go and sell that thou hast, and give to the poor.'

The key word there is 'sell'. Sell what thou hast, not accept that what thou hast will get nicked.

## 11th March, *Ash Wednesday*

'Remember you are dust and to dust you will return.'

I said it maybe 20 times, imposing the ashes onto the heads of the congregants. Then Nigel applied the cross shape to my own head.

At the school, I ashed maybe a hunderd little heads, trying to make sure, with the Muslim kids, that I put just a smudge, not a cross.

Before I was ordained, when I was working for the council, I thought of the first three months of the year as January, February, March. Now I think of them as Epiphany, Candlemas, Ash Wednesday.

I live in a sort of phantom year. I have a vicar's year that exists in parallel to the secular one. Sometimes you feel cut off. On the other hand, you feel an extraordinary bond with members of your faith.

Late tonight, at the bottle bank, I was in the queue for the clear-glass bin behind a rabbi. I didn't know he was a rabbi (he was in civvies) till he said, 'We're in the same business.'

His name was Michael Yudinski and he works at Hackney and East London Synagogue. He told me today was Purim, the festival that commemorates the saving of the Jews in ancient Persia from extermination. I asked him the theological significance of Purim and he said, 'God moves in mysterious ways.'

He was very amused when I told him that today was Ash Wednesday.

'To me, Purim, to you Ash Wednesday, to everyone else . . . Wednesday!'

That just about summed it up, I thought.

## 14th March

China, that's what it's about, said the Archdeacon. There's a huge demand from China for lead, hence the stripping of church roofs all over the London skyline. Apparently, they've even nicked the roof off the Mine Shaft, a day spa in Bond Street the Archdeacon frequents. What's a day spa?

I don't like it when the Archdeacon associates St Saviour's with bad news. I'm aware that in the time I've been here, we've had a window broken and some lead nicked. Neither of these can be blamed on me, but neither is an achievement. I'm aware that I haven't yet made my mark. Rev Roy, my mentor, always said a vicar's great gift was stealth. When you started work in a new parish, the first thing you should do was nothing. Keep doing nothing for six months. Learn the lie of the land before you 'build your own castle on top of it'. I'm not sure he's right, though. I've been here four months. Surely by now I should at least have a drawbridge and moat.

So I told the Archdeacon I was letting a Muslim children's group use the church for their classes. I was engaging in an interfaith dialogue, helping to hack down the forest of prejudice. I thought those were ideas he'd approve of, but no. He said he saw only 'shrubberies of prejudice'.

'Is that because,' he asked sarcastically, 'I live in a log cabin of denial?' (I knew not to answer. When he gets in this mode, it's best just to listen and look blank.)

His day spa is probably pretty much like 'a log cabin of denial'. Healthy and spartan, with a sauna and a Scandinavian feel.

Anyway, he said, as long as they paid, it was fine. In his view, Muslims 'liked men in cassocks'. They could relate to our sartorial style.

After he left, Colin popped up in the gallery, where he'd been hiding. Vigilante man Colin was waiting for lead thieves to fall through the roof so he could bash them with what he called his 'shovel of justice'.

Hadn't we just been through this with the broken window? And, in that case, should he not have bashed himself with the shovel of justice?

## 15th March

Alex is with Faiza and her other (female) colleagues on a girls' night out. It's great that she's made friends in London so fast. I'm not surprised, though. People always like Alex.

No boys' night out for me. Nigel and the Archdeacon are my male colleagues and I just can't see us having a pint in The Monarch after a game of one-and-a-half-side football.

I promised Alex I'd make myself a mushroom risotto, but I got sidetracked by the Chinese next to Tony's Kebabs. Excellent duck chow mein, though I sensed a slight aroma of cod, as they also do fish and chips. That's good though, isn't it? It's a bit Chinese and a bit British. It's an interfaith takeaway.

I'm preoccupied with interfaith and ethnic matters since Nigel said I was turning our church into 'a hotbed for radicals'. He was being ridiculous. Faiza runs prayer classes, for children, just like our Sunday schools. He said *he* didn't think they'd be hotbeds for radicals but he was worried that other people would. That really annoyed me. Possibly because it's exactly what I said to Alex. Why is it so aggravating when your worries are fed back to you?

I ended the conversation, which was wrong. I see that now that I've got some noodles and beer inside me. I should have explained to Nigel the common bonds of Islam and Christianity. The Abrahamic inheritance, monotheism, Jesus being a prophet in Islam and Mary being honoured, too. I should have disseminated information, as a priest is supposed to do. But then Nigel knows everything already.

I'm haunted by that thing about Joan's mum, the idea

she'd have dropped down dead if Joan had brought home a black man. Joan's mum didn't have information about black culture or black people. I bet she'd never even spoken to a black person. It's so easy to fall into that stereotypical thinking if you don't engage with people. All Muslims are terrorists, you think, knowing no Muslims.

I'm not saying it's only 'other people' who think in a stereotypical way. Look at the man who sold me my Chinese takeaway. As I stood at the counter, watching him shove my cartons into a bag, I found myself wondering if he'd nicked the lead off our roof. I was trying not to think, All Chinamen are lead thieves. What does that mean, though, trying not to think? If you're trying not to think something, it's too late, isn't it?

Shit! Just heard Alex pull up in the car. Must clear away the foil containers and make my plate look risotto-ish. I don't want her thinking that when she leaves the house I revert to the bachelor condition.

## 16th March

We're the Church of England. The Mother Church of the Anglican Communion. We can trace our lineage back to St Augustine in the sixth century AD.

That's what I want Faiza and those children to feel. We're their gracious hosts and we welcome them as a mother should.

It's great. Muslims will use my church to teach their

children how to praise God. A non-Christian God. Which is odd. Not wrong, but odd. Maybe it wouldn't feel so disconcerting if I actually *knew* any Muslims. But I don't.

I don't rent the church to Jews or Catholics. I certainly don't rent it to Scientologists. So why am I renting it to Muslims? Because the Jews and the Catholics and the Scientologists haven't asked, that's why.

## 17th March, *St Patrick's Day*

We were all set up for Faiza and the children when Nigel spotted the evidence. Colin had spent the night in the church. There was his mattress, there were his beer cans, there was his potty. Full. I told Nigel to deal with the potty while I dealt with the cans, but he said it was my church and my potty. And so it was that I welcomed Faiza into my church with Colin's piss in my hand, the piss compounded by Nigel telling her, 'We don't have a problem with your classes,' which of course suggested we *did* have a problem.

Faiza tried to lighten the mood with a joke about her not coming to our church to teach kids to build bombs so they could destroy the West! I told her I was from Suffolk, which came across as a baffling non-sequitur. What I meant was, I was from Suffolk so I knew what it was like to be a Muslim, in the sense that I, too, was a member of a minority group. A minority group in London, that is, not in Suffolk, where Suffolk people are in the majority. I carried on babbling in this vein. I thought it was better than silence, but I was probably wrong.

Then Khadijah the teacher arrived and Nigel and I did the best thing we could, which was to go and sit a long way away and not say anything.

So far, so bad, for our interfaith bonding. Piss and clumsiness everywhere. Watching Khadijah at work with the children somehow made it worse. She had such a natural rapport with them and they were so responsive. You could tell that Islam was woven into their everyday lives, whereas for our lot, the good old C of E crowd, it's just something you do on Sundays if you can be bothered.

When it was over I went up to Khadijah and Faiza and told them how inspiring I'd found their visit. For a moment, there really was a common bond, the sound of trees of prejudice falling in the forest. Or shrubberies collapsing. But then it was as if one of those trees fell on my head, because we all spotted one of Colin's wank mags. Faiza pointed out that it was inappropriate to have such a magazine in a church, let alone a church full of children. I apologized for the offence caused to her as a Muslim and a woman and a Muslim woman. (I thought that just about covered it.) She told me that in Islam it's wrong for women to use their bodies for personal gain. And then, just to make the conversation lighter and more fun, she told me her uncle earned a packet from selling magazines like that in his shop.

Lord, is it wrong to blame others when things go wrong? Given that I'm as flawed as any other human being? Because of Colin, Faiza thinks the Church of

England is a hotbed, not a hotbed of radicalism but a hotbed of beer cans, wank mags and piss, all of which are utterly foreign to the Holy Spirit.

Faiza's such a bright-eyed and positive person, Lord. A good person who made me look weak and bad. Not bad, maybe. But certainly weak. I know it's a dialogue not a competition, but it feels to me very much like Islam has won the conversation. Lord, what can I do to restore my pride in our church?

## 20th March

I went into the classroom to talk to Year Six about death but I never got to it. I asked if there were any questions about last week's story and I was bombarded with them, each question more inappropriate than the last. How come Mary was a virgin when she gave birth? Does that mean God did it to her? Was I a virgin? Was Miss my girlfriend? Did I fancy Miss? I did fancy Miss, didn't I?

Since Miss was standing next to me, in a smart grey double-breasted waistcoat and a crisp blue shirt, I felt duty-bound to defend her. I told the kids I didn't fancy her and would not have her disrespected in this way. And then I added, forcefully, that sex between Ellie and me – obviously I called her Miss Pattman – or anyone else was a beautiful thing and not to be mocked with stupid questions.

On my way out of school I told Ellie I was taken

aback by how sexualized they all were. Surely she and I weren't like that when we were 11? She suspected I might have been. But I knew she was teasing me. Because I wasn't like that, I know I wasn't. In Year Four, I sneaked a look at a dirty magazine in the toilet. But that's the point – sex was furtive and hidden and dirty, not out in the open and shouted about to vicars. I'm not arguing for repression or advocating shame. But there's a case for saying that, in a classroom with a vicar, repression and shame are more appropriate than what we saw this morning, when I yearned to put sex back in the toilet.

Ironically, Ellie felt that it was *me* who'd gone too far. Me who'd talked too much about sex to them and banged on and on about her and me not having sex. I went quiet. Was she serious?

To ease the tension, she told me she was 'a tiny bit upset' that I'd told the whole of Year Six I didn't fancy her.

That made everything far more tense. What was that meant to mean? I sensed, as I sometimes do with Ellie, that I'm a sort of joke figure. She doesn't take me seriously. Against that, she's relaxed enough with me to tease me. There's a warmth in her manner which I find quite gratifying.

Then something happened. Right there on the wall of the school, by the gates, was a planning application for a gentlemen's club called Cheeky's. A strip club, potentially opening opposite a school. A primary school at that.

I was outraged. Why was I so outraged? Ellie wasn't particularly bothered. After all, this Cheeky's place wouldn't be open during the day. I told her that wasn't good enough. A strip club wasn't appropriate, not opposite a school. What sort of example did it set her young girls? Did she seriously want drunk men hanging around outside the school gates with erections?

'Not if they should be inside teaching geography,' said Ellie.

I told her that young girls shouldn't be encouraged to use their bodies for personal gain. It was a genuine inter-faith moment, not that Ellie knew.

The forces – the force of Islam, the force of Christianity – were with me. Ellie could make all the smart remarks she liked. I'd found a cause worth fighting for. I made her agree that we'd fight it together. She suggested we go to a branch of Cheeky's to see what we were objecting to. I agreed. You can't complain if you don't know what you're complaining about. Outrage without knowledge is meaningless. It's just prejudice. She's also curious to see what it's like. As I am. We can be curious together.

My plan is to see the show with Ellie, then write a letter to the Council Planning Application Department, which I'll publicize throughout the borough. No council can afford to ignore a priest and a head teacher. We have too much clout.

The Archdeacon won't ignore it either. He'll know I'm making my mark.

## 21st March

I nearly wrote that I have a crusade, but crusades mean Muslims fighting Christians. This is the opposite. We are one. Let's just call it a campaign.

Since I defeated Darren the Invader, with a little help from Colin, my faith in the value of my own convictions has increased. My faith in my faith, as it were.

What I've learned from seeing that planning application is that vigilance is key. Not in the sense of Colin watching the roof with a shovel. You have to have your eyes open all the time, otherwise you literally miss the writing on the wall. The planning application on the wall.

If I'm going to make a difference, I need to notice everything. I can't serve the community if I'm not streetwise.

Alex is worried that my Cheeky's campaign will make me look judgmental when I'm not. I told her she was missing the point. I *want* to be judgmental. I'd go so far as to say my vocation demands it. People looked to me for moral judgment and for once I was providing it. Even if it meant a trip to Cheeky's with Ellie. (Alex is much amused by the vicar-in-a-strip-club thing. Fair enough. I'm not going to be put off by that.)

She doesn't want me to be judgmental like Darren's judgmental, in that Evangelical alpha male way. I understand. She married me for my tolerance and my reasonableness. My *niceness*. That blessing and curse.

As she left for work, Mick arrived, wanting money to go to Southend to see his mum in hospital, when exactly a week ago he asked me to give him money to identify her body. Two grannies is acceptable, but I'm damned if he's having two mums. It made me feel so angry that he was so thick. But then Mick turned the tables on me and made *me* feel thick.

He said I had to give him money because of the sign on my wall. I didn't know what he was talking about but there it was, a chalk mark on the wall next to the front door. A bit like an arrow sticking out of a chimney. How come I'd never seen it? Apparently it means 'soft touch for cash'. There was more. He pointed out the trainers hanging from the cables, which meant 'crack for sale in flats'. I pointed out the child's glove on the gate, another thing I'd never noticed. What did a child's glove on a gate mean? He said it meant some kid had lost its glove and someone had picked it up and put it on a gate.

But that wasn't the important thing he said, which was that he'd assumed I knew all this stuff. Mick had assumed his vicar was streetwise. I'll endeavour not to let him down. If you're not streetwise, you're out of touch. You're thick.

Chalk-marks on walls. Islam. Lap-dancing clubs. That's the world in which I live and minister. I have to know my world.

## 22nd March

Colin also thinks I'm judgmental. It's true I'm against his pinching bottoms. But now he's got it into his head that I'm against everything. Drugs. Sex. Prostitutes. Prostitutes opposite schools. I explained that they weren't prostitutes, it was a lap-dancing club and all I was doing was opposing a planning application. It's not like I was smiting people with stones.

I was interested to know what he thought of lap dancers, suspecting he had information. He said they were 'poor girls smuggled in from exotic places'. Their mission was 'to sell their fannies for cash' so they could train to be lawyers. He thought the whole thing was shameful. But he loved it when they bent over and wiggled their beautiful bums in his face.

I arranged with Ellie to go to the Holloway branch of Cheeky's next Saturday. I told her I was looking forward to it. We'll support each other when they put their bums in our faces.

## 23rd March

On her way home from work, Alex found a cassette player in a skip. It looked very 1980s but, miraculously, it worked. So I listened to myself, aged 10, warbling 'That Yonge Child', overlaid with Alex shouting, 'You're so sweeeeeeet!'

Mum had recorded it over something else, like you did in the good old days of cassette, so 'That Yonge Child' was followed by the last few verses of the Wenhaston Boys' Choir singing 'Hail To The Lord's Anointed'. That was the first hymn I ever learned. It was lovely to hear it again.

He shall come down like showers
Upon the fruitful earth;
Love, joy and hope, like flowers,
Spring in His path to birth.

Even as a little boy I loved that image of His coming down like showers. It made showers sound like a weapon, like Christ was attacking the earth with rain. But the rain was a weapon of creation not destruction.

I worry sometimes that my thoughts are more destructive than creative. This afternoon, I felt like punching the wall, as I do this time every year, knowing the accounts have to be prepared for the Annual Parochial Church Meeting. Accountants don't have to give sermons, so why must I do accounts?

## 24th March

The Don't Let a Lap-Dancing Club Open Opposite Our School Campaign is up and running. Nigel just calls it Stop the Filth, which I find crude and woolly and a bit too Mary Whitehouse-ish. Nevertheless, I salute him for putting his back into it. He's already sent three letters to the Bishop, and today in church he launched a petition.

Adoha was all for stopping filth, though she couldn't quite grasp the nature of the filth involved. She thought it was a club for paedophiles and nothing could dissuade her. Anyway she was against it, whatever it was, and every signature was welcome. Thirty-four signatures is a good start. OK, three of them were mine. But that's fair enough. Once for me and twice for Mum and Dad, who both agreed a lap-dancing club shouldn't open opposite a school, even if it is 100 miles away from them.

It was good to get Steve Warwick on board, as the father of two girls at the school. He said he was glad somebody was making a stand and I thanked him. But that wasn't really enough – I should have taken him aside and asked him how he was coping with his mother's death. Before there were therapists or anti-depressants or bereavement counsellors, there were priests. I should have ministered to him.

## 25th March

I thought the three-of-us-in-the-marriage joke was a joke, but then Colin rang Alex from the police station just before midnight, when the two of us were in bed, so it pretty much felt like the three of us were in bed.

I knew as soon as she put the phone down that the news was bad, even though she said there was good news, too. The good news was that Colin had caught the thief who'd stolen the lead from the church. The bad news was that *Colin* had caught the thief who'd stolen the lead from the church. Resulting in Colin's arrest for aggravated bodily harm with a wheelie bin.

Apparently I'd told Colin to call Alex if anything like this happened. She thanked me for that then headed off to the police station. What could I say? Colin was in a cell, and when you're in a cell, you need a lawyer more than you need a priest. Unless you're about to be hanged.

## 26th March

Autonomy's one of the great advantages of my calling. The rhythms and structures of my day come from the patterns of prayer. I have duties, of course I have duties, but basically I'm my own boss.

So, after Morning Prayer today, I went to Waitrose. The Archdeacon was coming to the vicarage at 11, to talk about my 'Cheeky crusade', so I went to the branch near Moorgate and bought some Costa Rican High Roast, which I knew he'd love, or at the very least love more than instant, which he disdains.

Alex called me judgmental, Colin said I was against everything – now it was the Archdeacon's turn. He said I shouldn't appear too 'forbidding'. People hated that. I told him I was fed up with the Church in London being like some affable club that forgives everything and is terrified of taking a moral stand. A lap-dancing club was about to open opposite a school, and if I was striving to build a kingdom on earth, I had to fight everything hostile to that kingdom.

Of all the things I said, the thing he picked up on was 'striving'. Where did my 'striving' come from? Did it come from one of my new Muslim friends? Because the Arabic for 'strive' was – wait for it, wait for it – *jihad*.

Was I on a sex jihad? Didn't I know that God was not against sex?

But the problem, his problem, was nothing to do with God, as it so often isn't. The problem was the Bishop, who wasn't going to stick his neck out for my sex jihad when he'd just alienated several other bishops by welcoming a lesbian bishop from America into his palace. I couldn't understand the link between a lap-dancing club and an American lesbian bishop. But it doesn't matter whether *I* can or not. The Bishop can. And does.

And then the Archdeacon bade me goodbye and poured away his coffee. That coffee cost me £3.09, plus bus fare, and he poured it down the sink – except he didn't pour it down the sink, he poured it into the washing-up bowl, leaving me to pour the washing-up bowl down the sink. Am I paranoid or does he do these things deliberately?

He wished me an enjoyable night out at Cheeky's. Like everyone else, he was far too amused that I was going to a lap-dancing club at the invitation of a headmistress. It's as if all the adults I know are in Year Six, sniggering at the back.

I was hoping to watch *The Wire* tonight with Alex, but she came home with the DVD of a true-life crime, so we watched that instead. A CCTV recording of Colin slamming a wheelie bin with a lead thief inside it into a wall. Which apparently he did 19 times before the police turned up.

At one point – well, at several points – the lead thief tries to get out the bin and Colin punches him back in. I'd never actually seen Colin at work, as it were. (Apart from the headbutt, which I didn't really 'see' because it happened so fast.) It was terrifying. And confusing. Because of course he was doing it out of righteous anger. Out of loyalty to the church and therefore me.

Alex thinks he has no chance tomorrow as the magistrate's a dragon who won't be interested in Colin's religious motives. Plus Colin told Alex that the man in the bin is a member of a nasty gang who know where Colin lives. Do they mean that literally? Colin moves from hostel to hostel. Sometimes, he's not sure in the morning where he's going to be that night.

Dear Lord, can I ask you to offer some protection to Colin? I know he's testing but I'm worried he may be about to get a kicking from this lead gang and he was only trying to do good in his own way. And can I thank you for bringing Faiza and the Muslims into my church? Was their arrival down to you? I'm not sure, but I found their clear moral values inspiring and it's given me some sort of certainty for once and I like that feeling. And please give me strength for my trip to Cheeky's.

## 27th March

Colin's mattress was there again this morning, with a force field of smell around it, but no beer cans or jazz mags or potty. I actually wish there had been a potty because I spent the rest of the day worrying where it was, convinced I was about to put my foot in it.

## 28th March

Where to begin?

Ellie met me in the church at 8. I'd never seen her with mascara. It really drew attention to her eyes, which are her best feature. They're headmistressy, but at the same time there's a softness there if you look hard enough, which I was careful not to do. In her brisk way, she said she'd come for our 'evening of sex and nudity'.

We went off to Cheeky's on the Holloway Road by taxi, not because I was trying to impress her but because speed was of the essence. I was determined to get the whole thing over in an hour. Two at the most.

As I went down the red-carpeted stairs, I felt I was part of a long and honourable priestly tradition. I was going into the bowels of London, in search of fallen women. It was exciting and transgressive and a bit disturbing. What would Ellie and I find down there? Breasts. Legs. Laps. Though weren't the actual lap dances done in private booths?

What we actually found, which neither of us expected, was Steve Warwick. There was something I wanted to say to him, but in the surprise and awkwardness of seeing him, it went clean out of my head. Instead, I introduced him to Ellie, his daughters' head teacher, despite knowing perfectly well that he already knew her.

So there we all were, in a lap-dancing club, doing that very English thing of trying to make small talk, while ignoring the lap-dancing elephant in the corner of the room.

Steve, heroically, launched the most sexless conversation he could think of. He said he was looking forward to Sports Day. Ellie responded by asking him how his two girls were. Steve thought she meant his two lap-dancing girls, so he made a sort of *phwoar*. Then he realized his mistake and mumbled something about his daughters loving her school. Finally, he made his escape, just as I realized what I wanted to ask him: How was he coping with his mother's death?

That question might have helped him. He could have looked despairing. And we'd have thought, Of course, this lap-dancing club is part of his grieving process. He's come here to forget.

'Lovely chap, comes in regularly,' said the manager, who'd already greeted us with some jokey remark about not all vicars being uptight fuddy-duddies. 'He works in TV. *The One Show*? Do you watch it?' We agreed he worked on *The One Show*, though we didn't watch it ourselves.

The manager's name was Rod. He reminded me of Nat Jones. He had the charm and self-assurance that comes from making your own money, as opposed to the confusion and unhappiness you seem to get when you inherit it.

Rod was perfectly pleasant but I knew he was the enemy. He was a cocky, pink-shirted exploiter of women's bodies, who only cared about money. But then he said he knew why we were there and we had nothing to worry about. He was withdrawing his planning application. No Cheeky's would open opposite the school. He didn't want to upset people or make the locals unhappy. As a token of his goodwill, would we accept a bottle of champagne on the house?

So this was what victory felt like. Ellie and I, Nigel and Adoha, and everyone who'd signed that petition – we'd actually achieved something. I couldn't say good had triumphed over evil, because Rod wasn't evil. Evil men don't have the sensitivity to acknowledge their mistakes. Let's just say good had triumphed over lap dancing.

Ellie was all for leaving at this point – she said she had a 'mountain of admin' – but surely we had to celebrate our victory, especially as the man we'd defeated was giving us free champagne? Reluctantly, she agreed.

To sit there with Ellie and champagne and not enjoy myself seemed wrong. Equally, enjoying it also seemed wrong. I know that a man who looks at a woman with lust in his eyes has committed adultery with her in his heart, but I also know that there are an enormous number of receipts and invoices that I somehow have to find before I ask the treasurer to do our accounts for the Annual Parochial Church Meeting, and I only had to think of that to feel no lust, just dread.

We looked at the girl a few feet away. I couldn't take my eyes off her breasts.

'Quite a hard face,' said Ellie. So I looked at her face. 'She must spend a fortune on knickers,' said Ellie. So I looked at the knickers instead.

I asked Ellie how much those knickers would cost. Were they what she wore herself? She went quiet. It was wrong of me to ask that and I regretted it immediately. But in my defence I was a bit drunk and I did feel quite a bond with Ellie, because everywhere we looked there were nearly nude people and she and I were fully dressed.

I was wondering if she was ever going to speak again when a dancer called Leanne spotted her. Leanne turned out to be an old pupil, now fully grown. She asked Ellie if I was her feller. Ellie said, no, he's my vicar. She said it quite sweetly and possessively and I felt everything was all right again.

Leanne snuggled up to me. She wasn't embarrassed that she was virtually naked; she couldn't do her job if she were. The embarrassment was all mine. I concentrated hard on the whereabouts of those invoices, while she purged all her bitterness. Ellie had told her, teacher to pupil, that she'd never amount to anything. Now look at her; she was earning a packet, which had paid for her accountancy training, and she'd bagged herself a footballer boyfriend. Ellie congratulated her on all this, and I did, too. I couldn't not. She was making my ear hot with her breath while fingering my collar. She even asked me if I fancied a little private dance.

I wanted to do something for Leanne, but I didn't want to pay for a dance. Why didn't I ask her to help me with the accounts? Wasn't that better for her in the long term? You see loads of old accountants but you never see an old lap dancer? I could canvass Leanne for ideas about getting more money from the congregation through planned giving schemes, 'stewardship' as the C of E calls it. After all, Leanne was clearly an expert on squeezing money out of men.

When it came to it, I didn't go for the dance *or* the accountancy. I didn't think Leanne would take kindly to my helping her, or in any way suggesting she needed to be 'rescued'. That's the trouble with trying to do good – people don't want to be done good to.

Leanne got up and carried on dancing. It was just as Colin predicted. She waved her beautiful bum in my face and the only difference was that he said all the lap dancers were training to be lawyers.

I sank into a champagne fug of moral relativism. Yes, it was bad to have a lap-dancing club opposite a primary school. But what if it wasn't opposite a school? Was lap dancing bad *per se*? Leanne was in control of her body, especially her bum, which definitely would have followed me round the room if I hadn't sat there transfixed. She was also in control of her finances and her destiny. Leanne was an empowered woman, with this wonderful God-given bum she was right to share with others.

No. It was bad, it was definitely bad. She was exploiting her body for financial gain and exploiting my male weakness and lust. That was the conclusion I came to, and I wanted to leave before I came to a different conclusion. So I asked for the bill, forgetting there wasn't one. It was all on the house.

Ellie and I left.

\*

Outside, we found Nigel and Adoha and some other parishioners with banners saying 'NO NUDES IS GOOD NEWS', 'STOP THE FILTH' and 'CHEEKY GIRLS – GET THEM OUT'. I gave them the news: the filth had been stopped. They cheered. They thought I was responsible, which in a way I was. I thanked them. In our own small way, we'd won a war. And I was the general, thanking the troops and feeling the warmth of their gratitude.

I think Ellie felt we'd achieved something. She had more respect for me now. I wasn't just the man who asked that knicker question.

And then I came back to the vicarage and found Alex and Faiza giggling away. I couldn't say for certain that they were giggling about my lap-dancing jolly with Ellie the head teacher. But I knew what I had to do. I had to tell them my trip to Cheeky's had been thoroughly worthwhile, because we'd won our campaign. And then I had to look wistful and say that what I'd seen was all quite sad. Profoundly sad. The sense of lives being wasted and bodies being exploited. And I had to say all that without sounding like I'd drunk 5 glasses of champagne.

## 29th March

I came into church and saw Khadijah sitting in a pew on her own. I was very pleased. It's one thing to hire the church for a class and another to feel so at home that you walk in off the street and sit on your own, just to be silent and still. But Khadijah turned out to be Colin in a burka, disguising himself to avoid getting done by members of the lead gang wanting vengeance for the wheelie bin battering of one of their own.

Was this what interfaith had come to? I told him he was being grotesquely offensive. He should disguise himself some other way – grow a beard, wear a hat, get an eye patch. He asked if I was seriously suggesting he disguise himself as a pirate. The answer was yes. Because a pirate's hat and eye patch aren't a deep expression of his religious beliefs.

Colin took off his hood and was Colin again. And now I felt affectionate. Affection and exasperation – those are my default emotions where he's concerned.

He said Alex was a genius and it was no wonder I loved her. She'd managed to persuade the magistrate that he couldn't afford a fine, and that prison would only turn him into a criminal. (Did she really say that? As if he hadn't been turned already?) Well done, Alex. Doing more good than me. Again.

I thanked him for catching the lead thief, omitting to mention the violence, and asked him, gently, if he could now move his mattress out of the church, given that he no longer had to stake out St Saviour's overnight. And he replied, equally gently, that he liked sleeping in the church because it gave him nice dreams.

I let it pass and we went out to smoke Colin's ciggies, to celebrate seeing off the lead thieves and 'beating the pervs'.

For the first time I notice a huge billboard opposite the church, announcing the opening of a branch of Cheeky's. That smarmy pink-shirted flesh-peddler Rod was opening his club opposite my church. Did that mean he'd won? No. The war was about opening a Cheeky's opposite the school. A church is not a school.

Anyway, it's really good for Steve Warwick. He can sin and repent within walking distance.

Is that a joke or is it moral relativism? I don't know any more. I really don't. A priest can't hope for a victory over evil, that's all I know. About the best you can hope for is a score-draw.

## 30th March

I'd rather have been woken by a giant pitbull crapping on my car and crushing it. Instead I heard, 'And now "Thought for the Day" with the Reverend Roland Wise.' Again! How many thoughts does he have?

There's no escape, there's nowhere to go, no Roland Wise-free zone. Last week, he was on *Have I Got News For You* and *The Graham Norton Show* ON THE SAME NIGHT. I'd have switched to ITV News but Roland would probably have been reading it.

It's a lovely thing, my radio alarm, a present from Mum and Dad last Christmas. Mum sent me the John Lewis receipt for £17.99, in case I was unhappy and wanted to change it, which I didn't, till this morning. It has a Sleep mode, a Snooze mode, an Auto mode, a

Manual mode, but no Shut-up-Roland mode. I pressed every button I could find, twice. None of them stopped him. The man could not be silenced. It was like a sort of negative miracle. He just kept on broadcasting, thinking his thought for the day out loud, where I couldn't avoid hearing it. Every sentence contained a nauseating name-drop or a big fat ugly metaphor. I heard 'Salman Rushdie' and 'Alain de Botton', which are name-drops, I heard 'Beirut' and 'Mumbai', which are place-drops, and I heard 'radiator of life', the same idiotic metaphor he was peddling last time he was on 'Thought for the Day', or 'TFTD' as he no doubt calls it.

Alex witnessed the whole pantomime. She saw me pounding the buttons and shouting out, 'And he dies!' She saw me rip the radio alarm out the wall, which finally did the trick. A hollow victory. Roland will be back. He's the Christian equivalent of the Terminator.

Last night Tim rang, which was great, because he's supposed to be my best friend and he hardly ever rings, though Alex pointed out that I hardly ever ring *him* so we're equal. The point is, we're both very busy. And we know each other so well, we don't need to see each other much. In some ways, that's the mark of a close friend-ship, no?

At the end of our conversation Tim said, 'Well, I'd better let you go back to reading the Bible.' It's the thing he's been saying at the end of our calls ever since I was ordained. It's partly nervous, because he doesn't really know what I do, and partly genuine. Tim really thinks I spend most of my day reading the Bible, as opposed to preparing accounts or trying to rent out the church hall or calling the police about the theft of lead from the roof or visiting old people. So this morning, after 'Thought for the Day', I really did read the Bible. I got out of bed, plugged the radio alarm back into the wall and went into my study.

I found what I was after in Matthew 23.

'And whosoever shall exalt himself shall be abased; and he that shall humble himself shall be exalted.'

Ever since I've known him, Roland Wise has exalted himself. I couldn't say with certainty that Roland believes in God, but I know, because I've witnessed it for 15 years, that Roland believes, evangelically, in Roland.

Alex was very sympathetic. She said she didn't blame me for being envious of the man and hating him for his desperation to get on in the world and be Mr Pointy Head the Bishop.

'Mind you,' she said, 'he was bloody funny on *Graham Norton*.' This is what I love about Alex. Yes, Roland's a pushy tosser, but he's also great on telly. It's like what she said about Darren – he's a knob-end, but he's also very good-looking. You always believe Alex because she gives you the truth in all its forms, comforting and painful. What she says is never sugar-coated or false.

I relaxed and started reminiscing about the early, pre-TV and Radio Roland. He was always not drinking at the right parties and chatting up the Bishop of London, 'Ooh, Richard, you must come over sometime and I'll dribble all over you!'

Alex said I wasn't like that and that's why she loved

me. I do the things I was called to do. I serve my parishioners. I don't spend my time doing media stuff or clambering up the greasy pole. I agreed with her. I *could* do media stuff and clamber up the pole. But I choose not to.

I went off into the hall and put on my collar in the mirror and I asked myself the big question, *Why* do I choose not to? Maybe I'm not as good-looking as Darren, but I'm a sight nicer than Roland and just as intelligent. Why shouldn't I be TV and Radio's Adam Smallbone?

When I came out of that lap-dancing club with Ellie, and there were Nigel and Adoha and all the protesters, and I broke it to them that we'd won, I could tell from their faces that I had a touch of charisma about me. Why shouldn't I use that charisma to help humanity by spreading the Word of God and making myself and St Saviour's more prominent in the community?

For that matter, why can't I push my way to the top and become a bishop? When Jesus spoke of the humble being exalted, he wasn't referring to the C of E. Everyone knows the humble get nowhere in the C of E. The meek disappear. They inherit nothing. If I'm going to be exalted, I'm going to have to push.

The Church recognizes and understands the human condition. A man wants to better himself. What better than being a bishop? It's right there, in Timothy 3:1. 'This is a true saying. If a man desireth the office of a bishop, he desireth a good work.' Exactly!

It's time to build my castle.

I decided to come up with a five-point plan, which is just the kind of thing Roland would do to catch the eye of the Bishop. Then I'll talk it through with the Archdeacon, who can talk it through with the Bishop.

That will put my name in his mind. But I want him to know my face, too. And the best way to do that is to get it on telly. I shall use my contact.

I told Alex that Steve Warwick works on *The One Show*, which I bet the Bishop watches. How hard could it be to get myself on that show? She said I mustn't try, under any circumstances, to get myself on *The One Show*. But she would say that, wouldn't she? She was protecting me against potential disappointment.

On the kitchen table was the *Church Times*. We were both thrilled to see that Roland was not on the cover. Our only mistake was to open it up. There he was on page 2. Not to mention page 3.

'WISE WORDS – REVD ROLAND WISE SHARES HIS VIEWS ON THE MODERN CHURCH.' As if he'd ever keep them to himself.

Next to the headline was a half-page photo of Roly-poly, looking like a big smiley hungry bear. Plus his well-worn quote, 'We are all chained to the radiator of life.' He doesn't say that to help humanity. He says it to remind humanity that he's a personal friend of the brave former hostage Terry Waite, who was chained to the radiator of life in a far from metaphorical way. So it's actually pretty tasteless and tacky, though he says it like it's deep.

Alex said that in next week's edition Roland will be a naked centrefold.

I don't know if it was because she said that but the day then took an extraordinary turn for the gay.

I'd decided to order some new vestments, my predecessor having Poped off with all the good tat.

Nigel informed me that Father Winters at St Clems looked majestic in his magnificent gold and red chasuble from Norfolk & Cotes. I pointed out that, actually, he looks like Dumbledore, with his huge flappy wizard sleeves. Nevertheless, said Nigel, I should check out the Norfolk & Cotes website, the finest source of tat on the internet.

He wasn't wrong. Their website was astonishing. Not only was their range enormous, not only was everything available in every colour from avocado to zebra, but the photos were like something from the *New Gay Testament*.

I clicked on 'clergy shirts' and was confronted with a dreamboat dark-haired model vicar, right hand on hip, left hand on Bible, gazing up longingly in God's direction, while sporting a pink long-sleeved slip-in-collar clergy shirt. It turned out Nigel had the very same shirt in mint green. Me, I simply couldn't resist the emerald chasuble.

'Get back in the dressing-up box!' said Nigel. It's actually quite endearing when he loosens up enough to say stuff like that – we all know the aisle of a church is basically a catwalk. When I clicked on Add To Basket, though, I discovered the emerald chasuble was 'out of stock'.

'There's been unprecedented demand for it,' said

Nigel, who probably bought them all himself. So I opted for black. Straight black.

Nigel – as if it were a change of subject – told me he was very excited about launching his new Singles Only Suppers. He's sure they'll be more of a success than his Singles Only Breakfasts – apparently a lot of single men are depressed and not good at getting up in the morning. Nigel's calling these suppers 'SOS'. He made me promise to come to the first one. I couldn't say no. Nor could I say, why not just call them Desperate Lonely Gay Men Who Want to Top Themselves Suppers? So I said yes, in the hope he'd change the subject, and sure enough he asked me if I'd seen Roland Wise's article in the *Telegraph* that day. I begged him not to start on Roland, as I'd already had him in bed with me this morning.

It seemed that things could only get gayer. Was that bad?

No, there are no references in the Bible to monogamous, life-long, gay relationships, simply because they didn't exist, or weren't acknowledged, in the 1st century AD. If 'unnatural acts' are sinful, doesn't that include going against your own sexual nature, thereby making it a sin for homosexuals *not* to be homosexual? God is a God of love. Would God really advocate hatred of people who loved each other?

I want St Saviour's to be a place where such questions are asked, where debate is prized over dogma.

Prizing debate over dogma: that'll be point one in my five-point plan.

# 1st April

Colin, the least gay man on God's earth, wasn't at Morning Prayer, so I sought him out at the usual place, hoping for a ciggy and a chat. We had the chat but I had to decline his ciggy because it was, in fact, a spliff. He gave it to me anyway, because he wanted to go for a piss. At this point, inevitably, the Archdeacon appeared, inevitably because we'd agreed to have lunch in The Monarch to discuss my plan, but he'd decided to come to St Saviour's first, instinctively knowing he'd catch me in an embarrassing position with some class-C drugs.

The first thing I thought was, I hope the Bishop doesn't get to hear about this. I suppose that's the sort of thing you think when you become a careerist.

The lunch got off to a bad start. The Monarch doesn't serve the kind of food to which the Archdeacon's accustomed. He's a Gordon Ramsay man and I don't think Gordon would have much to say about The Monarch's scampi and chips, apart from, 'This is fucking shit.' The next problem was the Archdeacon had to leave as soon as he could, to go to a recording of *Just a Minute*, featuring Roland Wise. Blimey, I thought, Roland'll win *Just a Minute* easily, so many are the words that pour from his mouth. He'd probably win *Just an Hour*. The Archdeacon asked if I knew Roland. I said no. It was a small and meaningless and false victory. But it felt good all the same.

Without blinking, I told the Archdeacon exactly what

I stood for. I took a literary and critical view of the Scripture as divinely inspired but not inerrant. I saw the Bible as a metaphor, a brilliant record of humankind coming to understand itself. It was a really good attempt at some very big questions but it wasn't divine dictation, since it was written over many hundreds of years. He was bemused. This wasn't what he was expecting. He looked as if some dish had been delivered to his table that he hadn't ordered.

So I dived in with point one: to make St Saviour's a place that asked challenging questions. It wasn't the Church's role, I asserted assertively, to resolve issues for our congregation. Our role was to deepen them. I wanted to be a man with a message, a Christian message, based on the Gospel: that faith was beautiful but complicated, and that debate was far more enriching than dogma.

The Archdeacon was not keen. He told me that, in his experience, congregations preferred cornflakes to muesli, theologically speaking. My mind went blank. I just couldn't think of any other breakfast cereals with which to counter his argument. As a matter of fact, I think congregations prefer a full English breakfast to muesli *or* cornflakes. They crave the nutrition and variety of textures and flavours which only a non-dogmatic Church can give them. But I thought of all that much, much later, when he'd gone.

He much preferred point 2: my plan to move the coffee out of the vestry and into the nave, so we can accommodate more people. In fact, he suggested we buy a cappuccino machine, which he was sure would boost our numbers, especially as the stuff we currently served was 'muck'.

I've got used to his coffee abuse and didn't let it get to me. The fact was, the Archdeacon was actually quite impressed. He knew what I was up to and he gave me his support. I was new in London and I wanted to make my mark. Nothing wrong with that. I simply had to remember that there were 10,000 vicars and only 350 top jobs, so my chances of promotion in the C of E are about the same as in the Chinese Army.

Strangely, that didn't discourage me. We all know the 21st century belongs to the Chinese.

On my way back to St Saviour's, I stopped for some Jaffa Cakes, which always help me think. For some reason, Lisa wasn't on the phone. Maybe it was broken. And there was no one else in the shop. Why didn't I try to interest her in the church? I'd been promising myself I'd try that for months now. It wasn't too late to make my mark on Lisa.

'You're Lisa, aren't you?' I said.

'Yeah,' she replied warily, as if I was from the police and she shouldn't admit to anything.

'Do you go to church, Lisa?' I asked. There was a pause.

'That's £1.20,' she said.

That was my answer. My Jaffa Cakes answer. I took it as a no.

## 2nd April

They installed the cappuccino machine today. It's money well spent. That's what I'll tell them if they ask me at the Annual Parochial Church Meeting. I'll point to the new people it has brought into my church. So far, that means the man who installed it, but there'll be more.

But what's the point of installing it if people don't know it's there? Why be shy if you have something to offer that enriches people's lives, such as the Word of God or a cappuccino machine?

I got Nigel to stick a FREE CAPPUCCINO sign on the board outside, next to the times of services.

That's what Roland Wise would do.

## 3rd April

Alex said that when we made love last night I made weird sort of roaring noises, like a lion. I said I doubted that. She said it didn't make me more manly, it was actually quite camp. I promised not to do it again.

## 5th April

Take that, Archdeacon! Numbers were hugely up today. The cappuccino machine was a big success. Adoha has taken it to her bosom, I mean she literally hugged it when it arrived. She gives every cappuccino a chocolate-sprinkle crucifix stamp, which looks fantastic. I might get the *Church Times* to come and take a photo.

Ellie was wearing an off-white belted knee-length coat and a gold and black necklace, which perfectly complemented her black blouse. I always notice the way she's dressed because it's so refreshing. The C of E, sartorially speaking, is still in thrall to ladies in hats.

She asked if there was a loyalty card – 10 crucifix coffee stamps and you went to Heaven. I said I was sure she was going to Heaven anyway and I told her she looked lovely, which is just what Roland would have done. He's never been frightened to flatter people and neither am I, not now. That's how you get on.

Steve Warwick asked me if he could use the church for his daughter Phoebe's birthday party and I was ready with my answer – Can you get me on *The One Show*? Steve looked taken aback, just as Ellie had done. They don't expect me to be so forthright and confident, but they're going to have to get used to it.

Then he looked worried and asked me if I'd told anyone. Alex? Ellie? For a moment, I didn't know what he meant. Then I realized. No, why would I tell Alex or Ellie I'd bumped into him in a lap-dancing club? Anyway, Ellie already knew because she was in the lap-dancing club, too. For that matter, I'd only bumped into him in a lap-dancing club because I was in a lap-dancing club myself. He begged me not to say 'lap-dancing club' again. He said he'd do everything he could to help me get on *The One Show*, as if I was using the whole thing as blackmail. I wasn't. That was all in his mind.

## 6th April

The speed with which the TV world moves is extraordinary. Steve's researcher Becky called me today and said they want me on *The One Show* on Friday to talk about Lent. What it is and what's meant by Shrove Tuesday, Ash Wednesday and Maundy Thursday. I was thrilled. I said yes straightaway, though you're probably supposed to tell them you're busy on Friday, just so they want you more.

I'm going to be on BBC1, talking to millions of people. Mark 16:15: 'And he said unto them, Go ye into all the world, and preach the gospel to every creature.'

If that's not a divine instruction to go on *The One Show*, what is?

Becky told me I'd be on for five minutes, talking to Christine and Adrian. I said I was a big fan of both of them, which was pretty much a bluff, since I didn't know who either of them was. (I watched it tonight. Christine's pretty and Adrian's not is the basic set-up.)

Five minutes! That's longer than 'Thought for the Day', and the outreach – a word the C of E loves – is far greater.

There's so much I want to convey. Most people think Lent's the time Christians give up smoking or

drinking or cream cakes. They don't know we're repli-
cating Jesus Christ's 40 days and nights of fasting in the
desert in preparation for his ministry, or make the link
with the events leading up to the Crucifixion. They definitely don't know the etymology of Lent, from an old
English word meaning 'lengthen', since it takes place in
spring, when the days are getting longer.

I told Becky I'd like 40 days and nights to prepare for
my appearance, but would make do with three. She
didn't get the joke, which shows how much I'm needed.
She said I should be light, fun, fast and informative.


## 7th April

2.17 a.m.

I just saw Tony of Tony's Kebabs lock up his shop and
lower his iron grille. Tony always has the telly tuned to
BBC1. At 7 p.m. on Friday, Tony and his customers will
be part of my Lent outreach programme. It's inspiring.

I'm having an amazing night, the kind of night I used
to have at Bristol when I was cramming for my final
exams, all pumped up and motivated to show my new
girlfriend Alex I was really clever, far more clever than
Nat Jones, who just talked in a clever-sounding way. Up
three nights, doing my dissertation on the impact of the
Paris Commune on the history of socialism. Three
nights of Pot Noodle and coffee. As the dawn came up
on that final morning, I poured my coffee into the Pot
Noodle just to save time.

Light. Fun. Fast. Informative. I've written those words on different-coloured cards pinned to the wall. And I've been true to all of them.

This is how I'll begin: I'll thank Adrian or Christine, or both of them, and then I'll just look into the camera and recite the Eucharistic Preface, which I've spent the last 2 hours learning:

For in these forty days
You lead us into the desert of repentance,
That through a pilgrimage of prayer and discipline
We may grow in grace
And learn to be your people once again.
Through fasting, prayer and acts of service
You bring us back to your generous heart.
Through study of your holy word
You open our eyes to your presence in the world
And free our hands to welcome others
Into the radiant splendour of your love.

At first I worried it was too long, but the more I say it, the faster it goes. After the Preface, I'll expound on Jesus in the wilderness, then I'll go to the booze and the cream cakes, then the etymology of Lent (and Shrove) and then I'll hit them with the significance of the number 40 in Judeo-Christian tradition – the flood in Genesis being brought about by 40 days and nights of rain, the Israelites spending 40 years in the wilderness before reaching the promised land. That's light and fun and informative, isn't it? I also have 'Stephen Fry' pinned to the wall, because it would be good if I could make it all a bit *QI*.

My last act, after I've written all that and before I go to bed, will be to email Reverend Roy Richards of St Peter's, Stoke Bishop, and tell him to turn on his telly at 7 p.m. on Friday. I hope he still has that black and white telly in his cottage, the last telly in England that only works if you twist the indoor aerial and bang the top of the set.

I've been thinking a lot about Rev Roy in the last few days. He is my mentor and I am his protégé, and that's how it will always be, even if I become Bishop of London. Rev Roy recommended that I be ordained, a process he described as 'being changed into yourself'. He told me I wouldn't be changed into myself for my own sake. I'd be changed into someone who was able to articulate the divine will. He made faith and ordination credible. And he made the one follow the other.

Without him, I'd still be sitting on my arse in the Bristol City Council Housing Department, reading *Zen and the Art of Motorcycle Maintenance*. Rev Roy took me under his wing. It was often a rather drunken wing. Shambolic and sometimes over-flappy. But it was warm and it brought me here.

## 9th April

I recited the Eucharistic Preface to Alex at breakfast and she said it was lovely but on no account should I do it on *The One Show*, even if I can do it that fast. I should just answer the questions Adrian and Christine ask me in as normal a way as possible.

She thinks I'm currently abnormal. Hyped up. Strung out. I pointed out that I felt exactly like this at Bristol in those final weeks. She said I didn't roar like a lion then, and I asked her how she'd know – she didn't sleep with me for the first time till the August Bank Holiday after I got my results, and the fact that I got a very good 2:1 may have had something to do with that. So the hyped-up strung-out weeks were worth it.

She said I was being ridiculous. She didn't fall in love with my exam results, she fell in love with me. She thinks she'll get me back again after I've been on *The One Show*. I'll be normal again, if she's lucky.

I'm not sure I want to be normal again. Being normal gets you nowhere. No one has ever called Roland Wise 'normal'.

## 10th April

Just before the car arrived to take me to the studio, I felt serious but fun, authoritative but dashing, informative but accessible. But then I just felt shit. I asked Alex if I should have a drink to calm my nerves and she said she was going to have a large one herself, which worried me, because a person shouldn't need to calm her nerves before a show that she's only watching. So I had a whisky and I thought of Rev Roy, who was probably doing the same, not because he was nervous but because it was quarter past five.

The phone rang and I was terrified it was Adrian or Christine wondering where I was, but it was only Nigel wondering where I was. His Singles Only Supper Night had just begun (which was pretty sad in itself, considering the time). I told him I couldn't possibly get there because I was about to go on a national television, BBC1 flagship show with 7 million viewers. None of that meant anything to him. He seriously expected me to be in church instead, watching 14 lonely gay men get more and more depressed as they ploughed their way through Tesco's charcuterie and Nigel's vegetarian lasagne.

In the car, I went over and over what I had to say, till it was word perfect. Then I got to the studio, shook the hands of Adrian and Christine, and was fussed over by lots of Beckys, Cheryls and Naomis, which was lovely. In the Green Room, which was gratifyingly green, I had another drink, which had absolutely no effect, and I chatted to a sweet man called Craig who was about to open an Abba museum in Bedford. Then we were taken to the studio. On the way I kept thinking of *Dead Man Walking*, that film with Susan Sarandon as the nun and Sean Penn as the murderer on death row she does everything in her power to help, because the walk to the studio was just like the walk to the electric chair, except, being nun-less, I had to supply my own spiritual balm.

I sat down in the studio chair and told myself they weren't about to switch it on. The nervous paralysis that gripped my arms didn't really matter, because I wouldn't have to move my arms, I'd just have to move my mouth. The worst thing was the sweaty hands. What could I do about them? I decided the best thing to do was ignore them. Nobody wants to turn on their telly and see a vicar wiping his hands on his trousers.

'One minute everyone,' said a disembodied voice from the control room. It really did feel like he was saying I had a minute to live. My heart was really pounding now. But that was great. That was how I knew I was still alive.

I thought of Steve Warwick in the control room, and how he'd probably only agreed to my being on the show because he was worried I'd tell someone about meeting him in a lap-dancing club.

And then a person who was sort of half windmill, half man counted us down. Five, four, three, two, one.

I thought of Alex and Colin and the Bishop and the Archdeacon and Ellie and Rev Roy and Tony of Tony's Kebabs. And the thought of Tony seeing me on his telly as he sliced away at the shish filled me with a great love for all humanity, particularly the local humanity: my wife, my parish, my neighbours, my congregation. I was full of love when Adrian started talking.

He said 'good evening', he said 'tonight's show' and then he mentioned lots of names. And then he said mine. Then he said Lent. I was off! This was my chance and I wasn't going to waste it. I was going to say everything there was to say about Lent, and I was going to say it now, while the camera was on me. I remember saying

Shrove derived from the medieval word 'shrive', meaning to confess, and I remember thinking that wasn't the first thing I meant to say. What was the first thing I meant to say? Oh yes, I meant to say what 'Lent' meant. By which time I was saying the second thing I meant to say, though I still hadn't got to the first. And then I had, if not an out-of-body experience, an out-of-mouth experience. There were words coming out of my mouth but they didn't seem to come from me. I felt I wasn't saying them. I was just there, watching them come out.

After 10 seconds, or 10 minutes, I sensed that Adrian and Christine were embarrassed and I knew, I just knew, that I wasn't being light enough or fast enough, or fun enough or informative enough. I just wasn't being *enough*. So I tried to be more of everything and then Christine cut me off.

She, or was it Adrian, introduced Craig, then Christine, or was it Adrian, asked me if we were Abba fans in the Church. I laughed nervously, having no idea what to say, and then they said something about us vicars liking to dress up, ha ha ha, and then I said, yes, we're all completely gay in the Church. That was the definitive out-of-mouth moment. I could see those words in a speech bubble suspended above my head. I could see them in great big capital letters in a bubble that would never burst. Frozen for all time in the bubble. 'WE'RE ALL COMPLETELY GAY IN THE CHURCH.' And then I really did feel like a dead man walking. I felt as though I'd pulled some lever and electrocuted myself.

Anything I said now was said by a dead man. Dead man walking, dead man talking. Dead man shooting himself in the foot.

When the show was over I rushed off, without saying goodbye to Steve Warwick, let alone Adrian or Christine or Craig the Abba man or any of the Beckys or Naomis, who by 7.10 had forgotten me anyway. I got home and we watched the whole thing again, just so I could find out what I'd said after the bad thing.

I'd said we weren't all gay in the Church, I for one was married, but equally we were very accepting of gays, in fact there was a supper for gay men going on in my church as I spoke.

Why did he say that? (I mean, why did *I* say that.) Alex assured me I had nothing to worry about, it was obviously a joke, and anyway, nobody watched *The One Show*. I know she meant that to be reassuring, but it didn't help at all. Nothing could shake my certainty that everyone I'd ever met had just seen me on *The One Show*, along with several million people who'd never heard of me before, but now knew me as the vicar who made the we're-all-gay-in-the-Church joke.

When she asked what she could do to cheer me up, I told her to ring Bristol City Council and see if I could have my old job back. She took far too long to understand that this was just a 'joke'.

We went to bed. I couldn't sleep. I thought of getting up and going to Tony's Kebabs and apologizing for my abject performance. Maybe Alex was right, though. Maybe nobody did watch it. I mean, the customers in Tony's Kebabs actually watching me on *The One Show*, talking about Lent? While they waited for their doners? The idea was absurd. Who did I think I was, Roland Wise?

I should never have gone on that show. The whole thing was misguided. I don't know what I was trying to prove.

## 11th April

I told the Archdeacon it was just a light-hearted remark, there was nothing wrong with being gay, inside the Church or out, not that I happened to be gay myself. But he hadn't turned up in my kitchen to debate the Church's attitude to gays.

In his view, my remark was not about gays at all. It was all about *me*. It was me trying to get noticed, me saying something, anything, that would make a splash with the high-ups in the C of E, the generals in the Chinese Army. But through inexperience I'd said the wrong thing. I'd made a splash but it was the wrong kind.

'There has been blowback to your splash,' he said, ominously.

All I needed, he opined, was some media training. Did I know Roland Wise, he asked, forgetting he'd asked me that a few days ago. So this time I said yes. Yes, I'd been at college with Roland. We used to drink at The Bat & Ball in Cuddesdon, oh yes. 'I love Roland,' I said, nauseating myself with my own hypocrisy.

The Archdeacon loved Roland, too. I'd never seen him go gooey before. His face went all smiley and radiant, like some lovely old uncle, and he giggled to himself, doubtless remembering something Roland had said on *Just a Minute*.

He promised he'd send 'Roly' to come over and see me. Till then, I should avoid radio and TV and journalists.

Our tête-à-tête was over. All that remained was for him to pour his coffee down the sink and for me to go to St Saviour's to face the wrath of Nigel, which kicked off as soon as I walked in the door. He told me to picture the scene: 15 men sat watching the telly 'with charcuterie on our laps and our mouths wide open' (presumably to put the charcuterie in). All of them utterly appalled as I labelled the lot of them gay.

'Some of these men are *married*, Adam!'

I asked him what they were doing at his singles night in that case, since everyone knew it was a gay thing. Nigel protested, as he always does. Protested too much. It was not 'a gay thing'. There was a straight man there, for one. A straight and lonely man called Derek, who everyone now thought was a gay and lonely man.

I've never once said, come on, Nigel, admit it, you're gay. It seems to me that forcing Nigel to come out is as bad as forcing Nigel to stay in. The latter being official Church policy, according to many of my colleagues, as if a confused and celibate Christian is somehow better equipped to do God's work than a happy and fulfilled one.

So instead of grabbing Nigel's nose and tweaking it

till he shouted, 'I'm gay!' I said sorry. I was very sorry, but I was under pressure, and however it sounded, all I meant to say was that the Church was not homophobic and neither was I.

Nigel showed me the emails. He could have forwarded them to me electronically, but he'd printed them out and divided them into piles, which was incredibly Nigel of him. Half of them said I was homophobic and a disgrace. The other half said I was pro-homosexual and a disgrace. And one was from an Abba fan who thinks I'm stupid, but still gave me the link to the new Abba Museum in Bedford.

## 14th April

Roland Wise called and said he was free for supper tomorrow so he'd see us then. It didn't even occur to him that we might not be free ourselves, which as it happens we are. Roland Wise had a slot free, so he assumed we'd be thrilled to fill it. Especially as he'd 'blown out Mary Beard'. Surely, it was the other way round. Wasn't it?

Now I've been on *The One Show*, I must admit to having more respect for Roland. I understand now how hard it is when the show's about to start and the lights and cameras are on you. You need a cast-iron sense of self to withstand the heat and light. I don't think I have that supreme confidence in who I am and what I want to say. Not like Roland.

And I don't really want to reach out to people, not on

the scale that he does. When *The One Show* started, I kidded myself that I love the great mass of people. But I don't, not really, there are too many of them. I don't really want to embrace 7 million viewers.

Seven million is nothing, of course. Jesus wanted to reach out to everyone in the world. The poor, the sick, the needy, the high-born, the low-born, the prostitute, the King. It didn't matter who you were or where you were from. You get the sense, when you read the Gospels, that he had time for everyone, everywhere, always. 'Go therefore and make disciples of all nations.'

I'm not saying Roland Wise is like Jesus. That would be grotesque. I'm just saying that I think, in some ways, he's more like Jesus than I am.

## 15th April

When it actually came to preparing his supper, the evening filled me with dread. Just the thought of him ringing the bell and me opening the door and him standing there, on the phone to Kirsty Wark.

I thought of the Cell Group Weekend I'd had with him in Wales. The worst weekend of my life, rain bucketing down for 48 hours, that special sort of Welsh rain, all powerful and dark, and Roland and me and two other young curates locked up together in a National Trust cottage, like some horrific social experiment, playing Christian Top Trumps. It still makes me shiver.

Then our bell rang. It *tolled*. On my way to the front

door, I went past the mirror and put on my big yes-I-love-him grin. But it wasn't Roland, it was Mick wanting to use our toilet as one of Tony's Kebabs had gone straight through him. I told him to use the pub. He said there wasn't time as he was touching cloth, and then I saw a taxi arrive. Roland got out with a bottle of wine, which I could tell at 50 paces cost at least £15.99. So I shut the door on Mick, fixed my grin in the mirror again and just kept shouting to Alex, he's here, he's here, completely unable to stop myself overdoing it.

I opened the door. Roland greeted me with, 'Look at you, the modern man, all moved up to London!' Somehow it was impossible to say anything in reply. It was as if I was watching him on TV. I put out my hand for him to shake and he hugged me instead. The patronizing speech was 15-love, the hug was 30-love, and suddenly it was 40-love, as he told me a man was defecating on my lawn.

He came in and said 'hi' to Alex and then it was time for some anecdotes. He started with one about meeting Salman Rushdie in a Turkish bath. It was quite a funny story, but all I could think was, I've never even had a Turkish bath, let alone met Salman.

By the time we got to supper, I just focused on the fact that he'd been sent by the Archdeacon to help me. So the best thing I could do was open myself up to him. What did he think I should do? He advised me to get straight back on the media horse. Did I want him to get me on 'Thought for the Day'? I couldn't believe there was a man in our dining room who could get me on

'Thought for the Day'. I asked him if he was serious and he said – completely straight – yes, they did what he told them.

I sat there wondering what I could say on 'Thought for the Day'. I'd thought for years about being on that programme, but I'd never actually thought about my Thought. Then it hit me. Ask Roland! He suggested I say something from the heart, something intensely personal and sincere and authoritative and Godly and humane and wise and funny. (I assumed that it also had to be light and fast and informative.)

'No pressure then,' said Alex, trying to inject some humour. But Roland wasn't amused.

What was from the heart? I told him about this Scottish pianist on the homeless night, playing Rachmaninov and making me a cup of tea without tea. How moving that was, even though it went wrong, and how it made me think of my favourite MacNeice poem, about the importance of small, daily unnoticed acts of kindness. I'd often thought of using it as the basis of a sermon, but I never had, so maybe I'd been holding it back for a time like this. I wanted to say it was synchronicity, but then I thought, No, you mean serendipity.

'Great, use it, I'll fix it,' he said. It was great to be with a man of action.

He complimented Alex on her spaghetti arrabiata, which reminded him of a dish he'd once eaten on Lebedev's yacht in Portofino. I couldn't look at her because I knew what she was thinking. Ooh, get him, with his big Italian accent for *arrabiata*, then his big Russian one for

'*Lebedev*', then another big Italian one for '*Portofino*'. The thing was, I could happily take the piss out of him before he arrived, but once he was there it was different. I'd forgotten what it was like to be in a room with Roland. He had a power that was quite intimidating.

Alex returned the cooking compliment by saying how much she enjoyed him on *Have I Got News for You*.

'Yes, it's a fun show,' said Roland. And that was it. He closed down the conversation, because it wasn't the conversation he wanted to have, and then he drank another glass of red wine and looked even more serious. Did I want him to tell me how to overcome my nerves on live radio? I thanked him and prepared for a masterclass.

His lesson amazed me.

This is what Roland does when he's looking at the microphone and waiting for his cue.

He imagines all the people listening. And then he despises them. He reminds himself what a herd of stupid, ignorant, uneducated, graceless, E-number-chomping plebeians they are, desperately seeking some form of guidance in their sad little fruitless lives.

Alex went into the kitchen at that point and didn't return. Half an hour later, as she and I stacked the washing-up machine, Alex shoved the plates in very loudly, which she always does when she's furious. She said he was an egomaniac psychopath with a loathsome contempt for ordinary people. How could I envy a man like that?

I went into the living room and sat with Roland. Alex came in a few moments later and very much didn't sit.

She offered to call him a cab, in a very brisk voice, like she wanted him to wait for it outside, in the dark, on the lawn, next to Mick's poo. He brushed her away, preferring to stay for 'a couple more drinks'. So Alex said she was going to bed, another 10-ton hint. He kissed her hand and bade her, 'Goodnight, dear lady.' Then he wished her '*bonne nuit*' and '*gute Nacht*' and something that sounded like '*bakkalakkalak*' that was probably goodnight in Arabic.

We were alone. Me and Roland. And the bottle of whisky he'd spotted. I could tell we were going to have a heart to heart, even though Alex didn't think he had one. As soon as she left, he told me she was wonderful, which was very nice, though I couldn't help thinking he hadn't addressed a single question to her all night.

He told me I was very lucky, not just to have Alex but to have a lovely home. And then any resentment or envy or antipathy drained from my body, because the poor man started crying. He cried because I was so happy with my wife and my church. I'd made him realize he could no longer remember why he'd got ordained.

It all poured out. How he went on telly all the time because he couldn't say no, he had to please everyone, he was a compulsive court jester. I was a proper priest, and he was just a godless shitting empty priest with no thought or purpose or ministry. These were extraordinary things to hear.

Onward he went. And downward. Did I remember that weekend we spent in Wales? Wasn't that great? I put on my best grin. That, said Roland, was the last time he was happy. And then he started crying again, full of self-pity and self-hatred.

I couldn't just sit there and watch him cry. I had to comfort him as a friend and fellow priest who, as it turned out, felt a lot better about being a priest than he did. I told him he was intelligent and quite funny. (I didn't want to overdo it.) I said he was someone who'd just lost his way for a moment, the way we all do. I suggested that, in the morning, he and I go to St Saviour's first thing and say the Morning Office together. Just the two of us. To get him back to simple ministry for a moment.

And then I gave him another whisky and made up the bed in our spare room. An hour later, I heard him come upstairs, with some difficulty, possibly in a zigzag.

A few hours later, when I woke up, I opened the spare-room door gently and sneaked a look. This great bear of a man, scrunched up on a single bed, looking woebegone. A piteous sight.

## 16th April

We got to St Saviour's so early that when we knelt down side by side and prayed, we could hear the dawn chorus. The birds seemed like witnesses to a moment we'd never forget. I felt moved enough – unselfconscious enough – to recite the opening verses of MacNeice's 'Fanfare for the Makers'. The poet's words worked their magic. I'd never seen Roland look so gentle or humble. It seemed to me only right, since he'd opened up to me, that I open up to him. So I told him I used to be very jealous of him. He could have waved that away or been falsely modest, but instead he was honest. He knew I'd been jealous and it was OK, a lot of people were, which had made him very lonely. And then we looked at each other and Roland leaned in so I could hug him. It was nothing like the hug with which he'd greeted me last night. I was the big bear now, and Roland was the baby bear who needed warmth and protection. It occurred to me that Nigel should invite him to his Singles Only Suppers.

A few minutes later, as he hailed a cab, I thought he had recovered. When the cab arrived, though, he kept it waiting. He asked me to recite the whole of the Mac Neice poem, which I did, standing there in Shoreditch High Street, with the cab engine running. He was close to tears again. He couldn't speak. He just got in the cab, shaking his head, then lowered the window and held out his hand in a silent farewell.

*Later* . . .

I was in the kitchen. It was just after 8. *Any Questions* had just started. Roly, my new best friend, was on it. Good for him, I thought, because this was nothing like the last time I'd heard him on the radio, when I'd had to pull the plug out of the wall to shut him up. I didn't know then how much he'd suffered. Some people wear their suffering on the surface, like Colin, with his battered face. People like Roland, smiley Roland, keep their pain within. You can't see it on account of their dazzling surface. But it's there. I'd felt it. I'd felt Roland's pain.

Roland was asked if today's politicians are as obsessed with spin as they were in the time of Blair. He answered by quoting a poem. A poem by MacNeice, in which the poet spoke of the transformative power of kindness.

A poem, said Roland, he'd 'always loved'.

Thank you, Roland bastard breakdown Wise, for always loving the poem you didn't even know existed until I told you this morning.

And what did the poem have to do with 'spin'? Did Roland even know what he was saying? Maybe the great Roland Wise was having an out-of-mouth experience.

If stealing your friend's favourite poem is what you have to do to get on, I don't want to get on.


## 19th April, *Palm Sunday*

Forty of us and Basil the donkey, who'd travelled 50 miles from the Fun Farm near Great Bardfield in Essex, commemorated the triumphal entry of Jesus into Jerusalem by processing up the Hackney Road and into St Saviour's.

Unlike Gromford, the Hackney Road has seen enough traffic to last several lifetimes, so to *be* the traffic for half an hour felt like a real blow for humanity, a victory for the 2-legged over the 4-wheeled, a slowing down of everything. In Jerusalem, AD 33, a donkey meant peace. We moved at a peaceful pace.

Colin loved it when I told him every donkey had a cross on its back, because the donkey that carried Jesus to Jerusalem followed him to Calvary, where the shadow of the cross fell on it and every donkey thereafter. He proudly told passing children that Basil was 'symbolic' and not for riding. He also told Adoha, who he loves to wind up, that a donkey was one of the few 'vehicles' he'd never nicked.

When I was seven, I was a donkey myself, in a production of Britten's *Noye's Fludde*, trooping down the aisle of Orford Church in my donkey mask with the stuck-on ears, singing 'Kyrie Eleison'. So my sense of God is bound up with animals. Maybe everyone's is – everyone who grows up in the Church of England. 'All things bright and beautiful/All creatures great and small'. The idea that God made creatures was the first religious thought implanted in my brain. It never occurred to me that 'creatures' might include human beings.

The kids, most of them from Ellie's school (a couple of them excluded from Ellie's school), responded to Basil with a gentleness and wonder you don't often see in the playground. And I think they understood that it wasn't just a parade with a donkey, and a chance to hold a palm cross above your head as if it were a party balloon. It was a celebration of the Prince of Peace. Though it's Basil they'll remember.

'Rejoice greatly, O daughter of Zion! Shout, O daughter of Jerusalem! Behold, your King is coming to you. He is just and having salvation, lowly and riding on a donkey.'

What happened in the Hackney Road was inspiring, even if it wasn't as advertised in Zechariah 9, since not everyone rejoiced greatly, or at all. Many car horns were hooted in anger. Our police escort was asked, more than once, why they weren't stopping crime instead of 'flanking a bleeding donkey'. A staggering number of passers-by simply ignored us, or asked if it was something to do with Comic Relief.

'Like your horse, mate!' said one guy, striding out into the middle of the road to take a selfie of him and the donkey before Colin pushed him away. That's all it was to him – a photo opportunity.

Inspiring and dismal. Dismal but inspiring. It's striking how often those two adjectives meet in the Church of England.


## 20th April

A letter arrived from Rev Roy, alive and well and retired in Castle Combe. He's delighted I'm working in an inner London parish where my 'gentle nature and diplomatic skills will be severely tested but sorely needed'. He apologized for missing my appearance on *The One Show*, but his telly broke down two years ago and the TV repairman said it wasn't worth replacing, which he'd taken as a reference to the quality of the programmes. I must tell him if I'm ever on the radio, though. He wished me 'joy and renewal' for Holy Week. Then, in classic Rev

Roy-style, he signed off by telling me not to miss the special offers on Spanish wines at the Co-op.

## 23rd April

To St Paul's Cathedral for the Maundy Thursday Chrism Mass.

The Diocese of London covers 177 square miles and contains 413 parishes and 484 churches. (I know this because Nigel told me and I wrote it down, as I wanted to show him I cared. How does he remember stuff like that? He's a sort of Nigel-pedia.)

St Paul's, if you spend your life in St Saviour's, is overwhelming. Both are built for the glory of God but only one has a broken stained-glass window. (As of today, the Window Restoration Fund is 'only' £26,212 short of its target.)

The Bishop was great. He talked to us like men and women of the world, making us understand what it meant to renew the promises of our ordination. He gave us ideas, not clichés, as a leader should.

'Doctrinal purity is secondary to ministry,' he concluded, giving us something to talk about in the pub afterwards.

And there we were. All the vicars in London. What's the collective noun for vicars? A condescension? A snore? A humbling? A 'cathedral', I suppose. We definitely divide into types. There are still, even now, men who look like the younger sons of aristocrats, chaps who go into the Church because that's what the younger sons of aristocrats *do*. There are still a few heavy drinkers, too, beetroot-faced men I feel drawn to, as a protégé of Rev Roy. Then there are the groovy ones, who look like they used to work in advertising or the music business or financial PR, before a mid-life crisis propelled them into the arms of the C of E, but they've still kept their big moustaches or ponytails.

Mostly, though, priests look (and act) like prima donnas or depressives. Or both, given that prima donnas have such exalted self-regard that, sooner or later, it's bound to collapse. In that sense, Roland's not untypical. As the Bishop spoke, a great cloud of ego rose from our heads, enough to fill the dome of St Paul's. But it wouldn't be long before the cloud burst, leaving all the priests sat on a sofa, weeping, convinced of their own uselessness and the futility of it all.

I didn't go to the pub afterwards. I didn't want to drink with 483 vicars, whingeing in 483 different ways. But I encouraged Nigel to do so, as it's all part of 'getting on'.

At St Saviour's tonight, the Mass of the Lord's Supper was beautiful. Heartbreaking too. How could it not be lowering and elevating at the same time? The prospect of the Cross looming over everything, even while you're giving thanks for the gift of the Eucharist.

I was meant to wash 12 pairs of feet but I ended up doing 15, as Colin brought a couple of mates who fancied some of the action. As a parable of service, it occurred to me to kiss their feet. Ellie had nice ankles and turquoise nail varnish, but I thought if I kissed Ellie's, I'd have to kiss Colin's, too.

After the Mass came the Stripping of the Altars. Altar hangings, candlesticks, ornaments, candles, all gone. Holy-water stoup emptied. Blessed Sacrament removed from the tabernacle. Paintings and crucifixes veiled.

'Do you know of its origins in the exile of the Jews to Babylon in 587 BC?' asked Nigel, expecting the answer no.

'The temple was stripped and vandalized and the worship stopped. Of course,' he continued, 'that dereliction is seen in Christian thought as a prophecy of the destruction by human hands of Jesus Christ who, as the place where God and humanity meet, is essentially the new Temple.' This was fascinating stuff, only spoiled by his smile of self-satisfaction at the end. Nigel was silently giving himself an A star.

Then he said, 'It's like a building site,' and I found myself in agreement. It didn't look precisely like that – no building site has pews – but it was desolate and basic and unadorned. And 'building site' is a good metaphor. It certainly beats 'radiator of life'. It made me think of the bombed-out buildings in the East End after the Blitz. They were terrible, yes, but they made you think about the human capacity to make things good. Buildings were destroyed and then re-born. For a Christian, there's no metaphor more potent.

## 24th April, *Good Friday*

I brought the cross into St Saviour's and held it high and sang, three times, 'This is the wood of the Cross on which hung the Saviour of the World.'

These are the moments when a priest is, as Rev Roy says, everybody and nobody. You speak for the world, but your own self – your body and clothes and possessions, your home and the people you love, your ideas and memories, your 5-point plans – is nothing. You abase and negate yourself.

I felt I could fit through the eye of a needle.

## 25th April

The Easter Vigil started at midnight. It was the biggest crowd I'd ever had in St Saviour's, apart from Darren's crowd, which I don't really count.

I suppose I should say it was the biggest crowd I'd ever had outside St Saviour's, since that's where we began, gathered round our health-and-safety brazier-contained fire. What we got in the inner city, which I never got in Suffolk, was passing trade – people who are out and about at 1 in the morning because they're living in a 24-hour city, as opposed to Gromford, which is basically a 12-hour village, with everyone getting up when it's light and staying inside when it's dark.

'On this most holy night, in which our Lord Jesus

passed over from death to life, we gather in vigil and prayer. For this is the Passover of the Lord.'

A hundred people must have heard me say that, true believers and passing clubbers alike. All drawn to the flame. Then I lit the Paschal candle from the fire and led the crowd into the church, which was when the clubbers fell away. Once we were inside St Saviour's, everyone in the congregation lit a candle from mine. It's not just a symbol of the risen Christ, there's a comradeship in it, a fellow feeling of joy in the light of the world, which isn't surpassed by anything else in the Christian calendar.

Rev Roy was right. There *were* excellent offers on Spanish wines at the Co-op, which was why at half-past five in the morning, long after the Exultet, the Gloria, the Eucharistic Prayer and the Communion, a small group of hardened Christians and drinkers were still guzzling vestry-chilled Spanish Cava.

## 26th April, *Easter Sunday*

We sang my favourite hymn of all, 'Thine Be The Glory'. Only Handel could have written that tune. His music has the power to make you believe you can conquer death. The words are extraordinary, too. (Who wrote them? I must look it up or ask Nigel-pedia.) The angels rolling the stone. The 'folded grave clothes'. Those images are transcendent and earthbound, too. There's dirt and bones in there.

Thine be the glory, risen, conquering Son;
Endless is the victory, thou o'er death hast won.
Angels in bright raiment rolled the stone away,
Kept the folded grave clothes where thy body lay.

Alex wasn't keen on an Easter egg hunt taking place in our house. Me neither. But where could I hide them? Our 'garden' is as flat and featureless as a piece of paper. I'm not some country parson with a few acres, a rockery or two and many an egg-concealing tree. As it is, there were maybe a dozen kids running up and down our stairs and in and out of every room, in search of chocolate plunder.

I stared out of our bedroom window while Steve Warwick's daughters bounced up and down on our bed, doubtless crushing all the eggs I'd concealed under the duvet.

From the window I saw Mick dancing on the lawn to the music inside his head. The man's a good mover. Then he stopped and started shaking his head, which he does when he's stressed. Mick had trodden in some shit. His own shit, in fact. The shit he'd deposited in desperation the night Roland came to dinner. I'd failed to clear it up. I can't blame Alex, that wouldn't be right. My parishioner, my parishioner's shit.

I thought of opening the window and apologizing to him, but why should I apologize for not clearing it up when he hadn't apologized for doing it?

Apart from that, it's been a Holy Week full of 'joy and

renewal', just as Rev Roy hoped. I feel I've served the community well, or at any rate those members of the community who come to church.


## 29th April

Mulberry House.

I asked Joan if she'd had a nice Easter. She said, 'No.' I asked her what she'd been doing and she said, 'Nothing.'

I asked her how the man in the next room was doing, the man who'd had a top job at British Gas, and she said he was 'old'. So, to raise the general level of excitement, I told her about my Easter. The Chrism Mass in St Paul's, the washing of the feet, the Easter Vigil. We talked about the candle in the church being a symbol of the resur- rected Lord. For some reason, that stimulated her and she started telling me a story.

She'd fractured her leg in a car crash when she was 21. A lovely young trumpeter called Murray was driving her home from a party. She told me that in the Forties, after the War, people thought drinking *improved* their driving. She'd just started training as a dancer, which was already very late, but everyone said she was a natural and had the most wonderful legs. After the accident the doctors told her she might never dance again. But she didn't give up. 18 months later, she got her first professional engage- ment, and in 1951, she was in the chorus line of the first West End production of *South Pacific*.

'I came back from the dead, Alan!' That was the punchline. That was the Easter aspect if you will.

The visit made me feel extraordinarily lonely. Maybe it was just the 'Alan'. Or maybe it was being God's representative, in a God's representative uniform. Sometimes it can make you feel sort of invisible.

The day I decided to be ordained, I was up most of the night with my best friend Tim, in that terrible flat he had in Peckham, with the smell of prawn crackers coming up from the Chinese takeaway below. I told him all about Rev Roy's theory that everyone who wanted to be ordained had an external and an internal cause, and that Rev Roy was the external cause, because he'd spotted my potential and encouraged me and kind of put me on the path; and the internal cause was a revelatory experience I'd had in Wales while I was high on magic mushrooms. I explained to him my conviction that the Bible was a record of man coming to understand himself, and that within every human being there was the potential to love thy neighbour as thyself. I talked to him about theology and ethics and teleology and the importance of liturgy.

And then, at about four in the morning, Tim said, 'So, basically, you just want to be nice.'

I don't think I'm nicer than anyone else. I seem nice to Joan, though. Nice but invisible.

My gran used to love those thrillers by Leslie Charteris about Simon Templar, *The Saint*. They always had a skeleton on the cover with a halo. That's pretty much how I felt with Joan.

## 3rd May

We woke early and tried for a baby, which was lovely, but meant I slept through breakfast.

Fifteen minutes before I was due at the school, I woke up. Now I had to run down Hackney Road. The obstacles were tremendous. People, hundreds of people, most of them on phones, not even noticing me hurtling towards them. (Extraordinary the way talking on a phone makes a person blind.) Dogs. Cartons. Skateboarders. Vomit. Bollards. Black plastic sacks.

Sooner or later, it had to happen. I was running one way and he was running the other. Bam, we slammed into each other and ended up on the ground.

He was about 14, with a little bum fluff moustache. He was obviously running for the bus, because it pulled up at the stop behind us. I told him I was sorry, asked if he was OK, said it was all my fault and I hoped he'd catch his bus. He did too. I shouted, 'Well done!' He thrust his middle finger at me and said, 'Pacdo!'

I looked down and saw a woman's handbag. Adoha rushed up to me.

'Thank you, Adam. God bless you! That little bastard snatched my bag and ran for it. My hero!'

I told her no, the whole thing was an accident. The boy bumped into me. I just happened to be there. But Adoha wasn't having any of it. She'd seen the whole thing. I'd wrestled that little bastard to the ground and snatched her handbag back.

I said, 'No, no, really, it was nothing.'

'My hero!' she said. Again. And then she hugged me.

I got to school late and had to wait outside what was meant to be my own assembly.

I thought about the little bastard. His middle finger. His angry face. If I saw him again, what would I say? (Apart from the obvious 'Fancy bumping into you!') There was something so urban about him. A street kid, as opposed to what I was, which was a village kid. There was so much less aggression in a village. And so much less litter. The village green was exactly that – green. There were no brown and blue and white bits, no fast-food cartons and plastic bags.

If I saw him again, I'd tell him he needed to get out of London. Expand his horizons. Leave the mean streets behind.

'Adam! Oversleep, did you?' asked Ellie, coming out of assembly. 'Don't worry, I covered for you. I mentioned God twice. Do I have to do your job on top of my own?'

It was important for me to win back her respect. So I apologized and told her about the handbag incident – not actually saying I did anything heroic, but not saying I didn't either. I told her it had given me an exciting idea.

'So many kids round here have never been out of London. I bet half your kids haven't.' She shrugged, but agreed I was probably right. 'They need to see the countryside, Ellie. Some cows!'

'*Cows*, Adam?'

160

'Yes. Half your kids have no idea where cheese comes from. If they've seen a cow at all, they expected it to lay an egg. As the person in charge of their pastoral care, I'd like to take your kids to the seaside.'

'Are there cows there?' she asked. I told her there'd be cows on the way. We'd go to the White Cliffs of Dover.

They'd love it. The White Cliffs! A natural wonder that would give them, along with cows, a sense of history. They might even see France. This was ministry. This was incarnational. This was the widening of children's eyes and the (literal) expansion of horizons.

Ellie said the idea had 'considerable merit'. Or was I was trying to get her in the back seat of a coach? This is what she always does to me. She alternates betwen formal and withering and flirtatious. Somehow, it's all designed to keep me in my place. But it's also quite enjoyable.

I said, 'We'll take your 15 most difficult but deserving children. Chloe Craven will love it.'

Ellie thought I had no idea what 'difficult' meant. A Year Six boy had just been cautioned for attempted twocking.

I tutted. 'Oh well. At least he didn't suceed.'

She suspected I didn't know what twocking was. I said of course I knew.

I didn't, but I knew I was against it.

Soon as I got to the vestry, I went on the internet. Twocking, of course. From Taking Without Owner's Consent. I'm struggling to keep up – but I'm succeeding.

## 5th May

I was looking for a dog-collar, any dog-collar, preferably one without ketchup stains. I was feeling ebullient and excited about the trip.

I told Alex I definitely wanted her to come. White Cliffs of Dover. Saturday, 22 May. I needed another adult and she'd already been checked by the Criminal Records Bureau. And it would be a very nice way for us to spend a day by the seaside.

I thought I was being lovely and caring. But that's no guarantee, not in a marriage. In fact, I'd put my foot in it from many different angles. Even 'Criminal Rewards Bureau' was wrong – she told me it was now called Disclosure and Barring Service.

I was prioritizing my calling over her. Again. Proposing to spend a Saturday, the one day a week we had together (if I wasn't doing a wedding) going to what she called a 'shit bit of Kent' with 'fifteen children belonging to other people'.

She was sick of either going to vicar-type functions and feeling excluded, or not going and having people say 'What a shame Alex couldn't make it' in a passive-aggressive way. What did these functions have to do with anything anyway? How come the Church of England equated religious devotion with excruciating social events involving sponge fingers, which Alex had to make? My life was taken up with such things and such people, who made unceasing demands on my time because they had nothing else in their lives and constantly invaded our house, which meant we never had the time to devote ourselves to shagging each other 24 hours a day, so she could have a baby and not be a solicitor all her life.

'We had sex a couple of days ago,' I said.

While I'd been looking for a clean dog-collar, she'd been in the loo, discovering her latest pregnancy test was negative.


## 6th May

'You hero,' said Nigel as I walked into the vestry.

He showed me the headline in *Metro* – KUNG FU KICKER VICAR. There was a photo of me and CCTV footage of me 'wrestling the youth to the ground'. Then there was a photo of Adoha with the caption, 'He's my hero.'

Nigel was amazed. He didn't think I had it in me. 'Congratulations,' he said with fervour. 'I admire anyone who shows physical courage in the cause of goodness and justice. Our Lord is the supreme example of that, is he not?'

Whoa! I thought. This was way over the top.

'No, no really, it was nothing,' I said.

'It wasn't nothing, Adam,' said Nigel.

No wonder people craved good news – I was on the same page as a pitbull terrier that had hospitalized a 4-year-old girl. I didn't look like a man who wrestled bag thieves to the ground, but that only worked in my favour. I looked like a nice vicar who'd done something extraordinary. I saw myself as the readers saw me – a gentle holy man who'd done something that made us all feel good.

I changed the subject. I told him about the seaside trip. Let's hire a minibus, let's chuck the kids in, off we go!

'Are you sure it's a good idea? They'll go shoplifting and take drugs.'

Basically, Nigel thinks all kids are bag thieves who need wrestling to the ground. I assured him it was a wonderful idea; it would take them out into the open air and fill their minds with wonder.

'You can't just chuck kids in a minibus,' he said. He was certainly right about *that*. What we had to do before anyone went anywhere was consider all the child protection considerations, so that no child got lost or had sex with another child or had an allergic reaction. There were Risk Assessment and Parental Consent forms and PCC permission. We'd need to appoint a respected member of society as a child advocate, so that if any child was subjected to inappropriate behaviour, by someone connected to the church, they'd have someone to talk to about it afterwards.

I was dazed at the thought of it all. Could the kids even eat a stick of seaside rock unless they had access to a 'dentist advocate'? The joy was draining from my body. Regulation, the enemy of joy, was destroying my capacity to do ministry. Society was obsessed with health and safety, which was fine until you realized that was a euphemism for distrust and paranoia, which aren't healthy or safe, just controlling and negative. What a sadness for priests everywhere that no one trusts us any more. But then again, no one trusts anyone.

Adoha entered, blazing with excitement, thrilled I was now a hero to the readers of *Metro* too.

I denied, yet again, that I'd done anything heroic.

'I simply did what anyone would have done,' I said, but with slightly less conviction than before.

'You're so modest,' said Adoha. Maybe she was right.

'Over 3.4 million readers' it said on the front page of *Metro*.

Maybe I *had* done something heroic – 3.4 million people thought so. Wow. Plus Nigel. And Adoha.

She'd come to the vestry to tell me that she'd nominated me for a Pride of Britain Award. I didn't know what to say. What could I say? I said, 'Wow!'

Apparently, no vicar has ever won a Pride of Britain Award. I'm sure I won't win, though. It would be wrong for me to win. And anyway, all she's done is nominate me. It's not like I'm even on the shortlist yet. Not that I deserve to be on the shortlist. I don't even deserve to be nominated.

On the bench, Colin said he really fancied Dover. If he'd had lovely seaside trips when he was a kid, maybe his life might not have been so 'shite'. Could I think of some way to involve him? It would be really good for his CV.

I sat there, musing on Colin's CV. What exactly was in it?

'Well, have you thought yet?' asked Colin. He said he could drive the minibus. Turns out Colin's CV includes 3 years' driving a heavy haulage truck, a real 'fanny magnet'. With his big truck, he once pulled a woman in an Italian service station. He chose to overlook her 'massive Adam's apple'.

I told him I'd think about it. He said that was great. All he wanted to do was give something back, 'even though I never got anything'.


## 7th May

Adoha was thrilled to be appointed our child advocate. As she sees it, that gives her a licence to hit cliff-top paedophiles with the handbag I heroically saved.

This morning she accompanied me to school to meet the difficult but deserving 15.

I stood before them, Ellie by my side, and asked who was looking forward to the trip. No hands went up. I asked who'd never been to the seaside before. No hands went up. Just to humiliate me, Ellie asked if anyone had seen a cow. All hands went up.

I didn't believe that. They're deprived urban kids. The only cows they've are seen on a screen in a game called something like *Cattle Killing Fields 3*.

To get them excited, I told them the White Cliffs of Dover were a natural wonder with an incredible history, which provoked Courtney Gaines into asking whether you could shop there.

'No, it's a cliff,' I replied, which sounded incredibly lame. White Cliffs does sound like a shopping centre, granted.

'Is it outdoors?' she asked and, as ever, I had to respect the integrity of her question. I couldn't clip her round the ear for being facetious, not unless she was in the presence of some ear, nose and throat advocate.

Courtney said she hated outdoors, except when it was Bluewater, which was indoors too. I sort of knew what she meant.

Chloe Craven said that in her opinion, cows stank. Was this going to be a stinky trip? I ignored her. I didn't say, you were the first name on the list because you've lived in a series of foster homes, your mother's an alcoholic, your father is unknown, you're surly and sly but Ellie believes you've got potential because your short story about your pet rat showed precocious wit.

I told them all it would be a great day, with some military history, and without their TV and games. I tried to make that sound liberating, but of course they took it as deprivation. Why does goodness always sound like punishment?

Chloe said we couldn't *make* her go to Dover, which I suppose is true. But I didn't want to say that, so I brought on Adoha, lovely Adoha, everyone's favourite granny. Adoha said hello, which was enough for Chloe, who put up her hand and asked, 'Are you a man?'

It was the funniest thing the children had ever heard.

Actually, it *was* pretty funny, because despite the cliffs of her bosom she does have an exceptionally deep voice. But I'm pleased to say I stood there and looked thoroughly disapproving.

## 8th May

The Archdeacon thought it was all very well for me. While I was flying through the air in my Spandex and landing on villains in alleyways, he was going through the DBS checks with Ghastly Graham, the Diocesan Safeguarding Management and Risk Assessment Panel Group Officer.

I told him Colin was one of the adults who needed to be checked, knowing he'd tell me, as he duly did, that there was no chance of Colin going on this trip, Graham would turn him down flat. I pointed out that passing a DBS check merely proved you hadn't been caught. I'd rather trust my instinct than some police report compiled by a pen-pusher whose favourite word was 'No'.

The Archdeacon was scathing about my 'instincts'. But then he doesn't understand what the trip would mean to Colin. Does he have to do everything by the letter? Why call Graham 'ghastly' then obey his every command?

The self-righteous Graham or the sinner Colin. It was obvious who Jesus would favour. No DBS checks for Jesus. No health-and-safety forms for Jesus to fill in before he walked on water.

Such were my Jesus thoughts in the Archdeacon's taxi. But I kept them to myself. He was looking very enigmatic. Best to lie low.

'Stop here, will you!' he instructed the driver, who pulled up in what seemed to be a motorbike lane. I asked if it was safe to let me out here and he told me to trust my 'instincts'.

I avoided death by motorbike and went to the shop to buy some fags. Time to confront Lisa. The woman who, when asked if she ever went to church, replied, '£1.20.'

Today, though, Lisa couldn't get enough of me. As soon as she saw me, her face lit up. She even put her phone down.

'You're that hero!' she said.

I denied it, though I knew by now that didn't make any difference. Lisa said if all vicars were like me, she'd come to church all the time. Her mum was going to be so jealous that she knew the Kung Fu Vicar. Would I like a free lolly?

I would, I would; and I did, I did.

## 10th May

Adoha hijacked the end of Morning Service to announce I'd been shortlisted for a Pride of Britain Award for my 'heroic actions in bringing criminals to justice'.

Everyone in the congregation clapped and cheered, as she presented me with a bouquet and a bottle of champagne, paid for by my congregation. Alex looked radiant. That's the word. As radiant as a hero's wife.

'Heroic actions in bringing criminals to justice.' I wasn't heroic, there was only one action, and only one criminal, too. Basically, *in* and *to* were the only words that were true.

Roland Wise feels contempt for the people who adore him. That's what he told us at that supper. Not me, though. I felt warm. I glowed.

'Our vicar will be on television!' said Adoha.

What can I do? It's a bandwagon. I can't stop it now.


## 11th May

I've got to stop it.


## 12th May

Colin's DBS check came in. He's been brought to justice 39 times. Among other things, he has convictions for sexual harassment, making an indecent or obscene or menacing phone call and attempted kidnap. All occurred on the same day.

The Archdeacon's wrong, though. My instincts tell me Colin could safely drive our minibus to Dover and back, without endangering children or lives, as long as we keep him from harassing the lager.

But I'll have to break it to him that he can't be there.

## 13th May

Oh no. It's actually happened. I got the invitation.

The Pride of Britain Awards are at the Grosvenor House Hotel, Park Lane, London W1K 7TN.

The invitation is addressed to 'Reverend Adam Small-bone and partner'.

Alex was thrilled. 'Unless you want to take Colin,' she said.

For her, this is the reward for 14 years of sponge fingers, lonely weekends and weird men coming into her house to use the toilet. She'll have a glamorous night out with her 'hero husband', wearing a frock, seeing the stars, leading the same charmed life as presenter Carol Vorderman and special guests Samantha Cameron and Richard Curtis.

I looked at the nominees in my category. There's Megan Fairley, 11, from Gunton in Norfolk, who confronted a burglar at her home, despite having no arms, and Alan Cable, 34, a partially sighted salesman from Swaledale, Yorkshire, who saved a 7-year-old boy from the burning car in which his parents and sister died – and then adopted him.

I could take the armlessness and the burning car, but not Alan adopting the orphaned boy, which wasn't the heroism of a moment but the heroism of 50 or 60 years – however long Alan Cable is alive to love and care about this orphaned boy.

I cracked. I told Alex I couldn't go. I didn't deserve it, not compared to those people.

Alex told me to think of all the things I did that went unnoticed. This was a prize for that as well. She'd been too hard on me, she said. She should never have gone on about the sponge fingers, she was just in a bad mood because she'd failed another pregnancy test. I told her she hadn't 'failed' anything.

'Come here,' she said. I sat next to her on the sofa. I told her she had to understand that the incident with the youth and the handbag had been blown out of all proportion. But I sounded more unconvincing than ever, possibly because she was stroking my leg and telling me how proud she was of everything I did. She was even looking forward to the Dover trip, and now I was a hero, why didn't I take my pants off?

There were two reasons not to take my pants off. One, I wasn't a hero and, two, I had to check the parental consent, health-and-safety and day-of-departure forms.

They weren't good enough reasons.


## 15th May

'Thank you, Carol. Thank you, Britain. When I look at the other nominees, I don't feel I deserve this award at all. Never in a million years did I think I'd win!'

Lord, I'm rehearsing my winner's speech. Is that wrong?

'This award isn't for me, though it's my name on it. This award is for the Church of England and all the good men and women who work in it. The bravest people I know.'

If I dedicate my award to others, I can accept it, can't I, Lord? I'll be humble, I'll be brief, and I'll end with a joke. Something like, 'I'd like to thank my wife, Alex. And I'd like to thank God. And now my boring speech is over – thank God!'

No, that's rubbish, isn't it. It's false modesty and it's not even funny. Why's this happening to me, Lord? It's a nightmare. It's wrong. I know that and you know it, too.

On the other hand, this award has brought more people into my church. They want their vicar to be a brave and good man. And I am. It's official. It's really helped me and Alex, too. Who knows, it might have helped her get pregnant. It's different when a hero 'tries'.

Also, I can get Carol Vorderman's autograph for Nigel. He admires her so much as a mathematician and a woman.

Maybe a better way to end my speech would be something like this, Lord: 'Finally, I'd like everyone here tonight to stand and sing with me that wonderful hymn, "God Moves In A Mysterious Way".'

## 16th May

Colin was very upset, as I knew he would be. The attempted kidnap and obscene phone calls had happened a long time ago, when he was in love with a woman who drove him nuts. It wasn't a *child* who drove him nuts, so why couldn't he drive us to Dover?

I explained that the Diocesan Child Protection Officer had to take into account all his offences, whether they involved children or not.

'What about forgiveness and second chances?' I didn't know what to say. Colin has thirty-nine offences to his name, so we were talking about fortieth chances. No, forty-first. There's the headbutt too. In terms of forgiveness, it's as if he's actually going for the seventy times seven.

I said I was sorry but he couldn't come, and he told me that other people might think I was a hero but I wasn't a hero to him. That hurt.

And he's right. I'm not a hero.

There's still time for me to withdraw from the whole awards fiasco. On the other hand, I'm not going to win. That's what makes it all right for me to be there. I'm just making up the numbers.

No. It doesn't make it all right.


## 17th May

When I was 16 or so, Mum and Dad used to go on about 'the corridors of power'. If I got on the management training course at Price Waterhouse that would be the first step. They wanted their son to walk down those corridors and make them proud.

That all feels very dated, I'm afraid. It's steam rooms

of power now. Saunas of power. Today I went to a day spa in Mayfair to see the Archdeacon. In the changing room, every man looked like a CEO or a member of the Cabinet. Under all those white towels lurked a willy of power.

It was so steamy in the steam room I could barely make the Archdeacon out. Eventually I found him, sat next to him and sweated. He recommended I get a Renewing Herbal Rubdown from Claudio. If I asked him, Claudio would go 'very firm and deep'.

'Maybe you'll get a hero's discount,' said the man behind us, clapping a hand on my shoulder. It was Roland. Of course it was Roland, it was a Roland kind of place. He congratulated me on getting 'on the front foot', making it sound like I'd actively sought a Pride of Britain Award, running down the Hackney Road in search of a thief to upend.

Then the Archdeacon whispered his news. He'd been talking to the organizers and he strongly suspected that I'd be the winner in my category. He didn't want me messing up. This couldn't be another *One Show*.

'It's your second chance of fame. And it may be your last. Don't blow it.'

Now the sweat really started to pour. I said, for the last time, that I hadn't *done* anything.

'No doubt,' said the Archdeacon, unbothered. What mattered was that I didn't mess up my moment in the spotlight. There was the incalculable benefit of the public perceiving vicars to be heroes. And then there was the calculable benefit. My time onscreen was effectively a commercial for the Church of England. If the Church tried to buy that time, like an ad agency buying a slot to show an ad for McDonald's, it would cost them £430,000.

Luckily for me, the Archdeacon would be there personally to guide me through the whole occasion. 'Do you have a decent suit, though, Adam? I've never seen you in one. And what on earth are we going to do about your hair?'

What was he talking about? Who cared about my hair? Rowan Williams was Archbishop of Canterbury. And his hair was terrible. Every day was a bad hair day for Rowan. So what?

I sat there, hot and bothered, struggling to cope with the changes in my life. This time last year I was a country vicar, living in a cottage with beams. Now I was in a day spa with an archdeacon in charge of my hair.

## 19th May

Well, that'll never happen again. Alex usually gives it a trim, but the Archdeacon said no, I must go where he goes. Laurence of Bond Street. And thanks to the Archdeacon, who's a mate of his, I had my hair cut by Laurence. It was a bit like going into John Lewis and being served by John Lewis.

Laurence congratulated me on my nomination. It turned out he'd won an award himself, Men's Hairdresser of the Year, also held at the Grosvenor House. He told me it's important to put your statue down before you start your acceptance speech, otherwise you can't use your hands, and your hands are the most expressive parts of your body. He would say that, wouldn't he?

During my blow-dry, I thought about St Matthias. After the death of Our Lord, a new apostle was needed, Judas having betrayed his ministry. The followers of Jesus nominated Joseph Barsabbas and Matthias. Then they drew lots and Matthias won.

Matthias preached the Gospel to 'barbarians and meat-eaters' in the interior of Ethiopia. That's just about all we know.

Basically, Matthias was a foot soldier in the service of the Lord. A pretty much unknown soldier. So you sort of feel it was great that he was nominated and won. He wasn't just lucky, he deserved his good fortune.

This was a man who went out and preached the Gospel to barbarians. And that's exactly what I do every time I go to Ellie's school. Don't I deserve a stroke of luck? Even if I'm not the hero those people think I am, I'm still some kind of hero.

Laurence showed me the back of my head in his hand-held mirror. He'd done a lovely job.


## 20th May

Today I met a great man and was humbled in every sense.

I was sitting in the vestry, struggling with one of

Graham's forms. 'State your objectives,' it said. 'Specify your desired outcomes.'

Then came the questions. 'What health-and-safety issues do you expect to encounter?' That was easy: I'd encounter cliffs. Cliffs were definitely a safety issue. Though they weren't a health issue, were they? A cliff, if you walked along the top of it, actually promoted good health.

Suddenly Nigel appeared, breathless from running upstairs.

'The Bishop of London is here!' he said.

Why was *he* here? Nigel didn't know.

I'd last seen the Bishop in St Paul's Cathedral, addressing 484 vicars at the Chrism Mass. To have him in St Saviour's was an honour. I rushed down and Nigel bounded after me.

He was dressed down in black, not a strand of purple anywhere. But he didn't need robes. He had natural authority.

The Bishop said he was 'just passing' and thought he'd pop in 'to have a look at the cradle of heroism and meet the man of courage inside'.

I smiled. Nigel quivered in quite a canine way and virtually licked the Bishop's face. He said what a wonderful job he thought the Bishop was doing and, what's more, he, Nigel, had read all the Bishop's books, not just the one on how to pray, but the one on passing your GCSE Religious Studies. The Bishop thanked him and asked him to make a cup of tea. He was inviting Nigel to leave immediately, but Nigel didn't mind, he was thrilled to get any invitation from the Bishop, and rushed off to do his bidding.

The Bishop sat me down and told me how lovely it had been to have such an inspiring story come across his desk. What's more, he'd heard I ran a wonderful church 'when you're not making headlines'.

'So, tell me. What exactly happened?'

Up close, he had wonderful hair. Lustrous. Swept back in a captivating style. The Bishop was handsome in an old-fashioned way, like an airman from the Second World War. His eyes were astonishing. Pale and piercing. Eyes not made for small talk, if that makes sense.

'You took this mugger on? It's just so courageous. Incredible, really.'

'No, no, it was nothing,' I said.

I waited for him to say, no, on the contrary. After all, that's what everyone else had said. But the Bishop didn't say anything. He gave me the full benefit of those eyes and waited for me to expand. I was mesmerized. My mouth was dry.

Lying was not an option. Nor was exaggerating. Even being a tad evasive was out of the question. The man was steely. He had a steely goodness about him.

'It's a lie,' I said. 'I'm about to be given an award for heroism and I can barely run a school trip to the seaside.'

I waited for him to tell me what I should do. Then I

realized he was waiting for *me* to tell him what I should do. So I told him – I was definitely going to decline the award. Or accept it. One or the other. Maybe I should accept it.

Didn't people want a vicar they could believe in? A vicar who was good?

'Yes,' he said. He was telling me I should be a good vicar. I must decide what was good and do it. In this situation, there was just one thing I could do that was morally and unarguably *good*.

'You're absolutely right,' I said. 'I can't accept it. I'll go to the awards dinner and decline it.'

But that wasn't the one good thing to do. Not according to the Bishop.

'If you're declining it, wouldn't you want to decline it beforehand?'

I found it worked best if I didn't actually look at him when I spoke.

I told him – or rather, I told his left shoulder – that I'd promised my wife Alex a night out. I'd also promised Nigel I'd get Carol Vorderman's autograph. Maybe we could compromise. Could I go with Alex to the pre-drinks reception and decline the award after that?

Without a word, he shook his head.

I told him if I turned down the award, I'd disappoint a lot of people.

'Yes,' said the Bishop. It would be a real test. Did I have the strength of character to disappoint all those people? The organizers, the Archdeacon, my wife, my parishioners?

'That's where your courage will really be shown. You'll have to tell them all the truth.'

Of course.

He had the holy man's gift of making things clear. There was no other way but his.

'*Gloriam praecedit humilitas*,' he said.

The Bishop of London was talking to me, man to man, in Latin. It was a special moment, the kind of thing I'd tell my grandchildren, if I ever had any.

I knew what it meant but I wasn't sure where it was from. It might be Leviticus. No, it was Proverbs. Yes, it was Leviticus.

'Glory before humility,' I said, getting the easy part out of the way.

'Before glory goes humility,' he corrected me.

Bollocks! I couldn't have got it more wrong. What kind of fool translates 'humility before glory' as 'glory before humility'?

'Yes, of course, humility before glory. My thoughts exactly.'

He put a hand on my shoulder, to comfort me in my hour of stupidity. Then he stood up.

'Good luck with your school trip,' he said, clearly implying that school trips were more my level than Latin. Or goodness. And then he was gone.

A couple of minutes later Nigel entered. He'd made three cups of tea, using our best crockery, which I'd never seen before. It was white with pink roses on it. It had probably been in the vestry cupboard since 1894.

'Buggeration,' said Nigel. I couldn't have agreed more.

## 22nd May

By 7.30 a.m., Alex, Ellie and I were in the school car park, waiting by the minibus. Then Adoha arrived, still angry that she'd watched the Pride of Britain Awards without knowing I wasn't in it. Her whole family had come round to watch it with her, including her new grandchild, 10-week-old Rihanna. I'd disappointed a baby.

I told her to forget the awards. Taking deprived kids to the seaside was far more important.

What deprived kids, though? No kids had turned up. Maybe none of them were coming. It seemed I couldn't even organize a trip to the seaside.

I'd never been so happy to see Chloe Craven trudging towards us, head down, with her friend Courtney Gaines.

'You came!' I said.

'Nothing better to do,' said Chloe, keen to show no enthusiasm. Outside the classroom, with no peers to show off to, she looked smaller, younger and more vulnerable.

I made the executive decision to give up waiting for anyone else. So we got in the minibus and closed the doors.

Within seconds there was a knock on the window.

Colin. As animated as when he'd first laid eyes on Pip, Queen of the Smoothies.

There was the procedural world of forms, DBS checks and caution, then there was the spontaneous world of Colin, where you just turned up with a fag on, brandishing tins of lager.

I told him to get in – he could come as one of the kids. As soon as I thought of Colin as a kid, it was OK to have him along. It was only as an adult that he was banned.

I put my arm round Alex. Behind us, Nigel was remonstrating with Courtney, who'd just put Colin's lighter near the back of his head.

'Do not try to set fire to me, you little tyke!' shouted Nigel.

'Ha ha ha,' said Colin.

We hadn't even left the car park.

Alex and I agreed that it was a terrible idea to have kids if they were going to turn out like Courtney. Or Colin, for that matter.

We make that sort of joke a lot. We want kids but we want it to be all right if it turns out that we can't.

Nine hours later, we were back in the car park. We'd done all the things you're meant to do on an English day out at the seaside.

We'd taken our shoes and socks off and paddled off a pebble beach. We'd walked along a cliff, with children asking what the point of a walk was, and adults explaining that there was no 'point', you walked for the sake of walking and the pleasure of being outdoors.

We'd spent 3 hours or more on a motorway, arguing what we should have on the radio and what games we should play, with the children saying that all games were stupid, but wanting to join in once the games started. (Eventually Chloe started her own game, Count the

Cows, which proved to be the most long-running and popular game of them all.)

What was the highlight of the day? There always has to be a highlight.

I pointed out France to Chloe Craven. I showed trenches dug across the cliffs in the Second World War to protect the soldiers from enemy aircraft. Alex, who knows her birds, flagged up a kittiwake and a raven. Then we went to the National Trust café in the visitors' centre.

'How's your brownie?' Ellie asked Alex, the kind of boring question adults ask each other all the time. Alex said it was delicious. Chocolate and beetroot.

*That* was the highlight of the day. Certainly for Chloe Craven. She made an 'Euuurgh' sound that went on for ages, however much Ellie told her to stop. This was disgust, she couldn't cut it short, even if she wanted to.

For the next few hours, all Chloe and Courtney Gaines wanted to do on their day out by the seaside was come up with disgusting flavours for brownies, more disgusting than chocolate and beetroot, as if that was possible. Broccoli and sick. That was one they liked. And Colin thought doner and dogshit was brilliant.

Alex, me, Ellie, Adoha, Colin, Nigel, Chloe Craven and Courtney Gaines. We were one big, happy, not too dysfunctional family.

When Alex and I got home, we were surprised how tired we were.

'This vicaring thing's exhausting,' said Alex.

I went into my study and looked up the Ordination Liturgy. I imagined it as a form that stated objectives and specified outcomes. Had I fulfilled those objectives today? Had I achieved those outcomes?

'Priests are called to be servants and shepherds among the people to whom they are sent.' Yes. I literally shepherded two children along the top of a cliff. 'They are to resist evil, support the weak, defend the poor, and intercede for all in need.' Yes. Sort of. In the broadest terms. I supported the weak and defended the poor by taking two kids, both of whose mothers live on benefits, one of whose mothers was stabbed in the thigh by her boyfriend (with whom she still lives), to the seaside. Not to mention Colin. 'Guided by the Spirit, they are to discern and foster the gifts of all God's people, that the whole Church may be built up in unity and faith.' Maybe. Sort of. In the National Trust café, we discerned and fostered the children's gift for inventing names of brownies, which was an engagement with the world of the imagination. Was that part of a campaign to build up the whole Church in unity and faith? Marginally. Minimally. Theoretically. Basically, no. 'They are to proclaim the word of the Lord and to watch for the signs of God's new creation.' Not today. I don't think so.

I just know that what I did today was somehow good. That's it. That's the best I can say. 'Priests are called to do things that are somehow good.' It doesn't say that in the Ordination Liturgy, but it should.

## 26th May

Lord, what do you make of this? Alex and I were watching the finale of Season 2 of *The Wire*. I thought she was utterly absorbed by it. I know *I* was. Omar was busy swearing revenge against Stringer Bell when Alex said, do you pray that we'll have a baby? I told her I did. She said, so you think it's God's will if we have a baby or not? At which point, I pressed pause and said, well, everything that happens is God's will, so in that sense yes. Which is true, Lord. Then Alex got incredibly upset and said, so you think the Lord will provide us with a baby. Or not. Is that it? To which I said, let's be patient, we've only been trying for a few months, we shouldn't obsess about it. And she apologized for obsessing about whether or not we had a baby when I was trying to watch *The Wire*. Then she left the room. Leaving me with *The Wire*, Lord. Which I really wanted to watch. But now that felt like a sort of betrayal, as if watching it meant I didn't care. So I ejected it. That was the right thing to do, wasn't it, Lord.

## 29th May

What a wonderful thing. Out of the blue, we got a letter from Sir Jeremy Tripp of the Lunardi Foundation, a philanthropic organization dedicated to the maintenance and restoration of ecclesiastical architecture, enclosing a cheque for £2,000 towards our Window Restoration Fund.

We didn't have to fill in any forms. We just had to accept the cheque. I wrote Sir Jeremy a very grateful letter, saying how much we valued their contribution, and how important the window was to the church and its congregation. His donation meant we needed 'just £24,101 to commission the actual work'. Then I crossed out the 'just', as it sounded bitter. Then I crossed out the sentence altogether. The letter was better without it.

## 4th June, *Ascension Day*

I told the children that Ascension Day was the day that Jesus went up to heaven, forty days after he came back to life.

Jerome, a sweet Year Two boy, put his hand up and asked if Muslims went to Heaven too. I didn't want to give him an on-the-one-hand-on-the-other-hand answer. I've learned that children like black and white; they get confused by grey. So I told him, yes, Muslims go to Heaven if they follow the Five Pillars of Wisdom: saying prayers five times a day, giving money to those in need, making a special trip to Mecca.

Prayers, giving money, Mecca. Mecca, prayers, giving money.

I was three pillars in and I dried. I knew five, but two were suddenly elusive. It was horrible. Children expect you to dispense information with clarity and confidence. That's your job. They don't know, you know; you tell them, they know – that's how education works. Unless you believe education is there to give them the tools to find out stuff for themselves. Maybe these kids had been given the tools and already knew. I looked round. Were they tooled up? I asked them: 'Who here knows the other two pillars?' But nobody knew the other two pillars. They thought *I* did.

Surely I could remember five pillars. Come on, I could reel off twice that many commandments. Ellie chipped in with 'Ramadan', which was kind of her, but after some more agonized silence, I gave up and went back to Heaven. Yes, Muslims went to Heaven. Their Heaven, not our Heaven, though maybe their Heaven and our Heaven were the same.

The children looked up at me in confusion. Too much grey.

As I left the school, I was cornered by Matthew, the Year Five teacher, whom all the kids love because he's cool and good-looking and fantastic at football. (Kids can be very superficial, can't they?) He told me that the fifth pillar was, There's no other God but Allah and Muhammad is the messenger of God.

'I might be wrong,' he said, knowing he wasn't. 'It's your area, obviously.'

I didn't like the way he said that.

Back at St Saviour's, Colin was sitting on the bench with his eyes shut, not saying anything. He didn't even have a fag in his mouth. Craving a bit of conversation, I asked him how he was.

Annoyed was how he was, because I'd interrupted his meditation. Four days ago, he fell asleep in London Fields 'with a hangover the size of Texas and a mouth like a fox's arsehole'. But he woke up to bliss, because under the nearest tree was a group of lovely-looking people, sitting on picnic rugs, doing a 'therapeutic healing thing mantra' with a 'medicine healing dude'. Said dude turned out to be a Buddhist. So now Colin's a Buddhist too.

What is it with Colin? A few weeks ago, he was in a burka. Before that, he was an Evangelical in the grip of Darren and Pip.

Colin's a one-man multi-faith society. But I shouldn't be cynical and I'm not – not to his face, anyway – because he's only trying to give his life purpose and meaning, and what else is there? What's more, when Colin believes, he truly believes, even if it's only for a fortnight.

I told him I admired Buddhism but preferred a religion with a God.

'Who's this Buddha then, if he's not a God?' The expression in his eyes was like Jerome's – he was seeking knowledge. I was the teacher and he was in Year 49 or whatever.

I explained that Buddha was a spiritual teacher and Buddhism was essentially a way of life. Colin agreed. And he liked the way of life – it was peace-loving and all about not wanting stuff.

I offered him a fag but he not-wanted it. He told me he'd quit.

I watched the people passing on Shoreditch High Street. People of many nations and many faiths. We're the Church of England, but it's not the England of white men playing cricket on the village green. In my C of E school, half the kids are Muslims. I still haven't really engaged with the Muslim community in my parish. And I definitely don't know enough about Islam. (Just ask Jerome.)

## 6th June

Went to the War Memorial in the park opposite Tony's Kebabs. Nigel came with me, suitably impressed that Corporal Eric Andrews, my mother's father, was one of the ten men of the 1st Suffolks killed in the Normandy landings on D-Day, 6th June, 1944. Every year, wherever I am, I try to honour his memory.

All we wanted was a few moments' quiet contemplation. But the kids in the park had no idea what the big stone monument was, or why two men in cassocks were standing in front of it. They carried on shouting and riding their bikes and playing football, and just laughed when the ball accidentally hit Nigel on the head.

The worst of it, of course, was the littering. I kept hearing that sort of plok! sound, as another KFC or MacDonalds carton hit the ground. It's not very loud but it is to me. I can hear it at fifty paces. And when I heard it in that park, as I tried to remember my grandfather, it really seemed he died in vain.

# 7th June

The pectoral cross the Archdeacon wears was in full effect today. If his robes are the armour of God, his cross is his weapon.

I was worried he'd heard about my Pillars of Wisdom assembly, since he always knows everything. So I told him I was thinking of going on an 'Understanding Islam' course to improve my religious literacy. He recommended basic accountancy or assertiveness training instead. Undaunted, I told him I had care of all the Muslim souls in my parish plus, of course, all the Muslim kids in the school.

He said I didn't need to lecture *him*. He played interfaith football once a month with a lot of Muslims, Jews and Catholics. But no Anglicans – maybe that's why he enjoyed it.

'I'd like to get involved with that,' I said, to which he replied, 'Well, I can't stop you.'

Then, as he always does, he told me precisely why he'd ordered me into his taxi. His four-wheeled office, with the silent driver instead of the silent secretary.

Ellie's denominational inspection was due. No school in his diocese had ever failed a religious inspection. If mine did, the level of shame heaped upon me would 'make the Islamic version of Sa'ir, the blazing inferno, seem like a tea party'.

He knew I'd never heard of Sa'ir, the blazing inferno. He was just rubbing my nose in my ignorance and bashing me, metaphorically, with his pectoral cross.

## 10th June

I'm starting a football team. Five-a-side. To play the Muslims, the Jews and the Catholics. To build bridges with other faiths. And to get me running around in a muscular Christian way. Too much of my religious life is intellectual.

Is football a religion? No. It's hundreds of religions. If you're a fan, you believe in Arsenal or Manchester United or whatever. If you're a player, it's hard to see you've got a religion at all. You don't score goals for Arsenal because you *believe* in Arsenal, you score for them because they've bought you. You used to score goals for Man United, so they paid you to score them for Arsenal instead. It's like the Church of England buying the Pope because he's a guaranteed winner.

As I went into school to talk to Ellie about the inspection, cool Matthew was in the playground, luxuriating in his football skills and generally being worshipped. He did a lot of keepy-uppy while the kids looked on and adored him. How was that education? Sure, he was demonstrating his skills, but I didn't see him passing them on.

I thought I'd shout at him to put him off. Invite him to join my new Anglican team. The Five Anglican Pillars. But then I remembered that Matthew is a Catholic.

I walked into the school and was immediately concerned for the denominational inspection, because the school cross was on the floor, not on the wall where it should have been. The wall was covered in cardboard cut-outs of footballers. I sensed the hand of Matthew.

Ellie was in her office, so I strode in, handed her the fallen cross and reminded her that the denominational inspection was due, and she should make sure Jesus Christ was prioritized over 'Wayne Mooney'. It was just a slip of the tongue but she was most amused, thinking it indicated my general level of knowledge about football. And then cool footballing Matthew appeared in the doorway, virtually filling it with his physique and charisma. Was it OK for Year Five to visit the Science Museum after half term?

Ellie was annoyingly smilcy with him, so just to remind him why I was there – I'm more assertive than the Archdeacon thinks – I suggested that when they were in the museum he could teach the kids that science was not the answer to the origins of the universe, God was.

'I wouldn't want to teach them anything there wasn't firm proof of,' said Matthew.

To lull him into thinking I was trying to be his mate, I asked if he was responsible for the kids' footballer cut-outs, which really brightened up the place. When he said he was, I thrust the cross in his hands and asked him to put it back on the wall, in place of one of his cut-outs.

He wasn't expecting that. I feinted to go one way and then went the other. Very David Beckham. Or, as I'd say, David Peckham.

## 14th June, *Pentecost (Whit Sunday)*

Alex took it badly when I broke the news about the Vicars' Wives dinner. All the wives take turns cooking dinner for everyone and it's our turn. Which means it's her turn. I told her she'd enjoy it, she'd make new friends. It wasn't like the wives would want sponge fingers for dinner.

## 16th June

The denominational inspection is on 29 June, the Feast of the Apostles Peter and Paul. When I should be contemplating the martyrdom of these great men, I'll be contemplating my own martyrdom at the hands of the Archdeacon.

## 18th June

Roland Wise's column in the *Church Times* today said no priest should forget that religion was 'a competitive business'. I found that depressing – I've never thought of what I do as competitive. But I couldn't say he was wrong. There are a lot of churches and ideologies competing for people's souls, especially Colin's.

As we were tatting up for Midweek Service, Nigel

suggested I abandon my five-a-side plan, since no one had volunteered for my team, apart from Steve Warwick (who, let's face it, would volunteer to be the ball if he thought it would keep me from telling his wife about the lap-dancing club).

Why was no one volunteering? Did my congregation consist of wimps? Nigel pointed out that, no, it mostly consisted of 70-year-old women with hip problems, so I'd be better off starting an Anglican bowls team, because women played bowls, and it wasn't associated with crowd violence, like football.

What was he talking about? Of course it wasn't associated with crowd violence, it didn't have any crowds.

I didn't want namby-pamby bowls. I wanted to get stuck into my Jewish and Muslim counterparts on a football pitch. All males, competing on behalf of their faiths, but uniting their faiths too. The C of E was far too feminized. I didn't object to women priests or even women lesbians, but the whole idea of the five-a-side was to make us man up a bit.

Nigel suggested I ask Colin to join the team – he'd jump at the chance of some ritualized violence. Excellent. Now we had me, Colin and Steve Warwick. Two pillars to go.

What about Nigel? He said that wasn't a good idea, he was hopeless. I remembered what happened at school when you said you were hopeless, and told him he was playing in goal.

## 21st June

By chance, we were side by side on our bikes at the traffic lights this morning, both on our way to school. Cool Matthew sitting tall on his cool fixie, helmetless and motionless, as if he was posing for a photo. No, posing for a *statue*.

I wondered how long he was going to ignore me, then he turned and said, 'I just think the idea that God implanted free will in the brains of slowly evolving primates seems a little unlikely.'

That was it, then. That was the moment. Matthew had outed himself publicly as an atheist, a Roman Catholic atheist, but an atheist. And if he thought I wasn't going to fight the good fight just because the lights might change, he was wrong. You man up or you don't. And I did.

I told him of course it was 'unlikely'. The incredible, inexplicable, awe-inspiring beauty of God's universe was completely 'unlikely'. In fact it was miraculous.

'No one's ever invaded a country in the name of science,' he replied, as if that were any kind of response to what I'd actually said. He just had some atheist bile to get rid of.

'Why do people with faith make you so angry?'

'They don't just think they're weird,' said Matthew, and then he was off, soon as it went amber, just to be sure he'd beat me to the school gates.

'You're a miracle!' I shouted. I was quite proud of that, because you don't often get the chance to be genuine *and* sarcastic.

That's why he got angry. He couldn't accept that I genuinely believed in the miracle of existence. Like so many atheists, he was imprisoned in his world view, he couldn't get outside it, and living in his prison made him angry.

Of course he was a miracle. Just as the earth's core and the North Sea and England and London were miracles. The street and his bicycle were miracles. His brain was a miracle. His feet were a miracle. Surely he'd agree with *that*, at least – him with his footballing genius.

I wasn't going to let the man bother me, but when I looked in the school assembly timetable I was amazed to see he'd done an assembly on *The Selfish Gene*. Cool Matthew had stood in front of our children in a Church of England school and fed them a load of old Dawkins.

I went to Ellie to complain. Surely, Ellie would agree that Matthew was a bit of a dick, with his cool haircut, his keepy-uppy and his sitty-uppy on his bike.

'What cyclist in London doesn't wear a helmet? It's stupid.'

She shrugged.

'Is it so we can all get a better look at his hair?'

'Matty's assembly was very good; it made the kids think,' said Ellie. She just wasn't taking the denominational inspection seriously. For a start, she kept calling it 'Godsted'. And now this: appointing a teacher who'd lied in his interview, claiming he was a Catholic when he was a rabid atheist. The man should be fired.

'Absolutely not,' said Ellie. 'He's a brilliant teacher. He's taken my difficult Year Five and raised them six points in a year, which is extraordinary.' I was amazed that a woman as intelligent as Ellie would take his side.

There was a knock at the door. But he didn't even wait for a 'Come!' He just opened it and, ignoring me, gave Ellie a big hunky smile, and then said a load of stuff that I didn't even bother listening to. Until the end. I heard that all right: 'And don't forget, we've got dinner tonight with Mark and Siobhan, babe.'

'Babe.' He actually said it. That's how I got the nauseating news that my head teacher, a woman for whom I had the utmost respect, professionally and personally, was having a sexual relationship with Twatty Matty. She was letting herself get babed by the atheist Matthew Feld. And there he was, standing there, knowing it and loving it. And loving that, now, I knew it too. I ached to wipe the smug smile off his vacuous face.

I reminded him that he was working in a Church of England school with a Christian foundation, ethos and mission statement.

He said he knew that. It was a C of E school where 60 per cent of the kids were Muslim. And with one more grin at Ellie, he was gone.

I told her that she needed to take him in hand or he could jeopardize her inspection.

'OK, Adam, I'll take him in hand.' She smirked.

That wasn't a responsible attitude, so I warned her against letting her personal life cloud her professional judgement.

Ellie's private life is her own concern. Or is it? For a head teacher to have a sexual relationship with a member of staff may actually be gross moral turpitude. As a school governor, it may be my duty to ban it and cut off his pay. Why an arrogant, atheist, fixie-riding, footballing hunk like Matt? He uses gel. I can smell it. His hair has gel in it. Next time she runs her hand through his hair, I hope she gets stuck.

## 22nd June

'What the fuck is an interfaith curry?'

I promised Alex it was the last time I'd ask her to cook, and I was sorry it came in the same week as the vicars' wives dinner. But this was St Saviour's United's first game and I felt we should celebrate by reaching out to the Muslims, Jews and Catholics with an interfaith lunch. It was just a matter of omitting pork, shellfish and meat (unless it was halal). She said she would do a bland curry 'with no ingredients at all', which sounded perfect.

## 27th June

The long night of the vicars' wives.

The bell rang at about half past six. Alex sighed. What kind of vicar's wife arrived early? How much boredom could Alex take?

She went to the door and I heard, in the distance, the familiar sound of Mick hustling money. We hadn't seen him at the vicarage for weeks. I wouldn't say I'd missed him, but he's part of my burden and I don't want to shirk my load.

I heard Alex say, 'No, you'll spend it on drugs.' That's when it hit me: Mick could be our fifth player. According to the *Church Times* – which was running a series of articles on drugs, so priests would know what they were dealing with – crack, which I knew was Mick's drug, gave you an intense high and made you hostile. That was just what our team needed.

I went to the door and asked if he played football, which he didn't till I told him it came with a free lunch and 10 quid for the dead flowers he was holding in his hand. He gave me the flowers and I gave him a fiver, the rest to follow at the game. Tomorrow, 1 p.m. He promised he'd be there.

He left and the first vicar's wife arrived, wearing a dog-collar.

'It's not fancy dress, is it?' asked Alex.

'No,' said the woman. 'I *am* a vicar. But I'm also *married* to a vicar.'

I excused myself and went upstairs to write my sermon. Alex gave her a drink, then followed me up, begging me to tell her it wouldn't always be like this, which I did. That didn't convince her, of course it didn't, so I pointed out that the person downstairs was a woman, not a vicar. Hadn't she always seen beyond my collar to the man underneath?

'Yeah, but she's a vicar *and* a vicar's wife.'

'OK, then. She's *two* women.'

'This is going to be the worst night of my life,' said Alex.

But it wasn't. At three in the morning, they were still partying. Alex had definitely got through to the women inside them, because when I went down to complain about the noise, no amount of assertiveness shut them up. They were smoking and drinking and dancing and giggling like women. There's no other word for it.

Alone in bed, unable to sleep, I just kept wondering why Twatty Matty wore those stupid jeans that went all tight at the bottom and showed his pants at the top. Did he not understand the 'under' in underpants? And were his pants now lying all happy and snug on the floor of Ellie's bedroom?

I prayed.

Lord, let us beat the Muslims tomorrow. Or the Catholics. Or the Jews. Let us beat anyone. And let us be able to say, when it's over, what Paul says, looking back on his life in 2 Timothy 4: 'I have fought the good fight, I have finished the race, I have kept the faith.' That's sort of a bit like 'My Way', Lord, except that song's about praising yourself and this is about praising You and not letting You down.

## 28th June

I scared myself today. Maybe it mattered too much. I raced through Morning Service, sermonizing quickly, then rushed home to help Alex load the interfaith curry into the car. The poor woman was pale and incapable of speech on account of her vicars' wives hangover, but while I'd been vicaring at St Saviour's, she'd been vicar'-s-wifing at home and, amazingly, cooked a curry for 20.

We drove to Hackney Downs Park and met our team. Immediately, we were one man short. Colin, the well-known Buddhist, announced that he'd given up competitive sports.

'You can't do this,' I told him, 'you said you'd play!' But he hadn't, we'd all *assumed* he'd play, and you couldn't assume anything with Colin. He pointed out a ready replacement: Alex.

'She can't play, she's a girl!' I said, as if that weren't a good thing in a wife. Unfortunately, or maybe not, Alex heard me say it, after which nothing would stop her playing. So now we had our team: Nigel, me, Steve Warwick, Alex and the cloud of smoke swirling above the bins in the distance, which was the sign of Mick.

Then a taxi pulled up by the railings and out stepped our ref: the Archdeacon. White trainers, white socks pulled knee-high, black shorts and shirt. All ironed, even the socks. Shiny whistle nestling on the breastbone, hung from a purple braid. Hair by Laurence of Bond Street. Somehow, it felt right that he'd get not a strand out of place. He was a natural referee, dispensing punishment, detached from the fray.

He advanced towards the team captains with a Catholic/Jewish/Muslim word for them all.

'Bruno, *Giorno*! Faisal, *Assalamu alaikum*. *Shalom*, Maurice, Simon Schama sends his love.' Then he had a quiet, undermining word with me, telling me not to expect any preferential treatment. Today, his Bible was the FA Code of Conduct.

And then, on His and Her bikes, up rode Ellie and Matty. The head teacher and her big mistake.

'You playing, Ellie?' I shouted. 'Alex is playing.'

'No, she's our cheerleader, aren't you, babe?' said the man I hadn't asked.

'He's not a Catholic, Ref, he's an atheist, they've brought a ringer!'

But the Archdeacon was already blowing his whistle.

'First up, St Saviour's against Dalston Synagogue.'

What did I expect? The Jews played every week and trained on Tuesday night. They had talented players and talked to each other. They were organized and focused and all of them had season tickets for Spurs.

We had Nigel, a goalkeeper who abhorred physical contact, even with a ball. We had Steve Warwick, who wouldn't pass to any of us (though you couldn't blame him for that). We had Mick, who scored a powerful and sweetly struck goal that would have been a good advertisement for crack if it hadn't gone in our own net. Then there was Alex, who wasn't just a girl but a *hungover* girl.

Finally, there was me. I was angry. Why was that? I just felt like everything was stacked against me, which wasn't right, since I'd done all the stacking. I kept shouting at everyone else, instead of concentrating on my own passing and tackling and shooting and not falling over.

We lost 6:0. Next up was Canonbury Mosque against Our Lady's. Since 'Matty' was playing, this was my chance to sit next to Ellie and ask if she was ready for the inspection on Tuesday. Instead of engaging properly with me, she leapt to her feet and shouted, 'Great shot, honey.' How could it be a great shot when it wasn't even a goal?

'If you don't communicate a clear Christian ethos, you'll fail.'

She told me she thought the parents were far more interested in Ofsted. I had to explain that the diocese could make her take the test again and again till she passed.

'Adam. It's the weekend. Lighten up.'

After we lost 8:0 to the Muslims, we had our last chance. This was the game that really mattered. Anglicans versus Catholics. The only game that's really mattered since the time of Henry VIII. They'd already beaten the Jews and the Muslims. And they'd done it without guilt.

In the centre of the pitch, I organized an Anglican team hug. 'Let's give it everything,' I shouted, even though the four other heads were inches away. 'Do it for me, do it for yourselves, do it for St Saviour's. Do it for our kind, liberal God who loves women and gays. Not their vain, cruel God who loves gold and Nazis!'

'You all right?' asked Alex. 'It's only a game.' I told her, no, I wasn't all right, we couldn't leave without at least scoring a goal.

The game kicked off. Matty had the ball and I rushed to take it off him, but he turned his back to me and shielded the ball – was that even allowed? – then suddenly he whizzed round and ran past me, using his ridiculous speed. (Anyone can have speed, though. Speed isn't skill.) Finally, he passed the ball into the net as Nigel covered his eyes – 1:0.

'What the fuck was that, Nigel?' I screamed. 'Man up! Keep your eyes open!'

'Oh dear,' taunted Matty. 'Your God has forsaken you.'

He was wrong. Just a minute later, with only Alex between him and a second goal, since Nigel made no difference, Matty stopped playing. He was distracted by a sideways run from Alex to the fence, where she stopped, knelt and vomited. Matty went over to see how she was. So did everyone else.

Not me, though. I knew Alex would be fine – vomiting was just what she needed. I fought the good fight and carried on playing. I got the ball and ran with it to the gates (as it were) of Vatican City: the Catholic goal. Because it had no Catholic goalkeeper in it, I only had air to beat. I pulled back my favourite right foot and slammed the ball into the net. No goalkeeper in the world could have stopped that shot, even by being in goal.

The Archdeacon blew his whistle and pointed to the centre spot. Now came my celebration. I've seen goalscorers on the telly rip their shirts off. Not me. I'm an aeroplane man. I ran round the pitch in the manner of a Boeing, cruising at an altitude of several feet, roaring like a jet. 'Goaaaaaaaal!'

All the Catholics round Alex turned to look.

'What?' said Matty. 'We stopped playing!'

'No,' I said. '*You* stopped playing. Play to the whistle. Those are the rules. It's not my fault you stopped.'

Five Catholics advanced on the ref, jostling him and shouting abuse. The Archdeacon, to save his immaculate shirt, blew his whistle again. In the interests of averting a riot, he abandoned the game with the score 1:1.

We'd scored a goal. Amen. Victory! Well, a draw.

*Later . . .*

Alex says she'll leave me if I ever play football again. She couldn't bear the pumping testosterone. What was I trying to prove? Why all the bloke stuff?

I said that was rich coming from her, who'd got pissed on a Saturday night with her mates then vomited during a game. Wasn't that classic 'bloke stuff'?

'And why were you so nasty to Ellie's boyfriend? He was sweet. And very good at football.'

I explained that Ellie's boyfriend was seriously undermining my authority and jeopardizing the denominational inspection with his rabid atheism.

## 29th June, *Feast of Ss Peter and Paul*

*I was ordained 15 years ago. Blimey, what have I achieved?*

Inspection day.

As I shaved, I rehearsed my assembly in my head. It was so important that the children identified with the

Good Samaritan. I'd set the story in present-day Hackney, just to be more current and engaged. The denominational inspector would love that.

I got to the school bright and early to organize everything. I stuck up some of the children's fishes and loaves pictures. Straightened the cross, which was leaning.

Ellie came out of her office and said the inspector was here. Was I ready for my assembly? I told her I was. Were all the staff here? She said yes, apart from Matthew. But we'd start without him.

The bastard wasn't going to turn up for my assembly. Of course he wasn't.

'You gave a clear directive that every teacher had to be here for assembly. Mr Feld has deliberately failed to turn up in order to undermine me.'

This irritated Ellie so much, she strode off to talk to the inspector. I hovered by the door of the assembly hall, and then I saw that sweet boy Jerome, sitting on one of those bright yellow primary school chairs that are meant to make children happy. But Jerome looked sad.

'Hello there, Jerome, are you all right?'

'Mr Feld fell off his bike.'

'Oh dear,' I said.

So *that's* why he was late. Poor old Matty, eh? It was unfortunate. Uncool. But it was a bit enjoyable. For me at any rate. I relished the image of Twatty Matty getting unfixed from his fixie.

Jerome started sobbing. He's dead.'

\*

Don't hug Jerome, you can't hug Jerome. That was the first thing I thought. So I lent him my handkerchief. That was probably inappropriate too. Some kind of health-and-safety breach.

Then I felt the most terrible guilt. Five seconds earlier, I'd been loving the idea that Matty had fallen off his bike. I'd been sniggering at the poor man, when he was already dead. What a terrible tragedy for his family and friends.

Poor Ellie. She'd be devastated. How awful for her. I should offer to break the news to the children, to spare her the burden. Ellie adored Matty. She thought he was gorgeous. What a waste. A waste of Ellie, that is. At least she wouldn't be wasting herself on him anymore.

I told Jerome to go into assembly and join the other kids. He was glad to be released, but not sure if he was meant to give back the hanky. I told him to keep it.

He got up from his chair and ran off. So I sat in it. What was I going to do? Jerome was the boy who'd asked me if Muslims went to Heaven. What about atheists? Would Matty go to Heaven? Yes, I believed he would, and he wasn't there to argue. I had to comfort the children.

The Good Samaritan wouldn't do, not now, it simply wouldn't help them. I'd tell them the bugs story instead. The one Rev Roy told, at the nursery school, after one of the pupils drowned. I was there, as his pastoral assistant, when he told it.

I heard footsteps and looked up. It was Ellie. I could see she'd been crying but she'd composed herself. She's such an impressive woman.

'I'm so sorry, Ellie,' I said, which I was. And wasn't. 'Would you like me to tell the children?'

'No, thank you. I'll tell them,' she said. 'Come on. Let's go in.'

After she told them, she retreated to the back of the hall and sat on the bench, looking at no one.

I stood up. A few of them sobbed, very quietly, trying to be brave.

I told them it was very difficult to know what to say at a time like this. They wouldn't see Mr Feld again because Mr Feld – Matthew – had gone somewhere else.

'Matthew didn't believe in Heaven. But I do. I don't know what Heaven is, but I know a story that gives me an idea.'

'Some little bugs lived at the bottom of a river. Every now and then one of the bugs would crawl up a plant out of the water into the light – and never be seen again.

'One day, one special little bug felt a great need to climb up the plant. So he did. Up the plant he went and out of the water. And then he turned into an amazing, colourful dragonfly and flew around in the air all day, happier than he'd ever been in his life. But when he tried to fly back down into the water, to tell all his bug friends how great it was, he couldn't. Does anyone know why?'

I looked at them and waited. After a bit, Chloe Craven put up her hand.

'Because he wasn't a bug no more.'

'That's right, Chloe. He wasn't a bug any more. He

was a dragonfly now, wasn't he? And he really missed his bug friends, till he remembered that one day they'd all do what *he'd* done. Every single one of them, sooner or later, would climb up the plant and join him in the sun.'

I went to the CD player and found 'You Shall Go Out With Joy'. I knew it would make them feel better.

> And all the trees of the fields
> Will clap their hands
> The trees of the fields
> Will clap their hands
> The trees of the fields
> Will clap their hands
> And you'll go out with joy!

It wasn't the words and it wasn't the singing, though it all helped; it was the clapping every time they sang 'hands'. The ritual of it. Their little palms hitting each other in memory of Matthew. It made me realize that a minute's applause works better than a minute's silence, because silence goes in and noise goes out, and the children had to get it out. I felt for them. I grieved for their loss. A teacher they loved had died. They'd never forget him.

Ten minutes later, I went to the door of Ellie's office, which was uncharacteristically shut. I was about to knock when I heard crying, so I left.

## 6th July

It's been a week now.

The Archdeacon turned up today with the letter from the denominational inspector. 'In the light of the unusual events at this school on the day of the inspection' – What was he talking about? Didn't he listen to my bug story? Dying is not 'unusual', it's usual, that's the whole point – 'In the light of the unusual events at this school on the day of the inspection, it was not possible to carry out the visit as planned. However, the inspector considered that a Christian ethos was amply evidenced in the assembly that—'

'Congratulations,' said the Archdeacon. 'You have brought no shame on the diocese. On the contrary, you have made us proud. That poor unfortunate atheist Matthew did not die in vain.'

I hadn't thought about it like that. But it's true – Matty dying on the day of the denominational inspection was a bit of an atheist own goal.


## 8th July

It happened at a crossroads. A car going through a red light hit Matthew's bike full-on. He died of his head injuries.

His parents wrote to Ellie yesterday and thanked her

and her pupils for all the cards and letters and flowers. They very much hoped that one good thing could come out of this tragedy – Ellie could convince all the children to wear a helmet when they rode a bike. Their son might still be alive today if he'd worn one.

Ellie's holding a memorial service at the school, with pupils invited to share memories of Matthew and do drawings or write stories or poems.

Some teachers have suggested it might be nice to name the playground in his honour, because he spent so much time there teaching football to the kids. The Matthew Feld Playground.

Is it just me, Lord, or is that a really annoying and stupid idea? For a start, playgrounds don't have names. No child's going to say to a friend, 'I'll see you at break in the Matthew Feld.' Second, he only taught at the school for six months.

He was too vain to wear a bike helmet and he couldn't stop showing off. But the way people talk, you'd think he was Nelson Mandela.

I'm an unfeeling monster. I must be, Lord.


## 10th July

A night in with Alex. We've given up *The Wire*. We're on to *Breaking Bad* now. The weird thing is, watching all these TV episodes together feels like an activity. An achievement, even. As though we're getting in the harvest or mucking out the pigs or thatching the roof, when in fact we're staring at a screen, eating the odd bit of pizza. We did customize the pizza with some grilled peppers to make us feel like we'd done some cooking.

Alex thinks I should base a sermon on *Breaking Bad*, since it's basically about a good man doing bad things to provide for his family, who he knows he'll soon be leaving behind because he's dying of cancer. Can a man still be a good man if he cooks crystal meth? Or gets involved in the odd murder? Apparently I should start the sermon with those questions. We joked about this for a while, then Alex got worryingly serious. She said I had to promise her she'd be the first to know if I ever committed a murder. There was 'Thou shalt not murder', but there was also 'Thou shalt not keep it from thy wife'. It wasn't a proper marriage if you did. I promised her I would, but she didn't believe me. She says I've been remote lately, I don't say what's on my mind. I said that was probably true – I'd been really disturbed by the death of Matthew and that was making me remote. But when she asked why it had affected me so much, I said I couldn't really tell her, which she thought meant I was being remote again.

Just before midnight, when we'd done 3 episodes, the phone rang. The voice said, 'Adam! Nat Jones!' He couldn't believe he hadn't seen me for so long. What was it, 5 years? I said I understood. Our lives were very busy. I was the vicar of St Saviour's and he was number 25 in the *Daily Telegraph*'s 'Top 100 Great British Entrepreneurs'.

'My God, you know all about me!' said Nat.

'I do,' I said. 'I follow your career in the papers.'

'Fantastic. I'm actually number 24.'

I apologized. He told me not to, it was all meaningless. He ran around pursuing success and money, when he knew they'd never bring him the happiness that old friends like myself and Alex did, the friends you made at uni being the most important friends in your life.

All this was over the top but also par for the course. You don't make millions in public relations without putting masses of energy into your private ones. Nat was making me feel our relationship was special, even if we hadn't had one for 5 years. He'd always been an entertaining and generous friend, a huge personality.

He asked if I remembered Tuscany 1998, when he'd offered me a job in his firm and I'd turned him down. I said I did and started to apologize, but he cut me off. No, no – it was he who should apologize to *me*.

I had no idea where our conversation was heading, till Nat said financial PR was 'the work of the devil' and he didn't want to waste another second in its evil grip. God had entered his life and he now understood what his purpose on earth was. He wanted to come and talk to me about being ordained.

His intensity was intimidating. I said, yes, I'd love to talk to him. Did he want to come to St Saviour's for a chat some time?

'How about now?' he asked, which completely threw me. I pointed out that it was midnight.

Nat apologized profusely. Of course it could wait till the morning. Could I meet him there at 8, before the Sunday service? I agreed, though it was massively inconvenient and I couldn't understand the urgency.

Then he got even more urgent. He told me to forget about the 8 o'clock meeting.

'What can I do for your church right now?'

I didn't understand the question, so he rephrased it. 'I'm getting rid of all my money. And I want to give some to your church. How much do you need? Tell me and I'll make out a cheque right now.'

Alex, who'd been watching my face throughout, said I looked stunned. Not happy, not appreciative, just stunned. She was right. The phone call had turned into some kind of miracle, and miracles tend to be stunning. I told Nat to hang on a moment, which felt rather good. I mean, it felt rather good to tell a multi-millionaire to hang on while I went to my study to find the folder marked 'Window Restoration Fund'.

I came back.

'Nat? You still there?' I asked, because I suppose that's what you do when you're experiencing a miracle, you check it's really happening.

'Tell me what you need, Adam.'

'£23,479.'

'You shall have it,' said Nat. 'Give me that figure again.' So I did. It seemed a colossal amount to me, but I felt that, to Nat, it was as if I was saying £11.99.

'I'm writing you a cheque. What's the address?'

215

I told him, very slowly, trying to keep calm, pronouncing each word clearly. Then I realized I hadn't even told him what the money was for.

'It's to restore a broken stained-glass window.'

'I have to go now,' said Nat.

Alex and I talked about it for ages, swinging between joy that he'd solved the problem and revulsion that a man could sign a cheque for that amount, just like that, before he even knew what it was for.

## 11th July

I wasn't at my best this morning. I hadn't had more than a few hours' sleep, on account of being churned up by Matthew's death, Nat's call and Alex saying I was remote.

Nat's excitement at finding God made me feel inadequate. Giving a sermon in St Saviour's wasn't exciting. For me or my congregation. On the other hand, it wasn't meant to be. A sermon was meant to make you think, not get you on your feet. I'd seen Ikon rapping from my pulpit about resurrected Jews and that was exciting but nothing else. It had no substance.

My sermon was based on the story of the healing of blind Bartimaeus. I asked the congregation to think about the idea that faith makes us whole. A wholeness that gives us the integrity to see other people as whole. So, for instance, when we see a person with a different skin colour, we see a person not a colour.

Halfway through, I began the reading from the scriptures: 'Then Jesus said to him, "What do you want me to do for you?" The blind man said to him, "My teacher, let me see again."'

I paused. I looked up from Mark 10 and out at the congregation. All the usual suspects were there. My loyal congregation, 20 or 30 strong. What were we doing? We were all going through the motions, comforting each other with routine and ritual. The content itself was sort of meaningless. It was just about being in this place, with each other. I heard Matthew's voice in my ear. *I just think they're weird.* Would it bother anyone if I stopped my sermon without getting to the miracle? Would anyone even notice?

I just couldn't see any point in carrying on. It all felt so *weird*.

Then I saw a young woman I'd never seen before. She had frizzy hair and glasses and looked very bright. She was even making notes. This new member of my congregation was concentrating on what I was saying, trying to learn something. She alone was reason enough to carry on.

'Then Jesus said to him, "Go, your faith has made you well." I gave it everything now, really belted it out. 'Immediately he regained his sight and followed him on the way.'

OK, there'd been a bit of a pause. I'd let it all go flat – a bit like that pause when I got to the Three Pillars and dried – but I got them back in the end. I really roused them.

Tonight, as we got into bed, the phone rang. I thought

it would be Nat, wanting to reschedule our meeting. I felt this was the second in a series of late-night calls. I'd probably end up being his mentor, just as Rev Roy was mine.

Alex answered. It wasn't Nat. It was his wife Caroline, a woman we barely knew. We'd met her at their wedding. Then at Nat's 30th on that boat in the Thames. And maybe a couple of times since.

She said she was very sorry to call us so late but she needed to talk to us.

At about half past midnight on Saturday, after Nat had said goodbye to me, he'd gone up to their bedroom, opened the window and climbed onto the ledge.

He stood on the ledge, clutching a downpipe, and shouted up at the sky. Nat told God, at the top of his voice, that he wanted to join Him.

Caroline begged him to come back inside for the sake of her, the kids, his parents, his friends and everyone who loved him. But he wouldn't. He just kept shouting that he was going to throw himself off, so she called an ambulance.

Nelson, their Labrador, provoked by the shouting, barked up at his master from the lawn. Nat's voice dropped to a whisper. He told Caroline that God didn't want him to jump, in case he landed on Nelson. And then he said, over and over, that he was a good man, he wanted to help people, he'd done nothing wrong and his faith would get him through. Caroline kept him talking till the paramedics arrived and induced him to come back into the bedroom. Then they sedated him and took him off to hospital.

Caroline had spent the whole day going through the dialled numbers on Nat's mobile. He'd called 50 or 60 people on Saturday night – I was the last – and he'd promised money to all of them. Some were charities, some were friends, some were religious organizations. One was Bono.

On the Friday, he'd had an appointment with the Serious Fraud Office. We would read in Monday's newspapers that he'd been charged with 79 counts of fraud and embezzlement. Basically, for the last 2 years, he'd been siphoning off clients' funds.

He'd only told her on Friday evening. All that time she'd had no idea. ('Thou shalt not keep it from thy wife.')

She'd found a cheque in his study, made out to St Saviour's, for £23,479. She was very sorry but we had to understand that this money was probably not Nat's to give. Alex understood. She told Caroline to tear up the cheque immediately. But Caroline insisted she'd send us a cheque from her own account, for £200. She felt honour-bound to do that. Alex felt that was unnecessary. In the end, she negotiated Caroline down to £100. And then she said Caroline must really need to sleep, and they said goodbye.

*We* couldn't sleep though. We talked for hours about Nat, just as we had the night before.

I looked for good and I found it. Nat was a man in spiritual crisis, wanting to atone for his wrongs, desperate to make something worthwhile out of his life. Hence his opening himself to God. Hence all those calls and all those promises of money to good causes.

Alex didn't see it like that. At his trial, Nat's counsel would mine God and those calls for all they were worth. Desperation didn't come into it. He'd calculated everything. He'd 'found God' and made those calls in the hope of getting his sentence reduced. There was nothing sincere about his conversion and nothing generous in his offers of money. What's more, she didn't believe he had any intention of throwing himself out of that window. Seriously, who abandons a suicide attempt for fear of landing on the dog? No, the window ledge thing was another bogus gesture of remorse.

I'd been used. Again. People used my church to try and get their kids into the right school. Or they used it out of habit, as their parents had used it before them, for ritual and routine, sponge fingers and fêtes, christenings, weddings and funerals.

There were so many more users than believers.

## 12th July

It was the perfect storm. Colin arrived at the vicarage seconds before the Archdeacon, then moments later Alex came in from work.

'Hello everyone,' she said, 'I was hoping you'd all be here in my kitchen.' The sarcasm was lost on Colin, who was busy looking for his favourite cheese, but not on the Archdeacon, who returned it with some of his own. 'Hello, Alexandra, have you been busy keeping murderers on our streets?' She said that was correct but, not to worry, she'd told them all to go to church to repent. It was like watching Roger Federer and the other one, the Spanish one.

The Archdeacon had come to show me my review on Godslot.com, a 'new irreverent Christian website' that sends anonymous people to review Sunday services and give marks out of 10 for the sermon. What mark did I think they'd given me?

Alex and Colin rallied round. Alex bet, without sarcasm, that they'd given me a 10. Colin hoped they'd heard 'that excellent one you did about sheep'. But they hadn't heard the one about the sheep. They'd heard my blind man of Bartimaeus effort. And they'd given me a -1. These people who sit in judgment on me hadn't even given me a 0. No, it was worse than 0. Worse than nothing. It was -1.

We all know that Jesus, were he living today, would be a blogger with 50,000,000 Twitter followers, thrilled that the Word could be disseminated so speedily and globally. That's all very present and engaged and relevant, till some troll from Godslot posts an instant review of your sermon, and the whole world knows, or thinks they know, that you and it were worse than worthless.

The Archdeacon read the whole thing out loud, of course. Not only did the reviewer insult me, they insulted my congregation.

The Reverend Adam Smallbone talked to his tiny and lifeless congregation about Jesus curing the blind man. It was without scholarship or insight, and the reverend seemed as bored by his own words as the congregation was. At one point, he stopped completely, apparently having lost the will to live. He wasn't the only one.

I didn't know what to say. Alex leapt in. Who were these sad green ink losers, typing anonymously away in their underpants? The Archdeacon explained that this was 'digital religion' and 'just a bit of fun'. But Alex wasn't having *that* – it clearly wasn't a bit of fun, or he wouldn't have come all this way to point it out to me.

The loser didn't wear underpants, I was sure of that. The loser wore panties. It was that girl with the frizzy hair and glasses, taking notes, the one I took for a new member of my congregation. As opposed to a four-eyed hitman.

The Archdeacon told Alex the idea of Godslot was 'to help Christians be self-critical'. She said I didn't need any help with that. And then she slapped Colin, who'd just got his hands on our best cheese and was about to cut himself a chunk. As if Colin was our surrogate son, which it often feels he is, for lack of a biological one. Or a dog.

When Colin and the Archdeacon left, I withdrew to my study, telling Alex I had work to do. I just wanted to be on my own. I sat there feeling angry for a long time at the injustice of it all. I've given so many good sermons. I know I have. I don't deserve to be judged on one; I deserve to be judged on them all.

And then my anger turned to apathy. What did it matter? Who cared? Would my numbers go down because of that bad review? No. They wouldn't. Everyone who came on Sunday would come again next week. Apart from the girl with the frizzy hair and glasses. And good riddance to *her*.

## 15th July

I woke up angry.

Yes, my sermon was flatly delivered, but there was an important idea behind it. Every day we hear or see something that reminds us people hate others for their difference. I took that thought and I linked it to the story in Mark 10 of blind Bartimaeus. I followed the advice of Rev Roy – when you're writing a sermon 'you listen to the world and you listen to the Word'. Who was listening to me, though?

I'm the Reverend Minus One. A reference not just to the quality of my sermons but to the size of my tiny, lifeless congregation.

## 19th July

Not angry now. More apathetic. What exactly have I achieved in my time at St Saviour's? Nothing.

I don't care. Let the world think of me as the Reverend Minus One. I couldn't give a toss.

Does God care, though? About me or my congregation or my life? Because if God doesn't care, nothing I do has any point.

Alex caught my expression in the bathroom mirror tonight and said I was having what she calls 'one of your little wobbles'.

She told me to take tomorrow off. Not be a vicar for a day. I reminded her that it's a calling and you can't be un-called, not even for a day.

Then she tried a different tack: I should go agnostic for a bit. In fact, I was already agnostic, wasn't I? Like all good priests.

That really upset me. My own wife doesn't believe that I believe in God. She thinks I'm an agnostic, as opposed to a believer who has doubts, as all believers do. And should.

I told her I couldn't bunk off tomorrow because I had to do school assembly. She told me to tell the kids God didn't exist. Given that kids are suckers for reverse psychology, that would get them flocking into church.

It was a smart idea. Very funny. But it didn't make me laugh.

This job demands your soul. If your soul isn't in it, who are you? You're a time-server or a hypocrite. You're using the church – using God – as a way to make a living.

I lay in bed, waiting to sense the presence of God. He's always been there when I shut my eyes at night and when I open them up in the morning.

## 20th July

My last assembly before the summer holidays. The kids can't wait to be free.

It was the first time I'd been in the assembly hall since Matthew's death, which haunted me. But it didn't haunt the kids. I saw nothing of that in their faces. The death of Matthew was a terrible thing but it was something that had happened, and a lot of things had happened since, and they were kids, so they lived in the present. Jerome, who I'd last seen sobbing, was laughing away because the girl next to him was trying to touch the tip of her nose with her tongue.

Chloe Craven, difficult but deserving Chloe, was telling a joke that lots of kids laughed at, possibly because it was funny, but more likely because they wanted to be in her gang. She was the one who dared to do and say stuff. They looked up to her.

Ellie was composed and sharp. As always. But you only had to look at her eyes to see that she was struggling with all her might to keep up a professional front. I admired her so much.

I began. 'Who here can remember who came down from the mountain with the Ten Commandments?'

Eighty children looked at me and silently said, 'Whatever.'

Eventually, Taylor Okonedo, that spiteful little turd, asked if it was the baby Jesus who came down from the mountain, knowing perfectly well it wasn't. I confirmed that it was Moses.

Then Chloe Craven spoke, as I feared she would. She was wearing her special Chloe smile. It's a scheming, disingenuous and undermining smile, but it's not actually against school regulations. Mostly, it's a sign to her followers, acolytes and 10-year-old disciples. *Watch this, it's going to be good.*

My ordination, my adulthood, my degree in history from Bristol – Chloe Craven could trump them all with that smile.

'You *sure* it wasn't the baby Jesus, sir?'

I said I was sure. When I was at school, they talked about 'dumb insolence'. But there's nothing dumb about Chloe's insolence. That's what worried me as I braced myself for her next remark. It would, in a smart and nihilistic way, deny the existence of God.

And I'd agree with it. That was my real fear. She'd deny the existence of God and, as the vicar in the room, I'd have to disagree with her and chide her for her insolence. What a hypocrite.

She spoke: 'But I thought the answer is *always* Jesus, sir.'

'NO, IT'S NOT! JESUS IS *NOT* ALWAYS THE ANSWER!'

My reply came out so loud that Ellie stopped the assembly. The children probably thought she did it to save them further punishment, but Ellie could tell how churned up I was. She did it to save *me* further punishment.

In her office, I asked her how she was coping.

'Don't worry about me,' she said, 'it's you we have to worry about.'

I couldn't believe she could be so professional. Didn't she want to cry on my shoulder?

'You've obviously had a bad reaction to your minus-one review.'

I told her it wasn't that. But I didn't tell her what it was. I was there as her vicar and a governor of her school. I didn't want to bother her with my doubts. Imagine if her maths teacher told her one day that he wasn't sure mathematics existed, maybe two plus two was four today but five tomorrow, who cared?

I said I couldn't take the feral apathy of the kids, which went down badly. They're her pupils, after all. Then I said that maybe I needed a new career. What about as a teacher? I'd be a good teacher, wouldn't I? I was just trying to be normal. I was trying to make conversation, like normal people do in their everyday jobs.

She strongly doubted I'd be good at teaching – I'd then have a roomful of feral and apathetic kids for 40 minutes, six times a day. I should concentrate on the task at hand, which was to take my terrible review as 'encouragement to do better'.

I told her to stop talking to me like I was one of her kids. In which case, she replied, I should stop behaving like one. And tie up my shoelaces.

I knelt down immediately. In fact, it was just a joke, because my shoelaces were fine. How could she make jokes, three weeks after her boyfriend had been killed?

Because she was being a bright and breezy head teacher, that's why. Normal. Professional.

From my vantage point, I had a wonderful view of her footwear. She was wearing little boots, bootees I supposed you'd call them, black bootees. I told her they were lovely and asked if they were new. She said they weren't and, keen to get rid of me, told me she had to sort out a venue for her fund-raising party in aid of the new school library.

I wanted to do something for her, so I told her to hold the party in the church. She couldn't give me any money. That didn't bother me. I'd shift the homeless meal because, important as that was, it would just be lovely to have the church used for something people *enjoyed* for once. In fact, why didn't she make it a vicars and tarts party? I told her I'd organize it. I was back to normal. Doing God's work. Yeah, right.

'Jesus said to him, Go your faith has made you well. Immediately he organized a vicars and tarts party and followed Jesus on the way.'

As I walked down Hackney Road, a policeman got out of a police car and asked if I was a vicar. The question was so surreal and stupid that all I could do was answer it. 'Yes,' I said. But then he did that policeman thing of looking at me like I was lying. I might be a vicar who was dressed as a vicar, but that didn't prove I was a vicar, did it?

He, of course, was dressed as a policeman, so I gave him a taste of his own medicine by asking if he was a policeman. Turns out the police can dish out the medicine but they can't take it.

He asked to see ID, which of course I didn't have. So I suggested he came to St Saviour's, which at least meant I got a lift to church with him and his colleague.

When we got there, Nigel, enjoying himself, said he could confirm that I was the 'one and only much cherished' vicar of St Saviour's. It turned out the police were investigating a series of incidents involving a man impersonating a vicar. He'd got out of a fixed fine for a litter offence. He'd gained entry to a coffee morning with the Bishop of London, then harassed him with questions about *The Da Vinci Code*.

I could see this was irritating. But was it actually illegal? The policemen weren't sure, though they knew it was wrong.

'Adam's been impersonating a vicar for years!' said Nigel, and the three of them laughed. Then the policemen left.

To get my own back, I put Nigel in charge of the vicars and tarts party. That immediately wiped the smile off his face and returned him to pompous mode. He considered such a party an inappropriate use of the church. I told him that when he ran his own church, he could make that decision. He'd just validated me as a vicar so I felt I had to remind him that it was actually *me* who did the validating. I validated him as a pastoral assistant, with the accent on the assistant.

I told him I was off to do some hospital visits, but I

wasn't. I went home, as Alex had suggested. I stopped being a vicar.

I didn't sense God on the way home. He wasn't on the streets and he wasn't in the shops and he wasn't in the faces of the people I passed. I felt like the Reverend Minus Ten. A man without a calling.

Speak to me, Lord. Can you do that?

## 22nd July

Why did you send that reviewer on my one bad day?
  Is that what I deserve?

## 23rd July

Why's the graveyard strewn with litter?

## 24th July

Why do Nazis always live till they're 96?

## 27th July

Why do African women get raped by boy soldiers every day while going to get water for their starving village?

**28th July**


**29th July**

Are you there, God?


**30th July**


**31st July**


**1st August**

I'm waiting.


**2nd August**

## 3rd August

## 4th August

## 5th August

## 6th August

I must not impersonate a vicar.
I must not impersonate a vicar.
I must not impersonate a vicar.
I must not impersonate a vicar.
I must not impersonate a vicar.
I must not impersonate a vicar.
I must not impersonate a vicar.
I must not impersonate a vicar.
I must not impersonate a vicar.
I must not impersonate a vicar.
I must not impersonate a vicar.
I must not impersonate a vicar.
I must not impersonate a vicar.

I must not impersonate a vicar.
I must not impersonate a vicar.
I must not impersonate a vicar.
I must not impersonate a vicar.
I must not impersonate a vicar.
I must not impersonate a vicar.
I must not impersonate a vicar.
I must not impersonate a vicar.
I must not impersonate a vicar.
I must not impersonate a vicar.
I must not impersonate a vicar.
I must not impersonate a vicar.
I must not impersonate a vicar.
I must not impersonate a vicar.
I must not impersonate a vicar.
I must not impersonate a vicar.
I must not impersonate a vicar.
I must not impersonate a vicar.
I must not impersonate a vicar.
I must not impersonate a vicar.
I must not impersonate a vicar.
I must not impersonate a vicar.
I must not impersonate a vicar.
I must not impersonate a vicar.
I must not impersonate a vicar.
I must not impersonate a vicar.
I must not impersonate a vicar.
I must not impersonate a vicar.
I must not impersonate a vicar.
I must not impersonate a vicar.
I must not impersonate a vicar.

I must not impersonate a vicar.
I must not impersonate a vicar.
I must not impersonate a vicar.
I must not impersonate a vicar.
I must not impersonate a vicar.
I must not impersonate a vicar.
I must not impersonate a vicar.

## 8th August

FUCK THE FATHER FUCK THE SON FUCK
THE HOLY GHOST FUCK THE CHURCH
FUCK THE CONGREGATION FUCK THE
BROKEN WINDOW FUCK DARREN FUCK
THE ONE SHOW FUCK THE SCHOOL FUCK
THE WHOLE FUCKING THING THE WHOLE
BARREL OF FUCKING LIES

Amen

## 9th August

## 10th August

## 11th August

Three fried eggs.
Nineteen fags.
Nine vodka tonics.
Ten episodes of *Top Gear*.
Two wanks.

## 12th August

## 13th August

## 14th August

## 15th August

## 21st August

It's 1.09 a.m. I'm alive. Alex is asleep next door. I'm still the vicar of St Saviour's. For all these, I give thanks.

## 30th August

I think I'm ready to talk about it now. The crisis. The meltdown. The *thing*.

Where did it begin? Probably at that Midnight Mass last Christmas. Possibly when I shouted at the scaffolders to fuck off, or when I couldn't stop blabbing on *The One Show*. Or when I exploded after Chloe Craven said, isn't Jesus *always* the answer? Then there was that time I froze during my blind Bartimaeus sermon. That was it, too, in another form.

It ended about an hour after the vicars and tarts party. Though I'm not sure a thing like that ends. I can't believe in 'putting the past behind you'. You *are* your past, surely? People, often American people, sometimes tell you, 'Today is the first day of the rest of your life.' Wow! Thanks for that. Does that mean the thousands of days before this one have had no effect on me?

The day the police stopped me, on suspicion of impersonating a vicar, I left the vicarage at about midday, telling Nigel I was off for my hospital visits, and got home 15 minutes later. I took off my collar and surplice, which was a liberation – of sorts. I no longer felt like a depressed vicar, just a depressed man.

I sat in front of the telly for hours. Nothing I saw had any effect. I watched a dating show called *Farmer Wants a Wife*, and normally, after laughing at it for a few minutes, I'd have got absorbed. I mean, it's not as if the show was called *Arms Dealer Wants a Wife*. We *love* farmers, we want them to be happy, for their sake and the sake of our food. But I didn't give a toss about any of these farmers or any of their prospective wives, or any of the jokes about being 'hen-pecked'. So I switched off and went to the shop for some fags.

It was the first time I'd been to the corner shop without my collar and cassock. In the middle of the afternoon, walking in a daze down Hackney Road in a T-shirt and tracksuit bottoms, I looked just like all the other unemployed men, which is what I was.

I decided to treat myself to some Jaffa Cakes. I'd watch telly, smoke and eat biscuits. The telly, fags and biscuits wouldn't make me any happier. I knew that, but that wasn't the point. I didn't want to be made any happier. I wanted to sink down deeper into the mire.

The fags and the Jaffa Cakes came to £5.05. I only had a fiver, so I asked Lisa if it was OK if I gave her the five pence next time. Lisa shook her head. She showed no sign of recognizing me, which I couldn't believe. I reminded her that I was the vicar. She'd seen me in the shop countless times.

Lisa gave me her wary look, the one she gives everyone. She told me I was the second person trying that on. There was a vicar impersonator going round shops, asking for free food to give to 'orphans'. She'd had him in earlier and told him where to go.

'At least he *looked* like a vicar,' she said, with a glance at my T-shirt and tracksuit bottoms.

'Lisa, come on, I'm the Kung Fu Vicar from *Metro*. You gave me a free lolly!'

'If you're a vicar, what you doing smoking fags?' she asked. As if real vicars didn't smoke fags because they only did good, even to themselves. Real vicars were sexless goody-goodies, devoid of human frailties. They were never five pence short.

I told her I smoked because I liked it. And then I said, sod it, if that's the way you want it, I'll put the Jaffa Cakes back on the shelves.

I went to the shelves but I didn't put them back. I just stood there holding the packet. Then I angled myself so I couldn't be seen by the security camera and stuffed the Jaffa Cakes down my tracksuit bottoms. Then I walked out of the shop.

I felt angry, strange and excited as I walked down Hackney Road. I felt the thrill of being bad with every step, as the packet chafed against my flesh. Left inside leg, right inside leg, left inside leg, right.

After a while the thrill wore off, so I stopped and looked in a shop window. The shop was abandoned, so there was nothing to look at, but that didn't matter, that was good, there was no one in the shop to see what I did next. I took out the Jaffa Cakes. I was a vicar removing a packet of stolen Jaffa Cakes from his tracksuit bottoms. I was living in a Godless world.

When Alex got home, she found me on the sofa, looking undead. She asked what I'd been doing so I told her. I'd just won 60 quid on Party Poker by bluffing every hand. Before that I'd eaten a packet of Jaffa Cakes. Before that I'd stolen them. Before that I'd watched *Farmer Wants a Wife* and somehow, in this busy schedule, I'd found the time, energy and conviction to have a wank.

'Have these things restored your faith in God?' she asked. I said they hadn't.

She apologized that she hadn't been around to help with the wank, but she'd been busy with a section nine procedural application for a Somali family's tribunal. I asked her if she thought she'd win and she said of course. And I knew her optimism was my cue to rise up off the sofa, to go out and make the world a better place. Instead I watched three repeats of *Top Gear* on Dave.

Did Alex think of herself as a lawyer or a woman impersonating a lawyer? A lawyer, of course. It wasn't like that for me. Not any longer. When I stood up in front of Chloe Craven and her gang, I felt *exactly* like a man impersonating a vicar, because anyone can tell the stories, anyone can stand up and describe what happened on Mount Sinai or in the Gardens of Eden or Gethsemane. But a vicar's not there to describe. A vicar's supposed to embody. I embody the Holy Spirit and live by the Word of God. What's the point of me if I don't? I'm meant to be suffused by His divine presence every waking hour, and it doesn't matter if I fail, we all know

I'll fail, the point is those children are meant to look at me and see, with their laser-like eyes, my soul, and know that it belongs to God. I'm a spiritual being. That's the job.

I thought of Roland Wise, sitting on our sofa, crying because he could no longer remember why he'd got ordained. He was just this court jester, pleasing everyone, but empty; he had no purpose. I thought him self-centred and self-pitying. But now I understood.

That Jaffa Cake night, I woke at 4 a.m. That's the worst time of all. At half past three you can tell yourself it's very late at night. At half past four, you can convince yourself you're awake very early. But at four you can't convince yourself of anything. You know you've fallen down the hole between night and day. You're nowhere.

I went down to the kitchen and made myself a cup of tea and sat at the kitchen table till it was time to get up and go to work, not that I did either. About five, I poured the cup of tea down the sink, un-drunk. I treated it like the Archdeacon treats my coffee.

Once upon a time I was suffused with His divine presence. I thought back to the day in 1999 when I had my revelation. There was me, Tim and his girlfriend Patty. The three of us were on a walking holiday in Wales. Pretty Patty, a vain girl who was always fiddling with her hair. Two weeks earlier she'd taken me to bed but hadn't let me do anything. What she'd wanted me to do was tell Tim, in order to provoke him. Much to my annoyance, it worked.

We ate the magic mushrooms at about midday in the bathroom of our B&B in Hay-on-Wye.

We had a drink at The Swan and then, as the mushrooms were really kicking in, we took the footpath that leads down to the Warren, a pebble beach on the Wye. I felt magnificent. Invincible. So much so that I skinny-dipped, even though it was October. I spent maybe two minutes in the water. I thought Tim and Patty would join me — we all knew I'd seen Patty naked — but they didn't.

The Wye was cold in a way that was sensational, meaning all my senses were involved. I could see, hear, feel, touch and smell the cold. It was wonderful.

On the other side of the river was a heron. It was the most beautiful thing I'd ever seen in my life, but not in a 'Wow!' way. Seeing this heron was nothing like seeing REM take their place on the Pyramid Stage at Glastonbury under the stars. That was a shared experience and very enjoyable, but it wasn't revelatory.

The heron took wing. It seemed to me it was flying on light, of which it was just a feature, as we all were. Me, Tim, Patty, the water, the ducks, the trees, the leaves, the insects. Every living thing. We were all made of light and we were all being loved, with an infinite generosity, by a presence that preceded all of us and united all of us, so that I felt a oneness with Tim and Patty and the ducks and the trees that was previously unthinkable, especially with Patty.

I didn't see the divine presence. This wasn't the moment I saw God, or found God, or even discovered I believed in God. It was the moment I discovered that *God believed in me.* That was the revelation.

The presence saw *me.* God saw me and illuminated me and understood me and forgave me and was ever-present everywhere I went. From that moment, I wanted to do His will. 'I heard the voice of the Lord saying, "Whom shall I send, and who will go for us?" Then I said, "Here I am. Send me."'

Because this wasn't an intellectual experience, because I didn't weigh up the evidence and decide that, on balance, I believed in the divine, people think that what I experienced was nonsense. My 'revelation' took account of the beautiful heron but no account of earthquakes or cancer. Therefore, it made no sense. Whereas I thought the opposite. God's divine presence made perfect sense, in the same way that God made everything else. He made sense and he made nonsense and he made suffering. God made suffering but He made you able to *cope* with suffering.

At four in morning, years later, I tried to re-connect with that day in the Warren. I knew I couldn't get back there in some mystical 're-birthing' fashion.

I could visualize the beach all right, and the river, and the heron, and Tim and Patty. I could visualize the place we went afterwards for tea, a restaurant called The Granary, near the Clock Tower in Hay. I could even picture the waitress, a school leaver with red hair, nervously dropping my carrot cake on the floor because, Tim said, I was 'smiling too much'. But that was it. That was as close as I got. Some snapshots but not the whole glorious panorama.

The thought of that day just brought me lower, because I couldn't understand how I'd got here from there. In 1999, I'd had a revelation of the truth of the divine, and now I was a time-serving hypocrite. I did a smiley thing every Sunday as I said goodbye to my congregation, all 18 of them. I smiled at the children at school assembly, I smiled at Adoha when she did the flowers for the spring fair and the harvest festival. I even smiled at Colin when he turned up at my house, with or without an invitation, though it was always without. I smiled at the homeless at the night shelter and I laid on an extra big cheesy grin when I went to the hospital and Mulberry House. I practically split my face at the Xmas carol service. I smiled because I was useless and irrelevant and I was trying to cheer myself up. But, more pertinently, I smiled because a smile is a technique for suppressing rage. The rage I felt that I was wasting my life on a God who either didn't exist or had no faith in me.

In 1999, I was overwhelmed. Now I was underwhelmed. He had filled me with His presence and now there was a void, which I filled for days with cigarettes, biscuits and shit TV. The great thing about being a priest is that I get my stipend even if I sit at home in my pants. So I did.

Between the Jaffa Cakes day and the vicars and tarts night, there were three Sundays. Every Saturday night I went to my laptop and found sermons I'd delivered earlier, in St Peter's Church, Gromford. All I had to do was recycle them. A bit of tinkering here and there, cutting a reference to 'this year's Olympic Spirit', changing the odd 'pheasant' to 'rottweiler', 'tractor' to 'four by four'. I thought no one would notice and they didn't. Why would they? The frizzy-haired woman had moved on. No one was going to complain.

I moped. I was remote. Alex tried to help me but she didn't have the power. She's done a course in mediation, which everyone thinks is the future of law: the settlement of disputes by discussion not litigation. But she couldn't mediate between me and God. Where was the discussion? I spoke to Him but He didn't speak to me.

When the bell rang one night, just as we were having supper, I knew it would be Colin and for once I was glad, because of all the people I knew, Colin was the one most likely to understand. The man is no stranger to despair. In The Monarch, I told him I felt like a remnant, the remnant of an illusion people used to believe in.

He asked me why I was 'being such a dickhead'. So I told him. I wanted God to overwhelm me, as He once had. Everywhere I went, I saw earthquakes, cancer, malaria, AIDS, dementia, apathy, thoughtlessness, anger, theft, addiction, violent dogs and litter. How could I believe in a God who'd created those?

What's more, I was sick of telling everyone what they wanted to hear. I was meant to be a good man. Was that what being 'good' meant? Smiling and not telling the truth? What was 'good' about not telling people what you really thought?

Colin was with me on that one. Colin, who always tells people what he thinks, urged me to do the same. If I told everyone what I really thought, I'd feel great again.

So I did. Starting with Colin.

I told him I thought he should stop coming round to the vicarage all the time. It was irritating. Was he satisfied now? Was he happy I'd told him what I really thought? Myself, I wasn't happy, I just felt worse.

He called me a bastard and left. Two days later, in the middle of the afternoon, when I was sitting on the sofa in my pants, smoking a cigarette and playing Party Poker, Adoha knocked at the door.

'Adam, you are in your pants,' she said, and it occurred to me that I'd never met anyone who stated the obvious quite so obviously. Then she did it again.

'And you smoke!' she said, as I took another drag from my cigarette.

I told her I didn't. I tried to make her disbelieve the evidence of her own eyes – pretty much the job description of a vicar. I dropped my cigarette on the ground and stubbed it out with my foot, even though I was only wearing a sock.

And then she started talking about some forthcoming funeral. She was thinking of doing a 'standing spray of lilies and gladioli'. Did I like that idea? God, she was boring me. OK, I thought, I'll tell you the truth. I'll do to you what I did to Colin.

'Adoha,' I said, 'I really don't care. I couldn't give a toss about flowers.' She told me I was not myself and

246

she forgave me. Not myself! She didn't understand. I'd never been *more* myself.

At 8.10 the next morning, the phone rang. I knew it was my mother because that's when she rings. 'Is everything all right?' That would be her first question. I always say, 'Yes, Mum.' I'd say 'Yes, Mum' if I'd just cut off my thumb with the bread knife.

I pleaded with Alex to answer it but she wouldn't – it was my mum not hers. The phone stopped ringing. Then it started again. Alex answered and said, 'Yes, Carol. Everything's fine. How are you and Peter?'

Mum was ringing to tell us that June and Graham Cooper's daughter Eliza, who I haven't seen since primary school, had just had twins. Also, Sheila McMichael, who I've never met, but used to be Chair of Ipswich Archaeological Trust when Mum was secretary – anyway, her son Alex (who I've also never met) had just had twins too.

One phone call, four babies. When the call was over, Alex asked if my mum was deliberately trying to undermine her. I said nothing. I was thinking that I didn't want to bring a baby into this world. It wouldn't be right for the baby or me. A pointless father bringing a child into a Godless world.

'Why do you keep rocking? It's driving me mad!' said Alex. Every time I sat in a chair, I rocked back and forth. In The Monarch, I even rocked on a bar stool. It drove her mad because it *was* mad. In my crisis, I was either slumping or rocking, comatose or manic.

I did some strange things, the kind of things that

made me wonder afterwards if it was really me that did them. Yes. It was. I did all those things.

I remember one lunchtime watching the news. An earthquake had killed hundreds of people in Pakistan. I looked on as mothers and fathers, brothers and sisters and sons and daughters wept at the deaths of their sons and daughters, brothers and sisters and mothers and fathers. Did this mean there was no God? I told myself that the cross was a sign of God suffering with a suffering world. In human pain, God was present, taking that pain on His own shoulders. I reminded myself that the ultimate healing comes with death, when we are made whole, and become one with God. I said these things to myself but they meant nothing. They were just words.

I didn't even have the energy to cry.

But then, just a few minutes later, I had a manic attack. It was the girl doing the weather. I just found the contours of her blue dress incredibly arousing. And I was very excited by the way she moved her hands, pointing out the areas of low pressure and such. And then she smiled and I knew she was smiling at me. She wanted me. I got up and walked across the room to the television, never taking my eyes off her. Then I got down on all fours in front of her and put my face against her face and I kissed her and it was nice, even though I couldn't see her any more, I could only see her massive pixels.

On 15 August, Nigel wore shorts. I remember because it was the Feast of the Assumption of the Blessed Virgin Mary and he brought in a book of Titian paintings, so we could admire the Master's rendering of the scene. The Apostles reaching up to the Virgin Mary on her cloud, supported by cherubs, while she in turn reaches up to God, who's watching over her, His hair flying in the wind as He awaits her bodily assumption into Heaven, before her body begins to decay. It's all a fore-taste of our own bodily resurrection at the end of time.

Nigel said it was one of the most beautiful works of the Renaissance, but I found it about as beautiful as his knees. It disgusted me, in fact. A grotesque pantomime, religiose, absurd. Cherubs – those flying Superbabies.Yuk.

Nigel had been looking at me with suspicion for weeks. He wanted to tell me I'd gone mad, but he couldn't quite bring himself to do that, for fear of the repercussions. Also, I was still doing my job, or a parody of my job, with something of 'dumb insolence' about me, as though I was doing it and mocking it at the same time.

'Don't ever show me that painting again,' I said. He slammed the book shut and said, 'I have no idea what's got into you lately, but I suggest you have it surgically removed,' which, as insults go, was not that bad, though it was marred by the smile of self-satisfaction that fol-lowed it.

I didn't feel like Twatty Matty when I looked at that painting. I wasn't trying, on behalf of science, to expose believers as fools. For me atheism wasn't a cause, it was a loss. I'd lost my faith and that made me sad. Or belligerent.

I plonked myself down opposite Nigel, slammed my trainers on the desk and got down to the serious business of necking a packet of cheesy Wotsits. Nigel was busy organizing the vicars and tarts party – tracking down guavas for the fruit punch and other such religious stuff. I enjoyed distracting him. And of course I rocked. Eventually, the rocking and the sight of the underside of my trainers got to him so badly that he asked if there was anything I actually wanted because he was busy. My assistant was trying to throw me out of my own vestry, because he was urgently trying to work out what prayer might be appropriate at the start of the party.

Prayer? At the start of a party? I questioned whether Nigel knew what a 'party' was. He tensed as the Archdeacon entered the room. I didn't. I'd done enough tensing in the Archdeacon's presence. If anything, I rocked even more.

The Archdeacon was impressed with the fund-raising potential of a vicars and tarts party, so much so that he asked if he could come. 'Who's going to be there?' he enquired, as if he hoped the answer would be Rageh Omaar and Kristin Scott Thomas. So I banned him. You don't check who's going to be there before you agree to go to a party. Who did he think he was? All those times he'd thrown me out of his cab, all those times he had to hurry me because he was off to a restaurant opening or a premiere or a recording of *Just a Minute* starring Roland Wise. I told him the party was sold out and that he'd have to go to one of his posh clubs for nobs instead. Or maybe he had a seminar on listed-building health-and-safety signage. Wasn't that how he spent his evenings?

For the first time ever, I got to him. I shook him to his Archdeacon's core. He told me I 'literally had no idea' how he spent his evenings. I thought he was going to lose it and tell me to fuck off, which I'd have counted as a victory. But instead, he composed himself and asked if he detected a 'certain lack of *esprit de corps*' in my current behaviour and mode of dress.

I denied it, of course. I told him, with fearless sarcasm, that I loved the vocation. And the people. Loved them. Absolutely loved them. *Laaaaaved* them.

'Have you still not got over your terrible review?'

He didn't understand. He had no idea.

Nigel laughed. In full sycophantic mode, he laughed as if the Archdeacon had said the funniest thing in the world. And I laughed, too, a big full-throated over-loud insolent laugh, which no one could mistake for the real thing.

'HA HA HA HA HA HA HA HA HA.'

I rocked in my chair. I literally rocked with laughter so hard that my chair fell backwards and I hit my head on the floor.

It hurt, it really hurt. But I didn't see stars. I saw a great shower of cheesy Wotsits, all orange and fluffy.

The Archdeacon suggested I go home, as I'd do less damage there. He hoped that the bang on the head would bring me to my senses, because he was tired of my adolescent and offensive behaviour.

*

A week later, it was the night of the vicars and tarts party, which was one of the worst nights of my life, but also one of the best. (See? On the one hand, on the other hand. I'm obviously back to my best, liberal Anglican self.)

At 7 o'clock, I begged Alex to go to the party as a tart. I wanted her to put on her full Vivienne outfit – the black belted mac, pink wig, matching pink bra and suspenders. Before we went to the party, we could have a quickie by the kitchen sink. We could finish off that one we were having, all those months ago, when Mick turned up to clean our windows.

She said all this sex stuff had nothing to do with her. It was just about my hyped-up sexual needs and didn't relate to her as a person; it was just a kind of generic lust I could aim at 'any passing woman'. What? She wasn't passing, she was my wife. It was *all* about her. Her as Vivienne.

She went upstairs to get away from me, and when she came down she was dressed as a vicar, in a white robe with black trimmings and a green sash. So I went up and put on my collar and surplice. And it seemed to me incredibly funny, laugh-out-loud funny, that I, a vicar, was going to a vicars and tarts party dressed as a vicar, because I'd never felt less like one. Then I went and put on a big black droopy Jason King moustache, the one I wore for Nat Jones' Seventies Party on that boat on the Thames when he turned 30. I found that the facial hair made me feel even more sexy.

And then it happened again. En route to the party, I

was stopped by the police and asked if I was a vicar, and much to Alex's embarrassment I told them I didn't know. Would they like to search my soul and tell me? She told the officers it was all right, I was just having a joke, and it wasn't funny, which proved I was a vicar because a vicar's jokes weren't funny. And then she made me show them my driving licence, with its photo of me in my collar.

We didn't talk for the rest of the way to St Saviour's. As soon as we got there, we split up. She just didn't want to be near me.

I'd missed Nigel's opening prayer, which apparently consisted of everyone shouting, 'Prayer! Prayer! Prayer!' at Nigel.

I got a glass of red wine. All I could see was the Pope. Nigel, dressed as a renaissance Pope, with his gold brocade and his robes and his foot-high mitre, looking absolutely vast, like a Pope shithouse. I'd never seen him so happy. Of all the things Nigel loved about the Church – the Liturgy, the Gospels, the scholarship – what he loved most was the dressing up, I thought. Fucking poof.

I had another red wine and I felt great. I could do anything.

And then I saw Ellie. I hadn't seen her for days. Weeks. She was my head teacher but these were the school holidays. Ellie was dressed as a nun. I'd never seen her in black. She looked lovely.

Poor Ellie. Her boyfriend had been knocked off his bike and killed. But that was weeks ago. By now she'd have realized that he was, in fact, a twat. As I'd pointed out to her. He wasn't half the man I was. But *I* was. In fact, I felt twice the man I'd ever been. That's how potent I felt.

She knew I was looking at her but she kept not quite returning my gaze. That was a sign. (This wasn't like the weather girl smiling at me. This was real.) Ellie was 20 feet away, provoking me by ignoring me. I realized she'd always wanted me. It all added up. That thing she'd said before we went to Cheeky's, when she'd told me she was looking forward to 'our evening of sex and nudity'. Her constant teasing. The dominatrix way she told me to tie my shoelaces.

And now she was available.

I took to the floor and danced for her.

So many men dance from side to side and back again. They go nowhere. But I wasn't a man, I was a god. I drew my stole between my legs sensually, like a Bulgarian lap dancer. I robot-danced my hands round and round in perfect circles. I did that move where it looks like I'm running on the spot, but I'm so at one with the floor that the floor appears to be running, not me. I was amazing. Travoltus, the god of dance.

I became aware that other dancers were drawn to me. Someone was on the right of my line of vision, wanting to be my partner. It was Nigel. He was strutting what he thought was his funky Papal stuff, grinning at me like we were lovers across the Anglican–Catholic divide, and it really annoyed me. I didn't want him crowding my space and blocking Ellie's view of me. I got rid of him, but when I looked at her again she walked off.

She'd obviously got fed up with my not making a move. So I waited till the DJ played a slow song. It was 'Can't Take My Eyes Off You', which was perfect. Sometimes, the song does the work for you.

I sidled up to Ellie, nice and slow, and told her the nun's costume was a little 'surplice to requirements', because I wanted my approach to be subtle and classy, as that's what Ellie deserves.

She didn't respond, so I said I hoped she wouldn't 'make a habit' of it. That definitely had an effect. She told me to stop it, it was embarrassing, my lovely wife Alex was her friend. Why was I doing this? Did I think she was up for it because her boyfriend was dead? Shame on me.

But if this was meant to put me off, it didn't. It seemed to me she was in denial. She knew she wanted me and it was no use her saying she didn't, or talking to me about Alex or Twatty, because we both knew we were powerless to stop the thing happening. All we could do was surrender to it. But we couldn't do that in the south transept, with all the partygoers looking on, so I suggested we go and have a quick one in the vestry.

I knew as soon as it came out my mouth that it was the wrong thing to say. What I ought to have suggested was a slow one. Slow as she liked.

She reached out and, with thumb and forefinger, ripped off my moustache. Then, with the very same forefinger, she poked me in the eye.

That hurt. That really hurt. What the hell was happening to my right eye? The bastard thing was cursed. First Colin headbutts it, then Ellie pokes it. Was this

Jesus at work, because I'd looked at her with lust? – 'If thine eye offends thee, pluck it out.' – No. Bollocks. I didn't believe in that nonsense.

The next thing I knew, Alex was shepherding me out of the church. It was that straightforward. She shepherd, me sheep. My wife knew all about the poke, even before it happened. She'd actually given Ellie permission to do it if I became too much of a pest.

Poor Alex. I pitied her, I really did. She was married to a foolish vicar. An unholy fool she couldn't control, though she could control everything else. So I told her to fuck off. *That's* how much she controlled me.

She told me I was drunk and should go home. So I shrugged and said OK. It seemed like I was doing what she wanted but I wasn't. I had no idea what I'd do next, but I knew I wasn't going home. I switched my phone off so she couldn't keep tabs.

I don't know what happened in the next few minutes. They're lost down some hole, that hole into which I wanted to throw myself. I just wanted to go as low as I could.

I remember I was by some lock-up garages on an estate, chucking a supermarket trolley around and kicking black plastic sacks, which spewed out pizza crusts. I remember singing 'Can't Take My Eyes Off You' so loud that some bloke actually came out on his balcony to tell me to shut up; he actually took time out from shooting up or sex trafficking to berate me, which was quite a compliment. So I sang even louder. I changed the chorus to 'Can't poke your eye out of you.' Which struck me as absolutely brilliant. And then I remember looking down at a pigeon that was pecking at a bit of pizza crust. And I vomited on it. As the vomit landed, I thought of Nat Jones, saying he couldn't jump cos he'd land on his dog.

I watched the pigeon fly away, flapping my sick over Hackney. Was sicking on a pigeon as low as I could get? No. I thought I could sink lower. How, though?

There was a void inside me now that could only be filled by a Tony's Kebab. I wasn't quite sure where I was, so I walked down a street and turned left, then left again, then I turned left again and found myself a few yards from where I'd started, near Tony's Kebabs.

Once I was kebabbed up, I felt ready for anything again. On the other side of the road, in what's laughingly known as the park, some kids were drinking and larking about by the War Memorial. There must have been 10 of them. The same kids that were always there, the kids that didn't stop shouting or littering when I stood at that memorial trying, in vain, to think about my brave grandfather, dying for his country on the beaches of Normandy.

One dropped his Kentucky Fried Chicken carton on the ground. His mate went towards it – to pick it up, I hoped. But no, he kicked it and the ugly thing went to join some other cartons nearby.

He shouldn't have done that, he really shouldn't. Now I knew what I was going to do with the rest of my night. I was going to go round London telling everyone who dropped any litter that they had to pick it up. And I was going to start here. Now. Right now.

I told Kebab Tony of my mission. I felt righteous and strong. He looked at me like I was mad, but that didn't bother me, because that kind of thing doesn't bother you when you're actually mad, it's only when you're not that you feel offended. Then I crossed the road and walked towards the kids.

'Hey! You! Pick that up!' I said to the kid who'd kicked the carton. And then I thought, No, that's not right, what about the kid who dropped it in the first place? So I turned to him and said, 'You pick it up, too!'

Then a third kid said, 'What's it got to do with you?'

So I told him to pick it up as well. 'All of you, pick that carton up. Now!'

'You looking for a fight, Vicar?' one of them said. Course I was. I wanted to fight 10 kids and I wanted to win. But I didn't care if I lost – that's what gave me my strength. My fearlessness empowered me. And I didn't need a gun or a knife or a brick or even my fists. All I needed to fight these kids was what I held in my hand.

A doner kebab. What a weapon. It's soft but its contents are hot. As the kids crowded round me and taunted me, I flicked it at their faces. They were shocked. They'd never been donered before.

I started swinging my arm around, whirling dervish style. I was seriously losing quite a lot of lamb now. I was pushed and shoved and I pushed and shoved, and then there was a policeman in front of me, asking me to put down my kebab, and all the kids ran off.

*

This was where it had all been heading. It had started in the shop, with the theft of the Jaffa Cakes, and it was ending in this park, with affray, assault and a breach of the peace. I'd be on the front page of the *Hackney Gazette*.

Alex would get me off with a caution or a fine. Maybe a suspended sentence. She'd tell the magistrate about a manic episode following a difficult few months in my new parish, which every vicar experiences. But maybe, just maybe, the magistrate would send me to jail. To make an example of a man like me, who was meant to *set* an example. Wasn't that the kind of thing they did?

Then there'd be the tribunal. 'Conduct unbecoming to the office of a clerk in holy orders.' The Archdeacon would ask what I had to say. I'd shrug. That would be it. They'd confiscate my collar and I'd have to look for another job. A defrocked vicar, nearly 40, smoker? I shouldn't have much trouble.

As the policemen led me away, I felt shockingly sober. Walking with a policeman to his car is like drinking 10 pints of water. I felt very low again, but I thought I understood: the whole thing had been a manic episode. Not just this night. Everything.

By that I mean my revelation, my ordination, my years at St Peter's and St Saviour's. In Hay-on-Wye, in 1999, when I was in my twenties, with no idea of who I was or what I was meant to do, newly split up from the only girl with whom I'd felt safe and loved, I'd gone mad and found God (been found by God) while high on magic mushrooms. Years of highs and lows had followed, years of divinity and banality, grace and uselessness, transcendence and boredom. And now it was all over. Mum and Dad were right – I should have done that training course with Price Waterhouse. I'd go on their website and see if they still did them.

We got in the car. The policeman told me he'd been looking everywhere for me. He'd gone to St Saviour's, which was full of vicars, but none of them was real. My wife had said I'd probably end up at Tony's Kebabs. Tony had identified me. He'd pointed me out.

The police car stopped on an estate. What was going on? He lead me to a lift in a block of flats. We got out on the fourth floor and headed down a walkway. He said the lady in flat 29 only had a couple of hours to live.

I asked him what exactly he wanted from me and he stared at me. Didn't I know? Hadn't my wife texted? The lady was about to die. She wanted the Last Rites. That's why they'd tracked me down.

I said I wasn't sure I was the right man. I'd been having a bit of a crisis and I didn't think I was strong and able. He didn't get the reference to Romans 15.

'*You're* not strong and able!' he said. 'Are you her vicar or not?'

I asked him to give me a moment and said I'd see him there. Alone in the walkway, I took off my white surplice with the green sash, my vicar's costume, to reveal my black cassock beneath. Now I was no longer a vicar dressed up as a vicar. I was just a plain vicar.

I felt confused and apprehensive. I felt ashamed at the way I'd treated Alex and Ellie, and stupid that my white surplice had a big lamb-coloured stain on it. I felt guilty that I'd nicked those Jaffa Cakes. I felt disgusted with myself for sinking so low. And my eye hurt.

So, there it was. I felt confused and apprehensive and ashamed and stupid and guilty and disgusted and hurt. But I didn't feel manic. Nor did I feel depressed.

I found myself reciting the section from Isaiah 6 that was read at my ordination: 'I heard the voice of the Lord saying, "Whom shall I send, and who will go for us?" Then I said, "Here I am. Send me."'

I walked to number 29. The door was open. In the hall was the policeman and an old man, who introduced himself as Norman. The flat had all the sweet odours of death: flowers, air freshener, skin cream. Norman gripped my wrist with both hands and said he couldn't thank me enough for coming round so late on a Friday night, as if death kept office hours. He was so sorry Val hadn't been to church lately, she'd been bedridden for a year now. I must be the new vicar because I wasn't the old one. I said that was right.

Then Norman, still holding my wrist, asked me how I was enjoying myself at St Saviour's. His wife was in the bedroom, dying, and Norman was asking me how I was enjoying my job. I welled up. I wanted to put my head on Norman's shoulder and cry my eyes out. I wanted to tell him I'd spent weeks on a sofa, filled with doubt and bile, and that I wasn't worthy of his kindness. But it was important not to say any of that stuff.

I asked if he had any oil. He was puzzled. Did I mean engine oil? I explained that I needed it to anoint Val's forehead and he apologized for his mistake, over and over. The policeman told him not to worry. Norman said he wanted to 'do everything right'. The policeman asked if he had any cooking oil. Norman wasn't sure. The policeman said, 'Cooking oil is your wife's department, I expect.'

'That's right,' said Norman, reassured.

The three of us went into the kitchen. The policeman found an egg cup. I poured some Flora oil into it.

Then Norman and I headed for the bedroom, leaving the policeman at the kitchen table. What did he usually do on a Friday night? Same as every other night. He confronted aggression, he dealt with fighters and binge drinkers. Me, for instance. And yet he also had the gentleness and grace to enter a dying woman's home and comfort the husband who was about to lose her.

I liked him, I really liked him. I wanted to know his name. What was happening? A moment ago I was near tears and now I was falling in love with a policeman. I was still manic, wasn't I? Could I go into that bedroom and read the Last Rites? Where was my grace? My calm?

Val was lying on her back with her head on the pillow, eyes closed, barely breathing. Norman sat down and held her hand. I stood on the other side.

Outside the room there was shouting and screaming, sirens and motorbikes and hip-hop. Inside, it could have been the sixteenth century. A dying woman, her husband and a priest.

First, the Laying on of Hands and Anointing. Then the Nunc Dimittis. Finally, the Commendation: 'Into your hands, O merciful Saviour, we commend your servant Val.'

As I spoke she became, to me, suffused with eternal light. To be in that room with Val was to be certain of a divine presence that couldn't sustain her in this life but which would keep her alive for ever.

We stayed with her. We knew we couldn't leave. Norman kept looking at his watch. When she died, he said, '11.47. The doctor will want to know.'

He stood up and I crossed to his side of the bed; he gripped my wrist again and told me she'd have been so happy to know I'd been there.

I was a priest again. I was everybody and nobody, ministering to human need.

I got home just after midnight. Alex wasn't there. As soon as I heard her arrive, I went into the hall and just kept saying sorry and I love you and I never want to hurt you again, but she said she didn't want to talk.

When we woke up in the morning, I didn't want to talk about myself or what I'd done – that would just lead to anger and strife – so I asked her how she'd enjoyed the party after I'd gone. I thought that was a safe and bland, trouble-free question.

She told me she'd had a phone call asking her to go immediately to a bar mitzvah in Bethnal Green. Who did I think that call was from?

She sounded irritated, which was the last thing I wanted. I didn't want to irritate her further. So my answer had to be right.

'Was it something to do with Colin?'

'No, it wasn't something to do with Colin,' she said, angry now. 'It was actual fucking Colin himself.'

He'd gatecrashed a bar mitzvah. Nobody dared question who he was. People thought he was probably there at the invitation of the Rabbi. Some interfaith thing. A reaching out of Jews to Anglicans.

They thought that because Colin was dressed as a vicar. He was the vicar impersonator, the one who'd got off the litter fine and gone into Lisa's shop asking for free stuff for orphans. And now he was celebrating the bar mitzvah of one Dan Hoffman.

He ate the meal, with lots of helpings, and was friendly and nice to everyone. But then – for a bet he'd made earlier with a man in The Monarch – he gave the bar mitzvah boy a pork pie as a present, which angered Mrs Hoffman so much she told him to get out. Colin said it was only a joke. Mr Hoffman came over and asked what all the fuss was about, which ended with Colin being exposed as a fake. Mr and Mrs Hoffman said they'd call the police. That's when Colin rang Alex. Alex and the Rabbi managed to persuade the Hoffmans not to get the police. Alex said impersonating a vicar wasn't a criminal offence, not unless Colin had used his vicar status to gain a financial advantage.

'What are you, meshuggah?' asked Mr Hoffman. 'You don't think smoked salmon, roast chicken, apple tart and petits fours cost money?' In the end, inspired by Nat Jones, Alex made out a cheque for £50 to Jewish Blind & Disabled, which Colin promised to 'pay back'.

The Rabbi, whose name was Michael Yudinksi, sent me his regards. Why couldn't I be more like him? He wasn't drunk and he didn't ask her to have a quick one in the back of the synagogue. He was funny and balanced and he wasn't self-pitying or manic or remote.

I went quiet.

## 5th September

The vicars and tarts night was 2 weeks ago. Basically, I've been quiet ever since. Alex and I have avoided each other – not aggressively, it's just, I can tell I hurt her very much and the best way not to hurt her any more is to say nothing and keep my distance.

Ever since we moved into the vicarage, I've talked about re-painting the bathroom. The previous occupants painted it a colour Alex calls 'Dying Flesh'.

As part of my continuing penance, I decided today was the day. Saturday, the classic day for DIY.

I didn't even eat breakfast. I just got in the car without telling Alex and drove off to Homebase for some white paint.

It took me an hour. Not the drive, the choosing. There was Cool White and Ash White and Flint White and Cornflower White. Grecian White. Jasmine White. Jade White. I wandered up and down the aisle, over and over again, trying to pick one Alex would like, and every time I settled on a different one. Finally, I asked a member of staff which one he thought was the closest to White White.

I came home and got straight down to business.

After 4 or 5 hours, with no stopping for lunch, I'd

done the undercoat. At that point, Alex came into the bathroom and asked why I wasn't speaking to her. I explained that action spoke louder than words.

'Yes, OK,' she said. 'Action, yes. Not *silence* speaks louder than words.'

I clammed up, which only upset her further, and then I decided it was time to go into serious detail, which I hadn't yet done. I mean I hadn't been through every item on the charge sheet. So I said I was sorry for my drunkenness and my moping and my abusive behaviour and my obsession with my own problems, and my neglect of her needs, and my sexual behaviour, both towards her and Ellie.

'And?' she said.

I couldn't think what was left so I said, 'And generally being me.'

'Yes,' she said. 'That's the real problem, isn't it?' Then she made a suggestion. If I wanted to say as little as possible and think about the mess I'd made of my life, why didn't I go off to a proper retreat? Instead of retreating to our bathroom and making her feel as though she didn't exist?

I said that under the circumstances that was a good idea.

She told me to look for a retreat in the countryside. Somerset. Norfolk. Wales, maybe.

'You might see another heron,' she said. Every so often, over the years, she's made some remark like that. She wasn't with me on that day in Hay-on-Wye. It happened during our four-month break-up. Sometimes I think she believes if we'd been together it wouldn't have happened. As if my being without her made me more available to God.

## 10th September

Thank you, Lord, for making a room available at such short notice in the Poor Clares Convent Retreat near Sixpenny Handley in Dorset.

Seven days of silence and contemplation. Perfect. And none of the nuns looks like Ellie did at the party, which is great. The food is better than adequate; there's nothing they don't know about rice. There are ornamental ponds, meditation gardens and icon painting for beginners. From my room, I can see cows. When did I last see a cow? Not since we went to Dover. There's peace to be found in contemplating cows. Even Chloe Craven will agree.

The library's small and dark but excellent.

## 11th September

I thought all day about the Lord. In silence. That's why I'm here.

## 12th September

Everlasting God, in whom we live and move and have our being: You have made us for Yourself, and our hearts are restless until they rest in You.

I wonder what's for lunch today?

*Later . . .*

Yep. It was rice. With vegetables. But different vegetables from yesterday.

There are rumours of cauliflower cheese. Well, not rumours. No one's actually said, out loud, 'Cauliflower cheese.'

It's more smells, really. Though it could be some sort of nasal mirage. Maybe it's the nuns. Do nuns smell of cauliflower cheese? I don't know who to ask. I know no one here.

I'm glad I bought some Kit Kats.

## 13th September

I woke at five, walked along the footpath east of the convent and mooched around near the cows, enjoying the sunrise. Alex was right. I had to get away. I'd been too long indoors. Physically and mentally.

At seven, I walked through the cloisters. The only sound was the squeaking of my shoes. I'd never realized how noisy they are – it just goes to show that in the clamour and chaos of the inner city, there's always a noise louder than your shoe squeak.

A nun approached me. I thought about saying good morning. I contemplated asking her if today might be the day when we welcomed cauliflower cheese into our hearts. But the beauty of a silent order is that I didn't have to talk to her at all.

I went to the library and read about John Chrysostom (347–407), Bishop of Constantinople, who we commemorate on this day. Chrysostom means 'golden-mouthed'. And the man lived up to his name. Some of the stuff he said about prayer really got to me: 'He commands each of the faithful who prays to do so universally, for the whole world. For he did not say, "Thy will be done in me or in us," but "on earth", the whole earth.'

In my meltdown, there was only me. I could never have prayed for the world because I thought I *was* the world.

I went back to my room and contemplated the nature of universal prayer for approximately 30 seconds, at which point there was a non-silent rap at the window. A grinning man in a straw hat was doing a little party jig and waving his bottle of single malt, shouting, not-silently, 'Retreat!'

It was Roland Wise. Of course it was. I let him into my room.

'Dear boy, I've just arrived. I'm staying in the kennel next door. How are you coping?'

I smiled and nodded.

'What DVDs have you got? I've got Diarmaid's *History of Christianity*. And *The Killing*.'

I shook my head to convey that I didn't watch telly on retreat. He thought my silence meant I was ill. Did I have laryngitis? I whispered that we weren't meant to talk.

Roland assured me it was the Lesser Silence in the morning. The Greater Silence didn't kick in until 5 p.m. I believed him, as I tend to do.

I thought I'd fallen out with him over the nicking of my MacNeice poem, but you don't fall out with Roland, he's irresistible – you sort of fall under him. He said he normally took his retreats in 'that chateau in Provence' but it was fully booked, so he'd come here. He'd invited Alan Yentob, but Alan had let him down.

He was keen to know what food I'd brought. I confessed to my Kit Kats and he trumped that. He had a hamper of Assam tea, potted goose, salted caramels, gooseberry cheesecake and Iberico ham. I confessed; Roland boasted.

But then he said, 'We shouldn't be doing this,' as if he knew it was wrong to come to a retreat and feast on expensive treats. Actually what he meant was that coming to a retreat was wrong: we shouldn't be skulking away here, we should be out there, tweeting and doing telly and radio and TED talks.

'The Church is never front foot enough,' said Roland, without irony. The man who comes to a silent retreat and talks, very loudly, about how best to advance.

'What have you brought to drink? I've got a couple of nice Rieslings and a Pic St-Loup.'

I hesitated. I didn't want to admit to alcohol. And I didn't want to share. But then I opened the drawer of my desk, the one decorated with two candles and a Bible. I revealed to Roland my bottles of gin and tonic. And then I opened the next drawer down and showed him the vodka and tonic.

'We may just survive this,' said Roland.

At seven, when supper – pasta with vegetables – was over, Roland came back to my room, still in shock that supper had ended 'two hours before Nigella starts *serving*'. We closed the curtains, in due deference to the nuns, and had a second supper, with wine.

After he left, I dived into the *Collected Works of Rufinus of Aquileia*, which had been thoughtfully placed in the bookcase where, in most Dorset rentals, you'd normally find a Pratchett and some John Fowles.

Rufinus wrote about the Desert Fathers, the Christian ascetics who followed the example of St Anthony: 'They live in separate cells, scattered apart in the desert but united in love for each other . . . they none of them take any thought for food or clothing or any such things.'

You couldn't say that about Roland. Just how self denying is a priest meant to be? Surely, if your purpose is to spread the Word of God, you need joy. It's a joyful calling. I mustn't go all hair-shirt just because I went over the top for a few weeks with my booze and my urges.

An unknown soldier in the service of the Lord, well up for salted caramels and Riesling. That's how I'd like to be remembered.

I might even write that in the visitors' book when I leave.

## 16th September

I texted Alex to say I was leaving and would be home around seven. She didn't reply. When I got back, I found a note on the kitchen table.

Helen and Sue and Maria and Howard invited me to go on a walking holiday in Shropshire so that's where I am. I'm leaving my mobile off for a week or so. I want to think about my life. Look after yourself.

I could probably write 10,000 words on that note, because I've studied it like a biblical scholar who takes a few lines from Matthew, Mark, Luke or John and obsesses over them so much that they become the key to everything. They are the truth, the whole truth.

I felt that Alex's note contained the whole truth about her and me.

I read it when I was angry and I read it again when I was sad; I read it when I was in despair and when I was drunk with optimism. And when I was just plain drunk. Each time I read it, I found something new to reassure me or make me even more convinced that Alex had left me. The words remained the same but I didn't, so their meaning changed.

The first time I read it was the worst. Not just its contents. Its location. This was what people did when they left each other – they wrote a note and put it on the kitchen table, so the other person would find it when he or she came home, by which time they'd be hundreds of miles away. In Shropshire, say.

It wasn't like we ever left notes for each other on the kitchen table. Maybe ones that said 'Back at 7.30' or 'Dishwasher salt', but never ones that said anything as drastic as 'I want to think about my life'.

When had she decided to go on this walking holiday? Was this something that had just come up, or had she been planning it for weeks? Alex didn't just drop everything and go on a walking holiday; she worked in a firm of solicitors and had to plan her leave in advance. She must have suggested that retreat to get rid of me, so she could slip off to Shropshire with Helen and Sue and Maria. And Howard.

Helen and Sue were friends from school. Maria was Helen's sister. Who was Howard? Why did she mention him last? *Oh, and Howard. Did I forget Howard?*

It wasn't Howard who'd invited Alex on holiday, no, it was Helen and Sue and Maria *and* Howard. Alex cleverly put him last to hide him behind the women. They were the cover, the decoys. Maybe I was meant to think Howard was with Maria – Helen and Sue and 'Maria and Howard' had invited her to Shropshire. If so, it hadn't worked.

Howard. What a shit name. He sounded like a really boring man, possibly from the North.

I couldn't speak to her. That's what hurt more than anything. 'I'm leaving my mobile off for a week or so.'

When had that week started? (The note had no date.)

273

And what did 'or so' mean? Was nine days 'a week or so'? Ten? Surely eleven was 'two weeks or so'. I had no way of knowing.

Alex was leaving me and leaving her phone off, so I'd have time to absorb her leaving me before I spoke to her next. Time to turn my anger into resignation.

'Look after yourself': it was obvious what that meant. Do that because, from now on, I won't be there to look after you.

I'd been remote, I'd been manic, I'd been obsessed with myself. I'd propositioned her friend Ellie. It made no difference that I was manic when I did that, or that I'd been poked in the eye for it. Those things didn't make it go away.

I went to the fridge and got a can of lager. Then I sat at the table and drank it. This was something I needed to do, in any event, after my three-hour drive from the retreat. Weirdly, I didn't touch the note. I just left it there, propped up against the salt and pepper, as if it would be bad luck to move it.

Now when I read it, it all seemed fine. Alex had gone off with some friends to Shropshire for a few days to think about her life. What had I just done? I'd just gone off to a retreat in Dorset for a few days to think about my life.

I went upstairs and checked in the cupboard: the tent was gone. You don't take a tent when you go off for a dirty weekend in Paris with Howard. She was in Shropshire, walking with her friends, including a friend I'd never met called Howard, and because she loved me she'd told me to look after myself while she was gone.

The next time I read it, woozy with tenderness, I remembered she'd said many times that we ought to go one day to Rodney's Pillar at the top of Breidden Hill in Shropshire. Her parents had taken her there when she was a little girl and she wanted to go back with me. It was one of those places we'd always planned to go: Madrid, Loch Lomond, Reykjavik, Rodney's Pillar. But that was OK, we had the rest of our lives to go to all of them and be happy.

For the moment we were apart. Now she was up Rodney's Pillar having doubts. I'd always said that doubt was important and I distrusted anyone who didn't have it. I had to allow her to have doubts about me, if I had doubts about *God*. The confident and loving thing was to let her get on with her doubting, knowing she'd get over it in a few days.

But I felt like shit.

## 17th September

I pulled out all the stops on the St Saviour's organ for maximum volume, but mostly I heard a bronchitic sort of wheeze. Or nothing. Some of the keys were quiet as the grave, probably because of the damp, which I'm told is even worse than dust for an organ. Today I received the forms from the Heritage Lottery Fund to apply for some money to repair it, under the Grants for Places of

Worship programme, which funds 'urgent structural repairs' to public places of worship. Is repairing our organ urgent? No, we use a CD player from a car-boot sale, so we get by. No one rushes into the church to ask us to play the organ, quick, or they'll lose their faith. Besides, there's still the window to repair. That's far more urgent.

Nevertheless, it saddens me that mine isn't more of a musical church. It's all there in Psalm 150: 'Praise him with trumpet sound; praise him with lute and harp! Praise him with tambourine and dance; praise him with strings and pipe!' Those aren't requests, are they? They're orders. Liturgy needs music. Although I'd question the need for a lute.

I dreamt about Alex last night. I bumped into her in the shop. She was at the counter, with a Kit Kat. I asked her where she'd been and she said she'd gone to Shropshire and she'd climbed up Howard's Pillar and sat on it.

I couldn't believe the crudity of this. I'd never think up something as basic and stupid as that, but there it was, I didn't think it up, I dreamt it. When I'm dreaming, I'm like everyone else – a basic stupid mass of anxieties waiting to be acted out, with puns.

Nigel joined me on the balcony, very excited. He'd had a letter confirming the dates of his selection interviews, for Ordination. Inspired by the organ, he said he was looking forward to having a large choir in his church. We really must stay in touch when we were both vicars!

For the first time since the note, I felt something that was nothing to do with me and Alex, which was a relief, even if that something was irritation with Nigel. He went on to say he couldn't decide if he'd prefer a nice rural parish in the Cotswolds or a church on Piccadilly. Or Knightsbridge.

I asked if he was sure he wanted to be a priest. He was. Very sure. In fact, he'd realized on his 'Towards Ordained Ministry' course how much better he'd be as a priest than all the other people there.

I advised him against saying that to the Bishops' Advisory Panel. They'd be wary of anyone who was certain they'd be called to God. Chasing preferment was frowned upon. It was right to be doubtful.

'Quite right, good point!' said Nigel. And then he actually wrote 'be doubtful' on the little pad he carries around, which made me want to laugh (and cry), because anyone who has to write it down can't do it.

'Don't you ever feel like some advancement, Adam? Nice cathedral job? Little bishop? Big canon?'

I turned away from him and played with the stops on the organ. I told him I wasn't interested in promotion, I'd joined the church to be a parish priest in a place like St Saviour's. And with that, I stabbed one of the keys with my finger and out came . . . nothing.

Nigel congratulated me on being very good at being humble. The Bishops' Advisory Panel would love me. At this rate, I'd end up as an archbishop.

I assured him my doubt was genuine. I certainly didn't tell him that at that moment I was doubting my marriage. Nobody must know.

*

After reception class – 'Stories Jesus Told' – Ellie tracked me down in the corridor. It's sort of OK with me and her now, though I doubt – that word again – she's forgiven me. Was Alex all right? She'd texted her but hadn't heard back. I said that was because she'd turned her phone off.

'Oh. Right,' she said. 'You mean it's broken?'

I said, no, it wasn't broken, it was just turned off. I'd already said more than I wanted to say.

'When's she going to turn it back on?' asked Ellie, in that head teacher's way she has, looking hard at you, expecting a straightforward answer.

'Why don't you ask *her* when she's going to turn it back on?' I said, immediately regretting my tone.

'I would,' replied Ellie, 'but her phone's off.'

I decided to say nothing, thinking that was the only way to keep my private life private.

'Is everything all right, Adam?'

I stood there mutely, hoping the subject would change.

'It's obviously not, is it?'

'I didn't say that!' I said.

'No,' said Ellie. 'You didn't have to.'

Why can't I ever be enigmatic, like the Archdeacon?

## 20th September

Look after yourself, Alex wrote, so look after myself I did. I couldn't face cooking a meal for one, so I went to the kitchen drawer and rummaged through the takeaway menus. There was a United Nations of crap food choices. I decided on an 'Animal Feast' pizza, but I ordered it with a salad, because maybe Alex would call me while I was eating it and I could talk about the salad not the pizza.

The guy from Pizza-U-Like said they were very busy and it would be 25 minutes.

I'd been here before. I mean, I'd been on my own in the house, feeling low, and I didn't want to go back to sitting on the sofa and smoking and drinking and watching *Top Gear*, and all those other depressed things I did. (Masturbation – the thief of time.) What I craved more than anything was sacred music. I'd decided we'd have a dedication festival at St Saviour's on the last Sunday after Trinity – even if we had no choir and no organ, it would still mean something to be together listening to 'Ubi Caritas' by Duruflé.

I listened to it on my headphones and felt protected from everything, as if I was wearing a crash helmet of music. I'd never thought of it as a love song before. Love songs usually mean Marvin Gaye, The Carpenters or Sinatra. Sexual healing, or birds suddenly appearing every time you are near. 'Ubi Caritas' is (loosely) based on Corinthians, but it's no less a love song for that. 'Where charity and love are, there is God.' It's a love song because it makes you think of God's eternal love.

Then I got stuck into the 'Jubilate Deo', the Britten version, with that amazing opening organ salvo, which I'd love to hear played on the organ of St Saviour's. After that, I was transported by 'Spem In Alium' from the same CD, *England My England* by the King's College Cambridge Choir, and then I went for 'Zadok The Priest' and 'Ave Verum Corpus'. It seemed to me I was listening to *God's Greatest Hits*. Then the doorbell rang.

I gave the pizza delivery man a £20 note, but he wouldn't take any money. I didn't understand until he took his helmet off. It was Colin. Colin, as I'd never seen him before: with a job. First Nigel, now Colin. Everyone was at it – seeking employment, being worldly, getting on with their lives. While I was in retreat, with my music, transported to a higher floaty plane.

He was elated. His job meant minimum wage plus pizza lunch with medium soft drink for him – and free pizza for life for me! So saying, he put my pizza on a plate, then took it into the living room and started eating it.

I put on 'Spem In Alium'. In his view, it wasn't uplifting enough for church, not like AC/DC's 'Let's Get It Up', which King's College Choir hadn't got round to recording yet.

He said he was sorry I was eating alone cos Alex had left me. I hadn't told him anything of the sort – I'd just said she'd gone off to Shropshire with friends. And I wasn't 'eating alone', I wasn't eating at all. And he'd forgotten my salad.

Colin was convinced that 'gone off to Shropshire with friends' was some sort of euphemism.

'What friends?' he asked, so I gave him the names, just to prove I wasn't making it up.

'Who's this Howard when he's not licking out four

women in a tent?' Obscene as that was, it was strangely comforting. Howard servicing all the women, not just Alex.

'Don't you see what this is, mate? It's a cry for attention. That's what women do all day.'

Colin's expert relationship advice was cut short by his radio, which made a sort of parping noise. He said 'Roger, Roger' into it a lot, angrily, and then 'P.O.B.', which I thought meant 'passenger on board' but maybe it meant 'pizza on board'. Anyway, it was a lie.

He said he had to go and I said that was fine, because Alex would be ringing me in a minute (which was a lie) and I had to make some supper for myself (which was true).

An hour later, I called her for the hundredth time from our bed. Her phone was still off. Then I fell asleep and dreamt that a man – Howard? – had his arm around my head. He seemed to be trying to kill me by squeezing my brain out from between my ears. But this was easily explained. I'd fallen asleep with my headphones on.


## 21st September

After school assembly, Ellie took me aside. Alex still hadn't responded to her messages. She wanted me to reassure her that any problems Alex and I might be having in our marriage were nothing to do with her. She'd been entirely innocent in that 'whole business'. She thought Alex understood that.

It was the first time she'd referred to the 'whole business' since it had happened. I felt excruciated, talking about it in a school corridor. I opened my mouth to speak, but then she shouted, 'Don't RUN, Courtney!'

'I didn't lead you on in any way, did I?' she asked without even looking at me.

'No,' I said. But that didn't seem to satisfy her; she still seemed upset. So I added, 'It's not your fault you're so attractive.'

She walked off.

I was only telling the truth.

Back in the vestry, I started writing Nigel's reference, to go to the Diocesan Director of Ordinands. Nigel kept hovering near me, stressing how my predecessor always encouraged him in his wish to have his own parish. He was sure my predecessor would have written him a glowing reference. (Yeah, I thought. To get rid of you.)

I just wished that, after our organ conversation, he wouldn't keep saying he was 'sure', especially as I'd already written, 'Nigel has many qualities but he's far too sure of himself.'

Nigel is dying to get out of St Saviour's and get on with his life. I'm the opposite. I don't want to get on with my life, I want to go back. I just want to be in my East London vicarage with my wife.

## 22nd September

*Nolo episcopari.* 'I am unwilling to accept the office of bishop.' When they offered you a bishopric 200 years ago, that's what you had to say. Then they asked you a second time and you refused a second time. It was only when they asked you a third time that you were expected, and entitled, to say yes. Presumably you were meant to look surprised as you did so. 'You sure you want me? Seriously? *Moi?*' (Actually, you probably said it in Latin: 'You sure you want me? Seriously? Ego?')

False modesty was built into it. We love false modesty in the Church of England. *Nolo episcopari. Gloriam praecedit humilitas.*

Today, after the service, when Nigel and Adoha and I were having coffee with the Archdeacon, Nigel brought up the subject of the vacancy for Bishop of Stevenage. Was he interested at all? The Archdeacon went for a loud and clear *nolo*. Then he put bells on it.

'I hunger to communicate the Gospel to the widest possible audience. But I fear my soul is unprepared for such a role, even if God were considering me for such a position, which I'm sure He's not.'

So that was a big yes then. Nigel and now the Archdeacon. Both moving on to better things, in Stevenage and the Cotswolds (or Knightsbridge or Piccadilly).

None of us had the power to make the Archdeacon Bishop of Stevenage. Nevertheless, he was definitely on the compassionate campaign trail, starting with the cup of coffee handed to him by Adoha.

'This coffee's lovely,' he told her. 'How do you do it?'

'It's just instant, Archdeacon.'

'Please,' he said, 'call me Robert!'

What was going on? The tricksy, waspish Archdeacon

had turned into cuddly Robert, who marvelled at the lovely way Adoha poured water on granules.

With his new-found humility, he turned the subject away from himself. He was delighted to hear that Nigel had put himself forward for ordination training.

'What do you think my chances are, pretty solid?' asked Nigel. You could almost see the cloud of smarm. It was like smarm incense.

'Yes,' I chipped in, enjoying myself now, 'how do you think Nigel could help his application, Robert?'

I knew the Archdeacon thought, as I did, that Nigel would make a hopeless priest – it was one of the rare bonds between us. To my delight, he suggested Nigel should go to the local authority youth drop-in centre to 'learn about teenagers' problems'. Oh yes, Nigel would love *that*.

'Good idea!' lied Nigel badly. He didn't just see himself as a theologian and preacher. He was a man of action, a drop-in kind of guy.

'I love teenagers with problems,' he said. 'Sweet!'

That was obviously a word he'd heard a teenager use, probably when he was looking at one through binoculars.

I asked 'Robert' who'd be interviewing Nigel now that the Diocesan Director of Ordinands had quit and had yet to be replaced. The Archdeacon said he himself would be standing in for the DDO.

'Did you hear that, Nigel?' I asked unnecessarily. 'Your interview is with Robert.'

Nigel did his best to look happy. But his best wasn't very good.

'Can't linger,' said the Archdeacon. 'Must go off and mop the loos in the palliative care unit.'

Did he actually expect us to believe that? I preferred him before he was 'Robert' – at least he didn't pretend to be self-sacrificing and nice. He was still basically unfathomable, though. He said 'palliative care unit' with the same lip-smacking relish he'd give to 'Gordon Ramsay restaurant'.

As I helped Adoha clear the coffee, she told me she was sorry about my news. I told her I didn't have any news and any news she'd heard was incorrect.

'You help so many people, darling,' she said. 'Now you must let us help you.'


## 23rd September

There's a treble solo about a minute and a half into the 'Miserere Mei' by Allegri that really does sound like a lark ascending to Heaven. I've taken to wearing headphones in the vestry so I can listen to *God's Greatest Hits* whenever I want. And it blots out Nigel. I've been wearing them in the shop, too, so I can't hear Lisa swear on the phone, and also when I'm walking down Hackney Road. I get quite a lot of people smiling at me. They've never seen a vicar wearing headphones before. It makes me feel very urban, like one of those people you sit next to on the Tube who's so into their music, they don't even notice how annoying they're being, with that *tsss-tsss* leaking from around their ears. I don't think I'm being annoying, though. Sit next to me and you hear sung Latin. You hear grace and transcendence. I'm doing you a favour.

As the days go by and I don't hear from her, I get more sad – I barely slept last night – but the one thing I don't doubt is that she'll come home. She has to. Her things are here. She can't go to work without getting her briefcase. It's on the table in the hall.

This evening I was intending to cook mushroom risotto. Enough for two. In case Alex turned up, which was not impossible. You can't walk in Shropshire for ever. Holidays end. Helen and Sue and Maria and Howard have lives to go back to. Assuming Howard isn't going on to a new one with Alex.

I was stirring the first of the stock into the rice when Adoha turned up at the front door, holding a casserole and telling me she knew I was a terrible cook. I told her to wait there and rushed back into the kitchen to turn off the rice and take the note off the table. I didn't want her seeing it.

Now I knew what Adoha meant when she said I must let her help me. Her help was compulsory. She didn't even have to ring me beforehand and tell me help was on its way. She just had to turn up at my front door with a casserole and I had to let her in and let myself get helped.

In the casserole were boiled beef and dumplings, which I don't like. But that was ungracious of me. Adoha was right, I'd helped people and I should let them reciprocate, allow them to minister to the minister. But I had to make sure there were no misunderstandings. I knew from the Pride of Britain 'heroics' that once Adoha got something wrong, she really got it wrong.

'The thing is, I don't know what you've heard from Colin but—' That was as far as I got.

'That bastard can't look after you like I can!' she said. Now I felt like a tug-of-love vicar. Adoha and Colin wanted me, and I'd better be careful who I chose (I was hoping to choose neither) because they were going to tear me apart. It was the Judgment of Solomon.

'It's very kind of you to come and feed me, Adoha, but Alex is coming home in a week or so.'

'Of course, darling,' she said, as if she were talking to a simpleton. 'Now. Where do you keep your serving spoons?'

After the beef and dumplings, there were profiteroles, because 'you need to put some meat on your bones,' and apparently the meat didn't do that, it had to be profiteroles. By the end of the meal, she was saying she really felt at home in my kitchen. 'No, please,' I wanted to shout. 'Fuck off now!'

While we were eating, we talked about the meal. While she washed up, we talked about where the stuff went after she'd washed it up. But when that chapter of the evening was over, I had no idea what to say to her. The awful truth was, I had nothing in common with her. But actually, what was so awful about that? What was wrong with having a relationship that worked in the church, but not outside it? God brought us together. Otherwise, there was nothing.

'Listen, darling,' said Adoha helpfully, 'I know how exhausting these things are.'

What things?

'If you want to watch television or go to bed, you go ahead.'

I thanked her and went ahead and watched television. What I didn't expect was her following me into the living room and watching it with me. Did that mean when I went to bed, she'd come with me?

Then I had a brainwave. I said that at ten I was due to call Alex.

'You go right ahead,' she said.

So I went right ahead. I picked up the phone in the living room and I dialled Alex's mobile, which was switched off, and I started talking to her.

'Hello, darling,' I said, 'it's me. What sort of day have you had?' I paused. How long was I meant to pause for, though? I suppose it depended on what sort of day she'd had. I decided she'd had a great day. 'Great,' I said. Then I said, 'Hold on a second, darling' – I wanted lots of 'darling' – 'I just have to say goodnight to Adoha. She very kindly came over and cooked me a meal. Yes, I know!'

I stopped talking into the phone and said, 'Goodnight, Adoha. Alex sends her love.'

Adoha nodded. She looked a bit hurt, as if she'd been rendered superfluous. Then she said, 'May I say hello to her?'

'May Adoha say hello to you?' I said to no one. Then I turned to Adoha. 'She says, no, sorry.'

I made a face as if to say, that's what Alex is like sometimes. She can be rude. But it worked brilliantly. Adoha got up and left. Just two hours after I wanted her to.

## 24th September

Tonight was very different from last night. It wasn't beef and dumplings tonight, it was tomato stew with fufu. This was proper ethnic Nigerian food. Somehow I felt I was doing some good by eating it. Being multi-cultural. Welcoming food of other nations into my mouth.

Fufu turned out to be a sort of dough ball for scooping up the juice from the stew. Adoha showed me how to do it. For the second night running, she didn't actually eat any food herself. She just watched me and made comments. When I got the hang of her fufu, she said, 'Good boy, Adam!' It was all quite infantilizing.

After a while, she went out to the kitchen to clear up, which she did with extraordinary dedication. Where had I seen her expression before? In church. She was abandoning herself to the task.

'You have to stop now, Adoha,' I said, concerned about her having an orgasm. 'I'm really grateful for all you've done, but you've got your own life, you mustn't overdo it. I can do this, I'm not old or ill or anything.'

'Are you ringing Alex now?' she asked, with a little edge, as if that would be a waste of my time.

'Yes,' I said. Why not? It had worked the previous evening.

I went back into the living room and dialled the

number. The charade was demeaning. But if it was what I had to do to ward off Adoha, I'd keep doing it.

'Hello.'

It was a wonderful shock. I hadn't heard her voice for days. Hearing it made me miss her more than ever.

'It's me,' I said.

'I know,' she said. 'Your name came up on the screen.'

'I wasn't expecting your phone to be on.'

'No. I just switched it on.'

'How are you? I miss you.'

'I've brought you more profiteroles, darling,' Adoha interrupted.

'Who's that?'

'Nothing. No, it's Adoha, she came round and cooked for me.'

'Oh, right. Do you want to ring me back?'

'No. Yes.'

'OK, bye.'

I put the phone down on the arm of the sofa.

'Never mind, darling,' said Adoha, looking at the phone like it was a tiny coffin. 'Eat your profiteroles. They will be a comfort.'

'I don't need comforting!' I said, too aggressively. 'I'm going to ring her back in a minute.' I stuck a profiterole into my mouth. The outside tasted dark and leathery and the inside felt like pus, but I made it last as long as I could, because I knew that as soon as it was over, she would ask me to eat another one.

We sat down to watch *Baby Face Brides*. She only left

when the programme finished at 11. I called Alex back, hoping it wasn't too late, which it was, as she was asleep in the tent she was sharing with Sue, so I'd woken both of them, and I had to wait while she put her clothes on and stepped outside. So – she wasn't sharing a tent with Howard. That proved nothing, though. They could be trying to conceal their affair from Sue and Helen and Maria. And, of course, me.

I didn't want to sound needy or demanding or hurt, so when she asked if I was looking after myself 'when Adoha isn't there', I kept everything low key. I said, yes, I was fine, then I talked about how hard it was to write a reference for Nigel. If I put the truth, it would prejudice his chances and he'd be devastated, but I couldn't really lie. She thought that sounded tricky but she didn't want to spend any more time talking about Nigel outside a tent in the dark.

She was sorry she had left me so suddenly. Did I understand why she had to go off and be incommunicado? I said yes, though she could tell I didn't and that she'd hurt me.

'Do you want to have a child with me?' she asked. I said, yes, of course, without even thinking about it. And she knew. She could hear it was just a reflex answer and told me I should think about it, because that's what she was doing in Shropshire: she was thinking about whether she wanted to have a child with me.

'What are you saying?' I asked. She said she'd just said it.

'I think you think God will provide us with a child. That's not good enough for me. I'm going to bed now.'

'When can I call you again?'

'We leave our phones off during the day. They spoil the walk.'

What wasn't good enough for her? She must have meant my not giving up the fags or cutting down on the booze. Not doing the things that helped fertility. Or maybe she meant my reluctance, my nervousness, my leaving it up to God if we had a child or not.

Lord, is it hard for a woman to have a child with a priest? Are we no good at being husbands or dads, is that it, because we give ourselves to You and have nothing left? Or is it nothing to do with being a priest at all?

Adoha has 5 children, Lord. And 19 grandchildren. Please let her spend the next few nights with them and not come back to the vicarage before Alex gets home.

She will come home, won't she, Lord? I believe she will, but I have my doubts.

Believing then doubting, believing then doubting. That seems to be my fate, doesn't it, Lord?

## 25th September

I wanted to call her about 100 times tonight but I didn't. She doesn't want me to.

It's been so many days now. No way is this 'a week or so'.

# 26th September

On my PC screen were the Church's criteria for selection for ordained ministry. In my headphones was Bach's 'Jesu Meine Freude'. Near me was Nigel, hovering. He really does do that a hell of a lot. Under 'any other relevant skills or aptitudes' I'm going to put 'hovering'.

The whole motet is sublime because Bach is the greatest genius who ever lived, but what's musically and dramatically so sublime is the '*es ist nun nichts Verdammliches*' when they sing that '*nichts*' twice. There is nothing – repeat, nothing – damnable in those who are in Christ Jesus.

Did that apply to Nigel, though?

According to the criteria, candidates should be 'self-aware, mature and stable' with a 'capacity to build healthy personal, professional and pastoral relationships'. He hadn't really built a healthy professional relationship with me. Maybe that was my fault. I'm the builder after all, and he's the builder's mate. Maybe I've just never let him build.

I wanted to be kind but that wasn't the job, I was meant to be accurate. OK then. Was his sense of vocation 'obedient, realistic and informed'? Well, it was informed, all right. He was like cleverest boy in school, the one who comes top but doesn't go to parties or do sport or resent the teachers or hate his parents. You respect that boy, he's top of the class, he knows all the information, but you don't want to spend time with him.

He's so much better at engaging with information than people.

What would it be like if I took off my headphones and told Nigel I was terrified my marriage was over?

It would be a breach of our vicar–assistant professional relationship. So what? Could Nigel cope with raw human need? No, he couldn't.

The music ended. I took off my headphones. Nigel suggested we go out together and get some supplies. We needed biscuits. It didn't take two people to carry biscuits, so this was evidently a social event – now that I was writing his reference, he was trying to build our relationship, but this was cowboy building, crude and rushed.

As we walked down the street, he told me he was going to help out at the homeless day centre and maybe clean some clothes for them, then he thought he might pop into the youth drop-in and offer them some solace about the job market.

'Don't over-egg it, Nigel,' I said. I stopped outside the Hackney Organic Bed Centre to stub out my cigarette.

I looked through the window. The Archdeacon was bouncing up and down on a bed. It was thrilling, like seeing the Pope on a trampoline. I so wanted to call Alex and tell her.

'Let's go and tell him all the pastoral things I'm doing today,' said Nigel desperately.

I knew it was a mistake. The Archdeacon was buying a bed and wearing a casual suit and a V-necked sweater. He was definitely not on duty.

As we approached, he was standing with his back to us, looking at the other beds with his companion, who put a loving hand on the Archdeacon's back. The companion was a man. A male man of the masculine gender. A geezer, a bloke, a guy, a fellow. A chap. *His* chap.

'Archdeacon, hello!' called Nigel and the Archdeacon turned and said, 'What are you doing here?' in a tone so sharp you thought he would add, 'And when are you going to fuck off?'

'I'm just going to the Homeless Centre to wash the needy,' said Nigel, trying (and failing) to impress.

The Archdeacon's chap was younger and taller and much better-looking, a real catch. He had fashionable black-rimmed glasses, an elegant grey suit and one of those almost-beards – that very dark stubble which takes a lot of tending so it never actually sprouts. He looked like an architect or a consultant, someone with poise and confidence, who put powerful people at their ease.

I had loads of time to study the man because the Archdeacon just stood there, failing and failing to introduce him to me and Nigel, until finally he said, with massive reluctance, 'This is my friend Richard,' and we all did a lot of firm handshaking and hellos in a thoroughly British manner, before lapsing into another silence.

The Archdeacon, rather touchingly I thought, attempted to relax himself and us by essaying a little joke.

'If you're about to start shopping in here,' he said to me, 'I think it's time we reviewed your stipend.' He

grinned, but it was a grin of fear, like the one a chimpan-
zee makes when it sees a snake.

'Are you going to buy that bed then?' I asked, looking
at them both.

Was that the right thing to say? I was definitely pre-
suming they were in this thing together – in this bed
together, as it were – and I was just letting them know
that didn't bother me.

'No,' said Richard, who made his excuses and told
'Bobby' he'd see him in the car.

So. There we had it. He'd gone from the sly and
intimidating Archdeacon, to the nice man who cleaned
palliative loos and loved our coffee and wanted us to call
him Robert, to Bobby. Gay Bobby.

He couldn't wait to get away either and, as soon as
Richard had gone, there was another ghastly pause
where we all made imaginary small talk. Then he did
another fear grin and said goodbye.

I felt I understood him now for the first time; all that
sly stuff he did, all those waspish remarks and odd little
looks, the way he had of wanting you not to know what
he was thinking – that was the key to him. Because what
he was thinking was, I'm a gay man who doesn't want
you to know, so keep your distance.

Twenty minutes later, as we rounded the corner of the
Hackney Road, the horn of a parked taxi hooted at me. It
was the call of Bobby. I said goodbye to Nigel and got in.

We stopped in a deserted industrial wasteland, all cor-
rugated iron and mounds of scrap, one of those bits of

East London apparently still recovering from the Blitz. It was all very Tinker Tailor Soldier Gay Priest.

He was back to his best, if that's the right word for it. Composed and conspiratorial and intimidating.

'Let's imagine,' he began, 'that there was a scenario in which I was being considered for an episcopal position.'

I knew he was about to go before the Crown Nominations Committee. Hot favourite to be the next Bishop of Stevenage. I told him I was imagining his scenario.

'Excellent. My concern is that if certain elements within the Church happened to hear about certain aspects of my private life, they might be open to misinterpretation. For instance, I'd hate for my friendship with Richard—'

'He seemed very nice,' I interrupted. 'So handsome!' (There was no reason I shouldn't enjoy this.)

'Yes. I'd hate for my friendship with Richard to be misinterpreted.'

'Church law clearly says that being gay is no bar to the bishopric,' I told him, knowing he knew that already. I paused. 'So long as it's a celibate relationship.'

I did a little pout and a tiny quizzical thing with my eyebrows. Oh yes! I was *really* enjoying myself now. I was out-archdeaconing the Archdeacon, toying with him as he'd toyed with me. For nearly a year, he'd been at it; he still called Suffolk 'Sussex', just to remind me I was from nowhere and could always be sent back there, where I belonged.

'We both know,' he said, 'that the Church isn't ready for an openly gay bishop.' I agreed that we both knew that, then asked if he'd like me to keep his friendship with Richard quiet.

'Thank you,' he said, ever so humbly, his face slightly cast down. I told him there was nothing I'd like more than to see him become Bishop of Swanage.

'Stevenage,' he corrected.

'Or Stevenage,' I said.

He offered to drive me back to St Saviour's, instead of doing his usual and dumping me right there, among the dead pigeons and plastic bags flying in the breeze.

## 27th September

Nigel was wearing his suit and tie this morning, though his interview with the Archdeacon isn't until tomorrow. I think he wanted me to do a dress rehearsal, because his first question when I arrived was, 'What do you think the Archdeacon will ask me?' I said I thought he'd ask about his personal relationships.

'I'm ready for that one!' said Nigel. It was question 14 on his form – Who might sustain you in your future ministry? – and he'd put, 'My dear mum and my girl-friend Cherry.' Did I think two people was enough?

This was nothing like discovering the Archdeacon's friend Richard. He wasn't really a surprise, because I'd always known, or at least suspected, that there was a friend like Richard hidden somewhere in the Archdeacon's life. But Cherry? This was like someone turning up in the vestry with the Turin Shroud. It was exciting, but did they honestly expect you to believe it was real?

'Your girlfriend Cherry?'

'Yes. That's a good answer, isn't it?' he said. I could see his point. He was applying for a job, so if he had to choose between a good answer and a true one, it was sort of no contest.

'You've got a girlfriend called Cherry?' I repeated, registering my surprise, because he'd never mentioned her till now. He said that was because he liked to keep his private life private.

But Cherry wasn't private any more. He'd outed her, on a form. Cherry was fair game now, so I asked what she was like. This was going to be fun.

He thought hard. Fair enough. I wouldn't know where to start if I had to describe Alex. Describing someone you love is hard – you're too close to them to be able to see them.

'What's she like? She's gorgeous, is what she's like. A real honey. A real honey babe.' Now he'd established, with knobs on, his heterosexuality, he got down to details. She had lovely legs and (for balance) a great personality. She was gluten intolerant, but that wasn't so bad, you could get special pasta for that now. She had blonde hair. She was 5 foot 6½ inches. (That was particularly convincing, I thought. An imaginary woman might be 5 foot 6; but a real one you knew intimately was 5 foot 6 *and a half*.)

Then, I'm afraid, Nigel lost his way. He said she had big breasts, but he said it without any enthusiasm, as though he'd heard her breasts were big but had never actually seen them, and anyway he wasn't a big breasts fan.

Then he added, as an afterthought, 'I'm a very lucky man.' But he'd never looked less lucky; he looked like a man who was convinced he'd soon be deprived of the one thing he wanted, the thing that gave his life meaning and purpose, which was the prospect of becoming a priest.

## 28th September

Last night I stayed on at St Saviour's and helped cook the meal for Night Shelter. I got back at about 11 and then got up at 6 to go back to church and serve breakfast. In all this my purpose was threefold: to serve God, minister to human need and be out when Adoha called.

Colin was there last night, being friendly to all the nervous newcomers who'd never slept in a night shelter. He told me that in a few months he will have saved up enough from his pizza job to rent his own place.

I thought about him when I woke up in my vicarage bed. I can't say I envied him, sleeping on a mattress in St Saviour's with 20 other men. On the other hand, I could have done with the companionship. Colin said as much as I left the church: 'Why don't you sleep with us, Vicarage, now you're single again?'

I don't know how many days I've been 'single' – well, I do, I just don't want to admit it. All I know is, every morning when I make tea, I make a pot for two, even if it means pouring half of it away, just in case Alex turns up. It makes no sense. Alex isn't going to leave Shropshire at four in the morning to get home in time for breakfast with me. But I do it as an act of faith.

I couldn't take her being away from me any more. Colin was right, the whole thing was a cry for attention. I'd get in the car, drive to Shropshire, find her, tell her how much I missed her and loved her, and beg her to come home. How was that for attention?

I looked it up online. It would take me about 3½ hours to drive to Rodney's Pillar from Hackney, probably more, since I was leaving in the rush hour, but it didn't matter. I had to go and find her. My music would keep me going.

The Subaru Legacy inched out of the vicarage gates just before eight. Then I inched up Holloway Road, Archway, Henly's Corner — it was a nightmare but that didn't bother me. I was a man on a (slow) mission.

By the time I got to the M1, it felt good to be alive. Ahead of me, before I turned off onto the M6, were 60 or 70 miles of uninterrupted pedal to the metal, a phrase I didn't even know before I watched *Top Gear*. Those presenters didn't understand, though. They talked about road-holding and torque and twin-turbo 6-litre engines, but they never mentioned the car feature that matters more than any other: music. Put a Bach motet in a Subaru and it feels like a Ferrari.

I was seriously on my way now. By lunchtime, I'd be 2,000 feet above sea level at the top of Breidden's Hill, taking a shot of myself on my phone in front of Rodney's Pillar, then sending it to Alex. Her phone would be off in the day, but as soon as she turned it on in the evening, she'd know I'd come to get her.

I stopped at Newport Pagnell for a well-earned cup of coffee. I'd done 97 miles in 1 hour 50 minutes. I felt like a hero.

Of course, I didn't know where she'd be in the evening. She and Maria and Sue and Helen and Howard would be in a pub, probably, somewhere in Shropshire, after their day's walk. Wherever she was, I'd go to her. She'd be mightily impressed I'd come all that way.

At Watford Gap, I had a pee. As I washed my hands, I saw myself in the mirror. I looked astonishingly determined.

I got back in the car and drove on. There was no turning back now. I was on the M6. I'd driven nearly 100 miles.

What exactly was I doing? Had I thought it through?

I was heroically driving to Shropshire to surprise Alex and tell her I loved her. There she'd be, with Helen and Sue and Maria and Howard, in some pub or tea shop or restaurant, or maybe in a campsite, when my Rodney's Pillar selfie popped up on her phone. How would that make her feel? Never mind how I felt, what would it actually be like for Alex? When she saw where I was, would she think, My hero! The idea was great – going all that way to tell her I loved her – the problem was the reality. I was going there to bring her back home, that was my mission, I was coming to take her away from her friends, without any warning. How would she like that? For that matter, how would Helen and Sue and Maria and Howard like it?

At Corley Services, over a tuna and tomato baguette, I prayed.

Lord, I want to show Alex how much I love her. Is following her to Shropshire an act of love or is it weird and sort of aggressive?

I got back in the car and stuck to the slow lane, as if getting there slowly would somehow help. I stuck in CD 3 of my *God's Greatest Hits* and got a shock. I'd forgotten what I'd put after 'Jubilate Deo', as a homage to Colin. AC/DC's 'Let's Get It Up'. Suddenly the car was full of sex music, sung by a man with an ugly strangulated voice that suited the lyrics perfectly. This man was going to get it up if it killed him.

I got off the M6 at the next junction and stopped in the car park of the Castle Bromwich Inn to make some calls. Within an hour, I was at the Second City Fertility Clinic, just outside Birmingham.

This was the thing to do. This, not turning up unannounced, was an act of love. If Alex was wondering whether she wanted a child with me, I owed it to her to find out if I was fertile. Why had she never told me to go to a fertility clinic? Because she was waiting for me to do it without being asked. To *want* to do it.

The woman asked if I'd abstained from ejaculation for at least 2 days. I said I had. I gave her my credit card and she gave me a sterile little pot thing.

I went into the masturbation room. Once I shut the door, I looked at my credit card receipt: £250, plus VAT. It was a lot of money, but it was worth it. They'd seen me within the hour, and they'd give me the results an hour after I gave them the sperm. I couldn't ring up the NHS and get all that done the same day.

Two hundred and fifty pounds, though. That was a hell of a lot of money. Two hundred and fifty pounds. Plus VAT. Shit, I had to stop thinking about the money! That and the VAT were making me completely limp.

I shut my eyes and thought of anything that might help. Ellie's bootees. Cheeky's lap-dancing club. Nothing worked. Course it didn't. I had to think about Alex. Anything else would be a betrayal.

'If thy dick offend thee, pluck it out.'

I thought of us having sex on the sofa. I got it up. For Alex. And for procreation, the divine purpose of the sacrament of marriage.

By 4 o'clock I was back on the M6, heading for London, and by 7.30 I was in Hackney, very near the vicarage, driving past Adoha, who was walking in the same direction, carrying a casserole. So I turned left and went to The Monarch instead. I stayed there for an hour, drinking 2 pints of bitter and texting Alex.

I told her all about my day, the whole 200-mile round trip, but I wrote it like a love letter. It had proper grammar. There was none of that LOL stuff. No 'sprem' test. It was so long it had to be broken up into 12 separate messages.

I told her that if I were her I'd think hard about having a child with me, but I loved her and I missed her and I was fertile – 54 million per millilitre. Just 10 per cent less than the national average. Current thinking was that smoking and drinking and obesity didn't affect sperm quality but, if she wanted me to, I'd wrap my lager tins and fags and pies in my Y-fronts and stick them in the bin – because boxer shorts were the only thing if you wanted to make a baby.

I told her that she didn't have to text me back if she didn't want to.

When I went to bed, she still hadn't texted.

I left my phone on all night, but when I woke up there were no new messages.

When I wrote that she didn't have to reply, surely she knew I didn't mean it?

This was torture now. Fucking torture.

## 29th September

In the church I put on the 'Sanctus' from Byrd's *Mass for Five Voices* and listened for a while, till a voice from 20 feet away said, 'Excellent choice.'

The Archdeacon had been there all along. I apologized for not having noticed him. He was unusually subdued. Contemplative. Genuinely humble.

'I just came in to think,' he said. I asked if something was bothering him and he said no, not really. But it was. Eventually, he told me.

'I've just seen the Crown Nominations Committee.'

'Right. How did it go?'

'They asked if I was in an "active gay relationship". I said yes. With a man I love more than words. I think that probably means I'll never be Bishop of Stevenage, don't you? Or even Swanage.'

I agreed that it did. He said he was reflecting on the fact that this was 'OK, really'. He could be as brave and nonchalant and waspish as he liked – it wasn't OK. We talk about 'wrestling with our consciences' and 'trying to interpret God's will'. In any other job, it would be called discrimination.

I left, hoping the 'Sanctus' would comfort him, and sat on the bench. I put my headphones on and thought about him, to the tune of Nina Simone's 'Our Love (Will See Us Through)'. Not an overtly religious song, but she was playing piano in her local church in North Carolina when she was just a little girl. And you can tell. Her voice inspires awe, it's so profound and deep. Which I wouldn't say of Kate Bush.

The Archdeacon had done the right thing. It was unthinkable that he'd deny the existence of Richard. Except it wasn't, was it, it was totally thinkable. In fact, he drove me in a taxi to a bombsite and told me to think it. Cherry was a non-existent girl I was asked to pretend was real. Richard was a real man I was asked to pretend did not exist. But when the panel asked the Archdeacon, to his face, if he was in an 'active gay relationship', he had said yes. He chose love over ambition. What was an 'inactive' gay relationship, anyway? Did you both sleep through the sex?

Colin turned up and started ranting. While delivering three Hawaiian pizzas, he'd had an altercation with a taxi driver. At the climax of this altercation, Colin hurled the three Hawaiians at his windscreen. It wasn't clear to me, and I didn't want to ask, if he'd ripped the Hawaiians out their boxes first and pineappled the windscreen.

'Guess what?' asked Colin. The taxi driver called Pizza-U-Like to complain about Colin's behaviour. And then, to Colin's 'total fucking disbelief', the shop sided with the taxi driver and sacked Colin. I was meant to be outraged. But what did Colin expect?

'That was my last chance!' screamed Colin. 'That was how I was going to sort my life out!'

'What you doing, you twat?' he asked, looking up at the roof of the church. To my shock, Nigel was sitting on the edge of it, his feet dangling over the drop.

By the time I got up there, he was sobbing. He'd been turned down for ordination training.

'How can they say I wouldn't be a good priest? How can they know what God wants? How dare they pretend they do?'

Poor man. I told him he wouldn't feel this now, but in time he'd be glad he hadn't been accepted, because God wanted him to do other things.

'What other things?' All he wanted was to be a priest, that's who he was, and now they were telling him he wasn't who he was, which made no sense to Nigel.

'If I can't do what I want to do, what do I do?'

I had no answer, so I told him that many were called but few were chosen, which didn't help, and then I put my hand on his back and asked if he'd let me buy him a drink, which did help. He let me support his weight as he leaned back and swung his legs over the edge, to safety.

That felt wonderful. But it didn't feel that way for long. Nigel turned aggressive.

'Did you give me a bad reference? Did you say I was boring?'

I told him, which was true, that I hadn't said he was boring. Just unfailingly punctual and organized. Which he said were euphemisms for 'boring'.

'What's the best thing you said about me?'

I racked my brain. 'That you were brilliant at working alone.'

He snorted. 'Was that in the question on teamwork?'

He stomped off towards the fire exit, then turned and jabbed his finger at me. 'You fucked me,' he said. 'You know I'd be a much better priest than you. That's the tragedy here.'

If it weren't for other people, Nigel's life would be perfect, and of all the other people in the whole world, I was the worst. I couldn't believe he'd actually said, 'You fucked me.' That was weird. He looked demonic when he said that. We might have to have the church roof exorcized.

I stayed and smoked another cigarette. The Archdeacon, Nigel, Colin and me. The Church of St Saviour's was like a convocation of lost souls. We were dazed and wandering sheep, all three of us, which was terrible, because the Archdeacon and I were meant to be shepherds; we were meant to guard and guide the Colins of this world, instead of which we were the blind leading the blind.

At the end of the day, when I got back to the vicarage, I found Adoha on the doorstep, waiting for me with her faithful casserole. Oven-ready. Just reheat.

How could I have thought bad things about Adoha? She was kind to me and she cared about me. She sat me down at my kitchen table and told me to do nothing. By now, she knew where everything was. She served me my lovingly prepared dinner – chicken, peas and rice – then asked me how I was coping.

'Badly,' I said.

'You are still missing Alex?'

I nodded. She shook her head. Someone had to give me a bit of a talking-to and she'd decided to take that burden upon herself. *Why* was I missing Alex? Alex had no interest in the church. She never came to the teas or did any flowers.

'You deserve a woman who will support you. How is your chicken? Not too hot?'

I took a mouthful.

'No, it's lovely,' I said, drinking a glass of water to soothe my scorched mouth in what I hoped was a casual way.

'You are better off without her, Adam.'

The roof of my mouth felt branded with an A for Adoha.

'Napkin,' she said. She stood behind me and slotted a clean blue napkin down my shirt front, smoothing it out so it sat happily on my chest, and then we heard footsteps and looked up.

Alex. So sharp and vivid and wonderful. The woman I loved.

'Hello, Adoha,' she said. 'It's really lovely to see you in my home. With my husband.'

I'd never loved her so much as I did in that moment. The way she was brave enough to stand there and say what was on her mind, so sarcastically but clearly that even Adoha understood. This was Alex's gift: she was always and only herself.

Within 2 minutes, Adoha was gone.

Within 5 minutes, Alex and I were in bed together, having a non-gay 'inactive' relationship, because there was too much to be said.

I asked her what brought her home. She started kissing me and stroking me.

'I missed you so much when I got your text.'

'I missed you all the time. Why didn't you answer?'

'I wanted to surprise you. I love that you stopped off in Birmingham for a wank.'

'My pleasure.'

She'd done a test herself. Just a few hours after mine. The test was positive. We were going to have a baby.

I felt like crying. She'd got what she wanted. What *we* wanted. And in some mystical way I'd helped by going to that clinic, even though it was, in the circumstances, entirely unnecessary.

After a bit she said, 'Are you upset you wasted £250 plus VAT?'

'No!' I said, though that was exactly what I was thinking. Because I hadn't seen her for days, I'd forgotten she had the power to know what I was thinking, even when – especially when – it was something I didn't want to think.

## 4th November

It's 2.13 a.m. I can't sleep, I'm too excited.

The curtains are open in the study. I've just seen the metal grille descend. Tony's Kebabs have shut for the night.

Today's the first anniversary of my arrival at St Saviour's. A year. I can't believe it.

This time next year, if all goes well, Lord, which I hope and pray it will, I won't be sitting here, because this won't be my study any more. It will be the baby's bedroom.

Before it's christened, no, before it's born – no, sod it, *tomorrow* – I'm putting its name down for Ellie's school. It's bound to get in. I'm happy to tick my own 'regular and committed worshipper' box.

Today we got a card from June and Graham Cooper, my parents' friends, congratulating us on our 'forthcoming happy event'. On the front of the card was a nativity scene.

'We thought this would be appropriate!' they'd written. What are they talking about? Which aspect of the virgin birth of the Christ child is appropriate?

Holy Visitor! There's a fox on the lawn. It's just standing there like it owns the place. What a magnificent creature.

It's staring at me. I can see it thinking, Who's the fox? You or me?

I know I'm not the only vicar who's been through a crisis. Maybe there's a Vicars Anonymous, where I can talk and all the other vicars will have to listen to me and nod and thank me for sharing.

Nat Jones wrote to me from Pentonville. He wants me to go and see him to talk about letting the light of Jesus into his life. I'll do it. Course I will. I imagine that in prison you need all the light you can get.

I feel so happy. I love Alex and I love my work. I'm doing what I was put on this earth to do. And we're only £23,197 short on the Window Restoration Fund.

Colin applied for a job as a refuse collector. I wrote him a reference and he got the job. He's delighted.

Colin will do the job fine for a bit and then he'll screw up and lose it. As he's done before. I'll experience severe doubt again. I may even have another 'episode'. But I'll survive it.

Roland's on the radio next week. He's doing 'Great Lives' with Matthew Parris. I don't know whose life he's chosen. Probably his own.

Everything is cyclical. Isn't that right, Lord? I'm talking to you while listening on my headphones to

'Turn! Turn! Turn!' by The Byrds, which is a very jingly-jangly 1960s folky-rocky sort of song, with words based on Ecclesiastes 3.

> To every thing there is a season, and a time to
>     every purpose under the heaven:
> A time to be born, and a time to die; a time to
>     plant, and a time to pluck up that which is planted;
> A time to kill, and a time to heal; a time to
>     break down, and a time to build up;
> A time to weep, and a time to laugh; a time to
>     mourn, and a time to dance;

I've listened to it about 10 times now and the line that gets me every time is 'A time to break down and a time to build up'.

The truth and beauty and simplicity and pain of that astonish me, Lord.

Alex is asleep next door with our baby inside her and I'm here, listening to the song.

The fox has gone. I'm going to have to stop now.

# He just wanted a decent book to read ...

Not too much to ask, is it? It was in 1935 when Allen Lane, Managing Director of Bodley Head Publishers, stood on a platform at Exeter railway station looking for something good to read on his journey back to London. His choice was limited to popular magazines and poor-quality paperbacks – the same choice faced every day by the vast majority of readers, few of whom could afford hardbacks. Lane's disappointment and subsequent anger at the range of books generally available led him to found a company – and change the world.

*'We believed in the existence in this country of a vast reading public for intelligent books at a low price, and staked everything on it'*
**Sir Allen Lane, 1902–1970, founder of Penguin Books**

The quality paperback had arrived – and not just in bookshops. Lane was adamant that his Penguins should appear in chain stores and tobacconists, and should cost no more than a packet of cigarettes.

Reading habits (and cigarette prices) have changed since 1935, but Penguin still believes in publishing the best books for everybody to enjoy. We still believe that good design costs no more than bad design, and we still believe that quality books published passionately and responsibly make the world a better place.

So wherever you see the little bird – whether it's on a piece of prize-winning literary fiction or a celebrity autobiography, political tour de force or historical masterpiece, a serial-killer thriller, reference book, world classic or a piece of pure escapism – you can bet that it represents the very best that the genre has to offer.

## Whatever you like to read – trust Penguin.